PENGUIN  CLASSICS

A TALE UNASKED

Born in 1258 into a high-ranking aristocratic family in Japan's capital (present-day Kyoto), LADY NIJŌ was largely raised in the court of Retired Emperor Go-Fukakusa, and at fourteen became his concubine. Their increasingly difficult relationship continued until 1283, when Go-Fukakusa abruptly expelled her from the court. Nijō subsequently became a Buddhist nun, and thereafter spent much of her time wandering Japan on pilgrimage. She died sometime after 1306.

MEREDITH McKINNEY is a translator of Japanese literature, both classical and modern. She lived in Japan for twenty years and is currently Honorary Associate Professor at the Australian National University in Canberra. Her translations for Penguin Classics include *The Pillow Book* of Sei Shōnagon, *Essays in Idleness and Hōjōki* by Kenkō and Chōmei, *Travels with a Writing Brush: Classical Japanese Travel Writing from the Manyōshū to Bashō*, and two novels by Natsume Sōseki.

LADY NIJŌ
A Tale Unasked

Translated by MEREDITH MCKINNEY

PENGUIN CLASSICS

PENGUIN CLASSICS

UK | USA | Canada | Ireland | Australia
India | New Zealand | South Africa

Penguin Classics is part of the Penguin Random House group of companies
whose addresses can be found at global.penguinrandomhouse.com.

Penguin Random House UK
One Embassy Gardens, 8 Viaduct Gardens, London SW11 7BW

penguin.co.uk

Penguin
Random House
UK

First published in Great Britain in Penguin Classics 2025
002

Translation copyright © Meredith McKinney, 2025

Set in 10.25/12.25pt Sabon LT Pro
Typeset by Six Red Marbles UK, Thetford, Norfolk
Printed and bound in Great Britain by Clays Ltd, Elcograf S.p.A.

The authorized representative in the EEA is Penguin Random House Ireland,
Morrison Chambers, 32 Nassau Street, Dublin D02 YH68

A CIP catalogue record for this book is available from the British Library

ISBN: 978-0-241-56246-8

Penguin Random House is committed to a sustainable future
for our business, our readers and our planet. This book is made from
Forest Stewardship Council® certified paper.

MIX
Paper | Supporting
responsible forestry
FSC
www.fsc.org   FSC® C018179

To Royall Tyler, friend and mentor

Table of Contents

Introduction

In 1938 a scholar stumbled upon an old manuscript with the intriguing title of *Towazugatari* (*A Tale Unasked*) tucked away in the Travel section of the Imperial Household Library in Tokyo, and decided to take a closer look. He discovered it was a late seventeenth- or early eighteenth-century copy of a much earlier work that was about very much more than just travel, apparently written by a high-ranking lady at the court of Retired Emperor Go-Fukakusa (1243–1304) and containing startling and detailed revelations of the sexual politics of courtly life. He also realized very quickly that *A Tale Unasked* was an impressive work of literature that surely ranked with the great women's diaries[1] of earlier centuries. Scholars were soon at work deciphering and transcribing the lengthy handwritten manuscript, and in 1950 this precious and long-forgotten classic was finally introduced to the public.

Internal evidence dates the completion of *A Tale Unasked* to around 1306. The memoir spans more than thirty-five years, beginning with a detailed account of the events leading up to the author Lady Nijō's first sexual encounter with Go-Fukakusa at the age of fourteen,[2] and coming to an end when she was an ageing nun of forty-nine. Despite chronological gaps in the story, it forms an episodic but broadly continuous tale of Nijō's twelve years as Go-Fukakusa's concubine at court until her expulsion in 1283 (Books 1–3), followed by a description of some key events in her seventeen years spent as an often itinerant nun (Books 4–5). Together, the two parts of *A Tale Unasked* give us not only detailed pictures of two starkly different experiences of life as a woman in thirteenth-century Japan, but provide a compelling portrait of a richly intelligent and vibrant sensibility finding its way through the sometimes daunting challenges of her difficult life.

Nijō

The author was born in 1258 into the high-ranking aristocratic Koga family, a branch of the elite Minamotos that traced its line back to a tenth-century emperor. Her mother, also of noble birth, died when Nijō was two, and from the age of four her father placed her in the court of Retired Emperor Go-Fukakusa to be brought up largely under his care, in a move designed to give Nijō every advantage in the high-stakes world of marriage politics that underpinned so much of broader court politics. 'Marriage' is a misleading word for the fluid relationships between men and women in this world in which a powerful man such as Go-Fukakusa had not only a primary consort but an assortment of lesser consorts, whose status was often dependent on the children they bore him. If Nijō's fate had taken a different turn, the son she bore him in 1273 might have secured her formal recognition as an imperial consort. Unfortunately, the child died at the age of three, and by then another blow had also severely undermined her position at court. In the previous year, her powerful father had died, and without the crucial support of his patronage to back her, Nijō's status at court was increasingly vulnerable. She was now solely dependent on retaining Go-Fukakusa's increasingly fickle favour as concubine. Remarkably, she succeeded in doing this for another ten years, until at the age of twenty-six she found herself abruptly and apparently inexplicably expelled from the court.

Her memoir takes up the story again in 1289. At some point in the intervening years, she had followed the established tradition for women who found themselves alone in the world and become a Buddhist nun, fulfilling an urge that her memoir tells us she had nursed for many years. Seizing the freedom that this new identity conferred on her, she now set off on a journey, first to the recently established centre of civil power in Kamakura, and later on a series of lengthy and sometimes arduous pilgrimages that took her to some of the more remote corners of the nation, interspersed with periods back in the capital. The final two books of *A Tale Unasked* describe this intrepid wandering life, filled with incident and often with pleasure as well as with the serious business of devotion and prayer, but perpetually haunted by her deep and sorrowing attachment to Go-Fukakusa. Occasional chance encounters with him down the years only served to reinforce her feelings for him, which culminate in a moving depiction of her despairing experience of his death. The memoir peters out around two years later when Nijō was approaching the age of fifty (then considered old). The date and circumstances of her death are unknown.

Go-Fukakusa

The man who haunted Nijō's life was already sixteen years old when she was born. The son of Emperor Go-Saga, he was born in 1243 and was himself made emperor a mere three years later when his father abdicated. The role of emperor had long since become purely ceremonial, and it was common to install a young child to perform the imperial duties while the previous incumbent took the title of Retired Emperor, which allowed him to wield real power and authority behind the scenes. Go-Fukakusa remained emperor until 1259, when Go-Saga made the controversial move of requiring him to abdicate in favour of his half-brother, Kameyama (then aged ten). Although Go-Fukakusa may well have been privately relieved to be able to relinquish his arduous ceremonial life and take up the more fulfilling role of Retired Emperor, the succession should have gone to a son of his and not to his rival half-brother, who was now in a position to place his own son on the throne to follow him in due course.

The bitterness that this caused, and the simmering question of succession inheritance, underlie a number of scenes in the first three books of *A Tale Unasked*, although Nijō never directly comments on the situation. Even after Go-Fukakusa had managed to win a promise that his own son would take his turn as emperor after Kameyama's son had stepped down,[3] the relationship between the half-brothers remained tense and rivalrous. The effect of this on Nijō was profound, for Kamey-ama did not hide the attraction he felt for her. Not only did she become a pawn in the complex manoeuvres between the half-brothers on several occasions, but rumours of a clandes-tine affair with Kameyama apparently played a large part in Go-Fukakusa's abrupt eviction of her from court. Nijō brushes off the suggestion of an affair but does not outright deny it, and there are signs earlier in the memoir that she was at least flattered by Kameyama's interest in her. After all, she was in no position to resist a powerful man's persistent attentions, and her ardent and adventurous nature also tended to make her easy prey; Go-Fukakusa's jealous suspicions were possibly well-founded.

The Court and Its World

Ever since present-day Kyoto had become Japan's capital in 794, it had been the seat of government and home to the imper-ial court, but by Nijō's day the importance of the court had waned and the recently established military government in dis-tant Kamakura now comprised the real centre of power. It was to the Kamakura authorities that Go-Fukakusa appealed in his struggle to wrench the line of succession from his half-brother's descendants, and it was those authorities who gratified him by making the final decision allowing his son to follow Kame-yama's on the throne.

When Nijō set off on her travels as a nun years later (see Appendix 2 map), Kamakura was her first choice of destin-ation, and her depiction of its intriguingly different social world is full of vivid detail. Nun though she was, Nijō maintained her unofficial status as a former aristocrat and member of the imperial court, and it is telling how eagerly those in Kamakura with cultural pretensions bowed to the authority of her opin-ion, and how inclined she was to look down on their boorish ways. Although now effectively powerless, the imperial court still crucially remained the nation's cultural arbiter.

The imperial palace itself, where the emperor and his court lived, plays a negligible role in Nijō's memoir. The world she describes as 'the Palace' belongs to the court of Retired Emperor Go-Fukakusa, a sprawling complex located in north-eastern Kyoto (see Appendix 1 map). Another important location for the events of her memoir was the Fushimi Palace, Go-Fukakusa's villa to the south of the city (near present-day Uji) where he retired for entertainment and relaxation from court duties. Like the other ladies of the court, Nijō's own periods of freedom from her duties at court were spent 'at home', which after the early death of her father was the home of her former nurse in the city centre. Children in upper-class families were largely raised by their wetnurses, and this bond remained close throughout their lives, but Nijō was far from fond of her nurse and did not much enjoy the time she spent there. The Palace felt to her like her real home, which added to the pain and dismay of her final expulsion from it.

The various ladies of the Palace, including Nijō, are described as being 'in service' to Go-Fukakusa. As well as tending to his needs and keeping him company as required, 'service' included sexual availability. Powerful men were sexually promiscuous. 'He never spent a night without a woman,' Nijō says of her beloved and now ailing father, with no hint of disapproval; the description is intended simply to indicate his former robust energy. Go-Fukakusa could choose whom he spent each night with, although his greatest allegiance was to his primary consort Higashi Nijō'in ('Her Highness' in the memoir). Besides the ladies of the court, he clearly had a predatory eye for other potential sexual partners, and it was the duty of whichever lady was serving him at the time to procure these women for him. Nijō several times describes such encounters with a coolly appraising and sometimes satirical eye. She understood his sexual tastes all too well, and would have had good reason to feel sorry for the women who failed to please him.

One of these unfortunate women, the timid and vulnerable Imperial Priestess whom Nijō had recently befriended, was not only a half-aunt of Nijō's but Go-Fukakusa's own half-sister, although this close blood tie does not seem to have troubled anyone involved. In fact, thanks largely to the combination of male polygamy and the alliances of marriage politics, all the prominent aristocratic and imperial families were related to each other, sometimes several times over. Go-Fukakusa's primary consort Higashi Nijō'in (eleven years his senior), for instance, was also his half-aunt. Her mother Lady Kitayama (Go-Fukakusa and Kameyama's grandmother) was also Nijō's great-aunt on her mother's side, as well as the grandmother of her lover Sanekane (referred to as 'Akebono' in her secret relationship with him). These complicated relationships sometimes mattered in the social politics of the court, but they usually played little part in private life.

Nijō herself had four children:[4] a short-lived son fathered by Go-Fukakusa, a daughter by Sanekane, and two sons by her subsequent lover 'Ariake', her private name for the abbot of Ninnaji Temple (who is generally identified as a half-brother of Go-Fukakusa). Her secret daughter was hastily removed at birth and brought up in the household of the father as an officially recognized daughter of Sanekane.[5] The fate of the other two children is not recorded, although Go-Fukakusa claimed he would accept Ariake's first child as his own. Nijō writes movingly of the strong maternal love she felt at their birth, but babies were automatically removed into the hands of a wet-nurse, and the extended period that Nijō spent alone nursing Ariake's second son after his birth was exceptional in every way. Late in life she says of herself, 'I essentially had no child to pass anything on to'. Clearly she had no ties to any surviving children. She truly was alone in the world.

Nijō and Go-Fukakusa

Nijō's only lasting bond was with Go-Fukakusa, and it continued until his death. Although there were many other women who claimed his attention, she depicts herself as his favourite, and certainly she seems to have been of considerable emotional importance to him. This is also attested by the jealousy and animosity that his primary consort Higashi Nijō'in felt towards her, which finally helped prompt Nijō's expulsion from court. Nijō's portrayal of events and of the relationship is surely skewed by her urgent need to emphasize her central importance for Go-Fukakusa and the depth of their bond, but we need not doubt that much of what she writes was substantially true.

Nijō was far from faithful to Go-Fukakusa. The opening pages reveal a stealthy courtship already underway with an unnamed man (Sanekane), which complicated her feelings during the subsequent encounter with Go-Fukakusa. Despite her protestations of innocence, both parties would surely have been well aware that she was destined to be Go-Fukakusa's concubine. Their flirtation later developed into a heady secret affair that culminated in the hidden birth of Sanekane's child, described in the memoir in moving detail, but the difficulties of maintaining secrecy and the compromises of Nijō's life at court finally caused her and Sanekane to become estranged, though he continued to be kind to her.

Sanekane strikes the reader as a genial and warm-hearted man; on the other hand, the desperate infatuation of Nijō's other clandestine lover, the Ninnaji abbot whom she calls Ariake, sometimes repelled and terrified, then finally enthralled her. The relationship with Sanekane appears to have remained largely undetected by Go-Fukakusa, although there are hints that he suspected it; but Go-Fukakusa's discovery and manipulation of the affair with Ariake, together with the rest of his increasingly capricious and abusive treatment of Nijō, makes confronting reading today. It is hard to judge how much her own often wilful and secretive behaviour may have contributed to the deepening rift between Nijō and Go-Fukakusa, but a modern reader can only feel repelled by his progressively arbitrary and degrading cruelty in the latter stages of their relationship.

Decadent though court culture clearly was by then, Nijō's depiction of Go-Fukakusa's behaviour is dismaying; but Nijō herself may also puzzle us. We can understand that her situation forced her to submit to Go-Fukakusa's whims, but why, given the treatment that she details, does she never express outright resentment of him? An answer is suggested in the scene of her expulsion from the Palace, when Go-Fukakusa casually dismisses her with a cruel sneer and walks out. 'How could I not bitterly resent him at this moment?' she says, at last expressing what we have long believed she must feel. But reading on we discover that her resentment is not of his treatment of her, but rather the betrayal in his abandonment of her.[6] For Nijō their continuing bond was paramount,[7] regardless of the suffering involved. This conviction remained unshaken through the long years of her exile from the court as a wandering nun when she never ceased to love him, and in the end it is what sent her running barefoot and grief-stricken through the dark streets of the capital after his funeral procession, towards the end of her life.

Nijō and Religion

'Though we may be reborn in different forms, our bond will never cease,' Go-Fukakusa promised her during their first nights together, and on his deathbed Nijō's father admonished her to 'remember that the bond of man and woman lasts indissolubly through future rebirths'. This Buddhist doctrinal teaching is based on the concept of karma, which establishes unbreakable connections between people through the cycles of rebirth. The idea of karma, which permeates *A Tale Unasked*, was central to Nijō's understanding of the world and her experience of it, as it was for everyone. Relationships are not arbitrary but are dictated by karmic bonds, and one's experiences in life are likewise the result of karma from a previous lifetime. Although she often wept with unhappiness and lamented her fate, Nijō never expressed the resentful bitterness of the victim, no matter how cruelly and unfairly Go-Fukakusa treated her. The belief that what happened to her was dictated by her karma prevented Nijō from feeling blame and resentment. Nor was she made merely passive by this Buddhist understanding of life, for the evil karma from a previous lifetime could be transcended through dedication to the Buddhist Way. Again and again during her years at court we see Nijō yearning to retreat from the world and take Buddhist vows, and for all the unhappiness of her expulsion, when she finally steps out into the world as a nun at the beginning of Book 4 she has achieved her long-cherished goal.

Nijō does in fact spend considerable periods in retreat from her life at the Palace with female Buddhist communities, and

A Tale Unasked provides a valuable picture of the nature of such communities at this time. There seem to have been numerous small nunneries in the vicinity of the capital, centred around a female teacher and following a daily routine of instruction and devotion,[8] which were willing to shelter women in need who arrived on their doorstep. Sectarian affiliations were often fluid at this time, and some of these communities may not have been formally associated with any larger temple community or sect. It is likely that these were the kind of places in which Nijō also frequently stayed during her later travels.

Nijō had few options when she left the Palace at the age of twenty-six. Her father puts it starkly in his deathbed admonition to her: in such a situation, her choice can only be to become a nun or else to 'make yourself a name among the brothels'. In fact, entering the religious life released her into a new freedom of which she took full advantage. Women in her situation would normally have retired to live in the kind of pious community described above, but though she mentions feeling tempted to do so once, 'I realized that I didn't have it in me to quietly devote myself to religious study.' Instead, Nijō joined the free-floating world of itinerant pilgrims who flocked along the roads at this time, pausing for sometimes lengthy periods to pray at religious sites in often far-flung places before moving on. These sites included both Buddhist temples and shrines devoted to native deities, although there was little distinction between the two.[9] Despite its hardships, Nijō clearly enjoyed travel and the encounters it produced, but her aim was serious. She had vowed to make a complete copy of the major Buddhist sutras[10] and offer them as a prayer for salvation both for herself and for her father, an undertaking that took her many years and which she finally triumphantly completed in 1305.

Nijō was particularly alert to the women she came across on her travels, and there are interesting cameo scenes of her sympathetic encounters with courtesans and prostitutes as well as women of higher classes. She sometimes needed to be wary of men – the somewhat confused description in Book 5 of her attempted abduction by a man in whose house she was staying exemplifies the kind of problem a lone travelling woman might face. In one of their rare re-encounters later in life, Go-Fukakusa expresses a common opinion when he says, 'It's quite acceptable for a man to travel hither and yon . . . but it's said that all sorts of things stand in a woman's way to hinder her in this kind of wandering practice', and he accuses her of sleeping with men she has met along the way. She indignantly defends herself in a lengthy reply that is surely partly designed to put to rest the reader's suspicions as well as those of Go-Fukakusa. She may well have been speaking the truth when she asserts 'I have foresworn relations with men and that is that', although some of the men she met in her travels were clearly attracted to her, and by the time she left Kamakura rumours of an affair were certainly circulating. For all the sometimes startling honesty of description in *A Tale Unasked*, there was surely much that Nijō chose not to reveal.

A Tale Unasked

Although Nijō completed *A Tale Unasked* when she was around forty-nine, it is unclear when she began it. In the final section of the version we have, she says that 'since His Highness's death I have ceased to feel the need to unburden myself to others', which suggests that much of the work was written before his death and with the motivation of telling her story, as the title implies. The lonely lack of anyone to 'tell my troubles to' is certainly a recurring theme throughout the work.[11] Despite her final protestation to the contrary, she surely hoped that posterity at least would hear her with a sympathetic ear.

There are indications that many of the earlier sections of the memoir may have been written close to the time at which the events occurred. The detail is impressive, although Nijō's gift for bringing scenes vividly alive on the page would no doubt have extended to skilful imaginative reconstruction from memory. More importantly, the style and tone of these earlier scenes sometimes seem to belong to a much younger person, while here and there the comments of a later self are slipped in, suggesting that Nijō may have been copying out descriptions preserved from an earlier time, editing and shaping as she wrote. We can speculate that with her natural narrative flair she had long found pleasure and comfort in keeping a kind of sporadic diary, that this gradually evolved into a version of *A Tale Unasked* as Nijō's urge to record her story grew, and that earlier parts were perhaps copied out again towards the end of her life and edited to become part of the final work.

There are a number of problems with the version of the text that has come down to us in the single surviving copy. We share the copyist's puzzled frustration expressed in the occasional inserted comment: 'The page has been cut with a blade at this point. If only we knew what had been written below', and we sense perhaps an earlier reader's violent disapproval of the excised passages. In other places the text occasionally suddenly breaks off, either because a tired copyist has laid down her pen and inadvertently taken it up again at a different place, or perhaps because she (or possibly even Nijō herself) decided that the content should be omitted. It is also likely that in places the text has become somewhat garbled through careless or successive copying, and larger sections or even perhaps whole books may also have become lost. Comparison with a second copy, if one existed, would no doubt reveal various other anomalies and omissions, but we are lucky to have the single copy that did survive in an obscure corner of the library stacks in the Imperial Household in Tokyo, since it seems that *A Tale Unasked* was seldom read or remembered, and perhaps actively suppressed, in the centuries after Nijō's death.

Nijō herself is unrecorded in history. This is not so surprising, given that she never attained official status as an imperial concubine, but it has encouraged some to suggest that *A Tale Unasked* might be fictional. There are some historical anomalies in its record of known events, and here and there the narrative timing does not convincingly hang together. If it is indeed a fictional work, it is a most extraordinary one, which not only invents a compellingly real three-dimensional protagonist along with all the gripping details of her long story, but persuasively embeds her deep within both the complex social and familial fabric of the court and the broader historical moment. Such absolute historical authenticity in a work of

fiction had never been attempted in Japan, let alone so successfully achieved. If it is a fictional work, it could only be called
a product of genius.

Most scholars are happy to accept that *A Tale Unasked* is
indeed a memoir; but this does not deny it the status of literature. Nijō was writing from within the centuries-old literary
genre of 'women's diaries', though she extended this far in
the direction of confessional realism. The literary models that
can be felt behind both what she wrote and how she wrote
it include above all Murasaki Shikibu's great early eleventh-
century novel *The Tale of Genji*, which had long since attained
the status of literary masterpiece. As was not uncommon in
writing of the day, faint or overt echoes from *The Tale of Genji*
permeate *A Tale Unasked*, adding an aura of literary sanction to
Nijō's tale. The writing itself can also be self-consciously literary. The work she claims as her primary inspiration is a version
of what is now called *The Tale of Saigyō*, a highly romanti-
cized poetic biography of the great twelfth-century poet-monk
Saigyō, whose elevated style she often emulates, and in the
early travel section of Book 5 Nijō's description of her journey
along the Tōkaidō Road largely conforms to the genre of poetic
travel journal. Throughout her memoir, particularly in evoking
a moving scene, Nijō reaches for time-honoured literary tropes
of poetic depiction to elevate the effect. Straightforward realism
was often not her aim, although the style continually varies, and
sections such as the extended description of the grand birthday
celebrations at the end of Book 3, or her later experiences in
Kamakura, suggest that Nijō was sometimes conscious of her
role as a recorder of important facts and events.

Nijō's real talent lies in narrative writing. Certain key
scenes, such as her first traumatic sexual encounter, the death
of her father, or the secret birth of Sanekane's daughter, are
masterfully paced and vividly written, and she has a keen eye
for telling detail. Such a judgement would have disappointed
her, however. Her aim was to produce a literary work, and
literature at this time meant above all poetry. For her, the
poems scattered throughout the memoir[12] constituted a vitally
important record of Nijō the poet, proud inheritor of the long

poetic tradition of her forebears. Unfortunately, changing poetic taste makes it difficult for us to appreciate what worth there might once have been in the poems. With the poetic quality of her prose Nijō is on surer ground; her sentences are sinuously beautiful in the classical manner. Above all, the sustained focus on feeling establishes *A Tale Unasked* as a work of literature. Being easily moved to tears was a marker of the refined and delicate sensibility of a literary persona. Nijō had good reason to weep, of course, but her tendency to 'soak her sleeves with tears' has a strong literary as well as autobiographical resonance.

Although lost and forgotten for centuries, Nijō's tale still speaks to us compellingly today. With its richly varied and at times deeply moving content, its impressive scale, its stylistic elegance and its startlingly modern honesty and relishing of incident and narrative realism, *A Tale Unasked* fully deserves the place it has belatedly achieved among Japan's literary classics.

A Note on the Translation

Nijō's prose style generally follows the classical pattern of lengthy and often allusive sentences that sweep the reader along through shifting time and events in a way impossible to replicate in natural English. While attempting to maintain the overall effect where possible, I have often imposed a shorter sentence structure and added paragraph breaks for ease of reading.

Names are seldom used in classical Japanese texts, people being referred to if necessary by their titles. I have simplified this while trying to preserve the important decorum of title use. Since Go-Fukakusa and his half-brother Kameyama both hold the position of Retired Emperor for much of the story, I distinguish between them by generally referring to Kameyama by name. Titles such as Abbot, Counsellor and so on, are approximate equivalents, since no exact equivalents exist in English. Nijō's naming scrupulously distinguishes between her two secret lovers in their private roles (Akebono and Ariake) and their public roles (respectively, Sanekane and His Holy Eminence), and I have preserved this distinction where possible. (See page xxvii for a list of the main characters cross-referenced with their titles.)

Japan at this time used the Chinese lunar calendar, in which the full moon is on the fifteenth day of each month. The new year (the first day of the first month) began on the first day of spring, which usually fell somewhere between our early February and early March. At birth a child was one year old, and one's age increased at each new year. Since the exact date of birth is often not known, precise ages are impossible to calculate, so I have retained the ages as given in the text.

I have based my translation on Iwanami's Shin Nihon Koten Bungaku Taikei edition of *Towazugatari*, annotated by Misumi Yōichi, while also consulting Shinchōsha's Nihon Koten Bungaku Shūsei edition, annotated by Fukuda Hideichi.

There are two previous translations of *Towazugatari*: *Lady Nijō's Own Story: The Candid Diary of a Thirteenth-Century Japanese Imperial Concubine*, translated by Wilfrid Whitehouse and Eizo Yanagisawa (Charles E. Tuttle, 1974); and *The Confessions of Lady Nijō*, translated by Karen Brazell (Stanford University Press, 1976).

NOTES

1. *women's diaries*: The usual translation of the term *joryū nikki*, although these works are often closer to a loose journal or memoir than to day-to-day diary entries.
2. *the age of fourteen*: A girl was considered an adult and legitimately able to have a sexual partner the year she turned fourteen. Here, as in the translation, I retain the age as given in the text (see A Note on the Translation above).
3. *his own son would take his turn . . . had stepped down*: This was the origin of a system of alternating succession between these rival branches of the imperial family that continued for approximately sixty years.
4. *four children*: She describes a fifth pregnancy, to Go-Fukakusa, but makes no further mention of it. Presumably the child was either miscarried or stillborn.

5. *hastily removed at birth ... officially recognized daughter of Sanekane*: It is likely that she was one of Sanekane's three daughters who became high-ranking consorts to later emperors.

6. *the betrayal in his abandonment of her*: See page 132.

7. *their continuing bond was paramount*: It was not exclusive, however. She and Ariake also speak of the deep karmic bond that will continue to unite them through future rebirths.

8. *instruction and devotion*: Devotion generally took the form of prayers, sutra chanting and copying rather than meditation. Zen had only recently arrived in Japan, though one of Nijō's relatives was Dōgen, the renowned founder of Zen's Sōtō Sect.

9. *there was little distinction between the two*: Native gods were considered to be local avatars of Buddhist deities.

10. *make a complete copy of the major Buddhist sutras*: Painstaking copying of holy texts was a common form of Buddhist devotion.

11. *a recurring theme throughout the work*: 'If only someone somewhere cared enough to ask', as one of her poems puts it.

12. *the poems scattered throughout the memoir*: It has been suggested that the pages that originally followed the final page of the work as we have it contained an anthology of her poetry.

List of Principal Characters

AKEBONO: Abbreviation of 'Yuki no Akebono' (Snowy Dawn), Nijō's private poetic name for her lover **Sanekane**.

ARIAKE: Abbreviation of 'Ariake no Tsuki' (Dawn Moon), Nijō's private poetic name for her lover who is believed to have been **Go-Fukakusa**'s half-brother Prince Shōjō, abbot of the imperial temple Ninnaji. Referred to in public situations by his title 'His Holy Eminence'.

CROWN PRINCE (1265–1317): Son of **Go-Fukakusa** and **Lady Genkimon'in**, he later reigned as the 92nd Emperor Fushimi.

GENKIMON'IN (?–1329): Second Consort of **Go-Fukakusa**. Mother of Emperor Fushimi.

GO-FUKAKUSA (1243–1304): Reigned as 89th emperor, 1246–60. Nijō's primary lover, referred to by her as 'His Highness'. Father of Emperor Fushimi and **Yūgimon'in**.

GO-SAGA (1220–1272): Reigned as 88th emperor, 1242–46. Father of Emperors **Go-Fukakusa** and **Kameyama**. Referred to by his title 'His Cloistered Excellency'.

HIGASHI NIJŌ'IN (1232–1304): Primary consort of **Go-Fukakusa**. Daughter of **Lady Kitayama**. Sister of **Lady Ōmiya'in**. Mother of **Yūgimon'in**. Referred to by Nijō as 'Her Highness'.

HIS HIGHNESS: See **Go-Fukakusa**.

HIS HOLY EMINENCE: See **Ariake**.

IINUMA (?–1293): Son of Taira no Yoritsuna, effective ruler in Kamakura.

IMPERIAL PRIESTESS: Kaishi Naishinnō, a half-sister of **Go-Fukakusa**, and Nijō's half-aunt. For some years she was imperial priestess at the Ise Shrine.

KAMEYAMA (1249–1305): Reigned as 90th emperor, 1260–74. Son of **Go-Saga**, half-brother of **Go-Fukakusa**. When his son Go-Uda was named as the next emperor, a succession dispute broke out between Kameyama and his rival **Go-Fukakusa**.

KANEHIRA (1228–1294): Takatsukasa Kanehira. Regent and Chancellor, who forced his attentions on Nijō with the connivance of **Go-Fukakusa**.

KITAYAMA (1195–1302): Mother of **Lady Ōmiya'in** and **Higashi Nijō'in**, grandmother of **Go-Fukakusa** and **Kameyama**. Wife of Saionji Saneuji and grandmother of **Sanekane**. Sister of Shijō **Takachika** and Nijō's great-aunt, giving Nijō tenuous imperial status.

KOGA MASATADA (1225?–1272): Nijō's father. A high-ranking noble who served in **Go-Saga's** court. Head of the Koga clan.

NIJŌ (1258–1308?): The author. Daughter of **Koga Masatada**, concubine of Retired Emperor **Go-Fukakusa**. Personal name Akako.

ŌMIYA'IN (1225–1292): The Empress Dowager, **Go-Saga's** primary consort, mother of **Go-Fukakusa** and **Kameyama**. Referred to by her title 'Her Cloistered Highness'.

SANEKANE (1249–1322): Saionji Sanekane. Nijō's lover 'Akebono'. A high-ranking noble who played a key role in the succession dispute negotiations between **Go-Fukakusa** and the government in Kamakura.

TAKAAKI (1243–?): Shijō Takaaki. Also called the Zenshōji Counsellor. Nijō's maternal uncle, son of **Takachika**.

TAKACHIKA (1203–1283): Shijō Takachika. Nijō's maternal grandfather, father of **Takaaki**, brother of **Lady Kitayama**.

YŪGIMON'IN (1270–1307): Daughter of **Go-Fukakusa** and **Higashi Nijō'in**. She later became primary consort of Emperor Go-Uda.

ZENSHŌJI COUNSELLOR: See **Takaaki**.

Timeline of Principal Events

Ages use the traditional Japanese counting system, in which a person is one year old in the year of their birth. A person's age is given in brackets after the name.

Dates for events not recorded in A Tale Unasked *are given in square brackets.*

[1258] Nijō, private name Akako, born
[1259] Nijō's mother dies
[1261] Nijō (4) goes to live in Retired Emperor Go-Fukakusa's palace

BOOK 1

1271.1 Go-Fukakusa first sleeps with Nijō (14)
8 Higashi Nijō'in, primary consort of Go-Fukakusa, gives birth to a daughter
9? Retired Emperor Go-Saga falls ill
1272.2 Go-Saga (53) dies
5 Nijō's father falls ill
6 Nijō (15) discovers she is pregnant
8 Nijō's father (50) dies
10 Akebono sleeps with Nijō
1273.2 Nijō (16) gives birth to a son
1274.1 Emperor Kameyama (26) retires, Go-Uda (8) becomes emperor
9 Nijō (17) gives birth to Akebono's daughter
10 Nijō's son dies

11 Go-Fukakusa sleeps with his half-sister the Imperial Priestess

Book 2

1275.3 Ariake confesses his love. Kameyama shows interest in Nijō (18)

   9 Ariake sleeps with Nijō

1276.9 Nijō (19) attempts to sever relations with Ariake

1277.3 Upset by her grandfather's behaviour, Nijō (20) goes into hiding
     She is pregnant

   4 She re-encounters the daughter she bore Akebono

   8 With the connivance of Go-Fukakusa, Kanehira sleeps with Nijō

1278–80 *No recorded events*

Book 3

1281.2 Go-Fukakusa discovers Nijō's (24) relationship with Ariake

  10 Pregnant with Ariake's child, she goes into retreat at Saga

  11 She gives birth to Ariake's son. Ariake visits. Ariake dies of the plague

1282.3 Nijō (25) realizes she is pregnant with Ariake's child

   4 Go-Fukakusa suspects her of an affair with Kameyama

   8 She secretly gives birth to Ariake's son and suckles him

1283.3/4 Nijō (26) is ordered to leave the Palace

  11 She begins a thousand-day retreat at Gion

1284.2 Nijō (27) makes an offering of a cherry branch at Gion

1285.1 Nijō (28) is invited to the birthday celebrations of Lady Kitayama

 2–3 She attends the three-day party

[Yūgimon'in is elevated to primary consort of Go-Uda after the birth of Prince Go-Nijō]

1286–88 *No recorded events*
[Emperor Go-Uda retires 1287, Fushimi takes the throne. Yūgimon'in is his primary consort]

Book 4

1289.2 Nijō (32) sets off along the Tōkaidō Highway
    3 She calls at Atsuta, Mishima, Enoshima
  4–6 She falls ill while staying in Kamakura
    8 She watches the Shōgun's procession in Kamakura
  12 She goes to Musashino
1290.2 Nijō (33) goes to Zenkōji
[Go-Fukakusa takes Buddhist orders]
    9 She returns to the capital
  10 She goes to Nara
1291.2 Nijō (34) meets Go-Fukakusa at Hachiman
    4 She goes to Ise and Futami
  6? She returns to Atsuta, finishes sutra copying and presents it
  1292 *No recorded events*
  [9] Ōmiya-in (68) dies
  1293 Nijō (36) meets Go-Fukakusa at Fushimi
1293? Nijō (37) returns to Futami
1293–1301 *No recorded events*
[1298] Emperor Fushimi retires. Go-Fushimi takes the throne
Go-Nijō (14) becomes Crown Prince
[1301] Emperor Go-Fushimi retires. Go-Nijō (17) becomes emperor

Book 5

1302.9 Nijō (45) goes to Itsukushima
She goes to Matsuyama
  11 She goes to Wachi and is almost abducted
1303.2 Nijō (46) goes to Bichū and on to the capital
1304.1 Higashi Nijō'in (73) dies

6 Nijō (47) learns that Go-Fukakusa is ill
7 She goes to Hachiman to pray for him
   She visits him on the 15th. He dies the following
   day. She goes to Tennōji
9 She attends Go-Fukakusa's 49th-day memorial
   ceremony at Fushimi
1305.3 Nijō (48) goes to the poet Hitomaro's grave
7 She attends Go-Fukakusa's first-year memorial
   ceremony at Fushimi
   She learns of Kameyama's illness
9 She goes to Kumano
10 She returns to the capital and learns that Kameyama (57) has died
1306.3 Nijō (49) goes to Hachiman Shrine and encounters Yūgimon'in
7 She attends Go-Fukakusa's third-year memorial
   ceremony
[1307.7] Yūgimon'in (38) dies

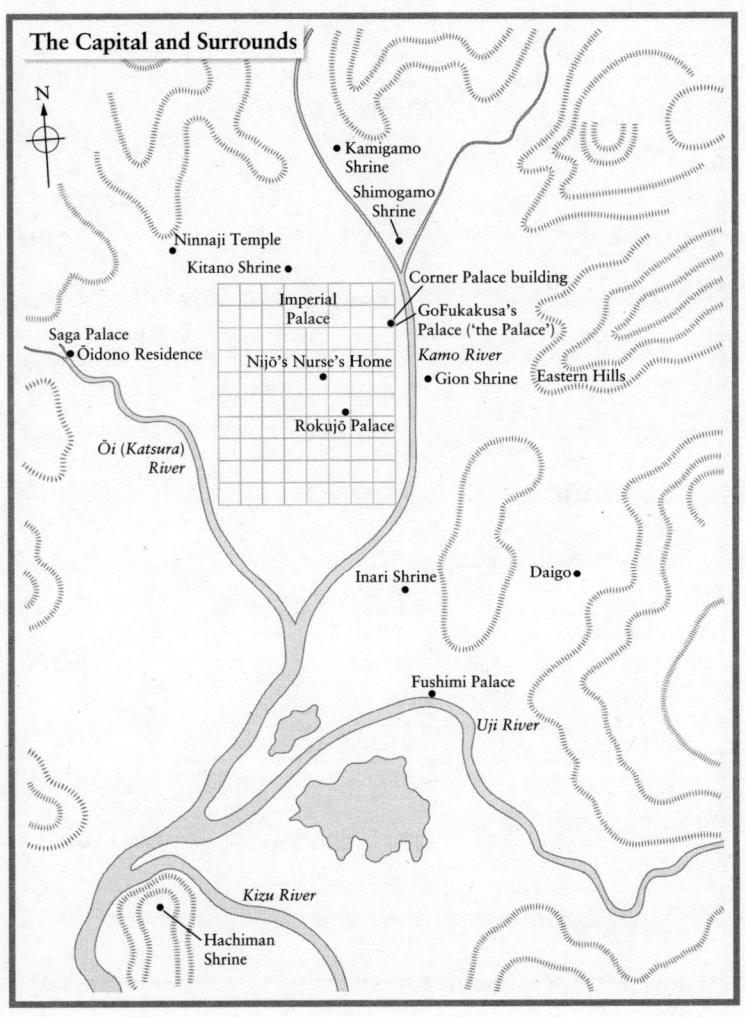

The Capital and Surrounds

N

- Kamigamo Shrine
- Shimogamo Shrine
- Ninnaji Temple
- Kitano Shrine
- Corner Palace building

Imperial Palace

- GoFukakusa's Palace ('the Palace')

Kamo River

- Saga Palace
- Ōidono Residence

Nijō's Nurse's Home

- Gion Shrine

Eastern Hills

Rokujō Palace

Ōi (Katsura) River

- Inari Shrine
- Daigo

Fushimi Palace

Uji River

Kizu River

- Hachiman Shrine

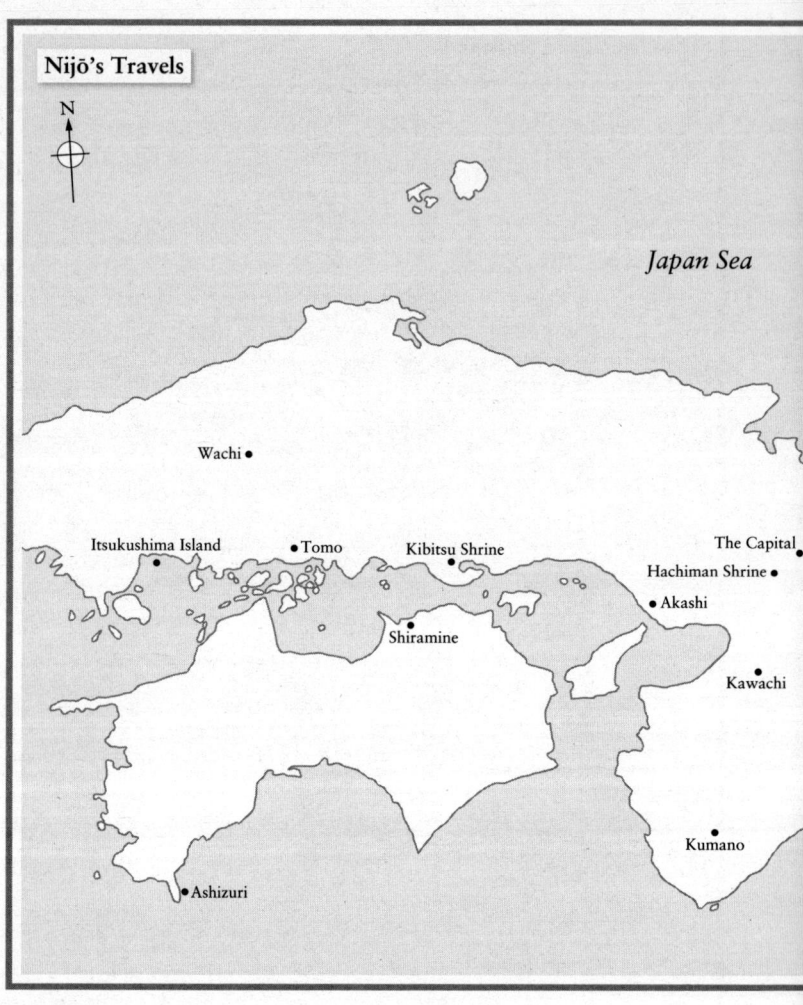

Nijō's Travels

N

Japan Sea

Wachi ●

Itsukushima Island ● ● Tomo   Kibitsu Shrine ●   The Capital ●
                                              Hachiman Shrine ●
                                              ● Akashi
                    Shiramine
                                              Kawachi ●

                                              Kumano ●

● Ashizuri

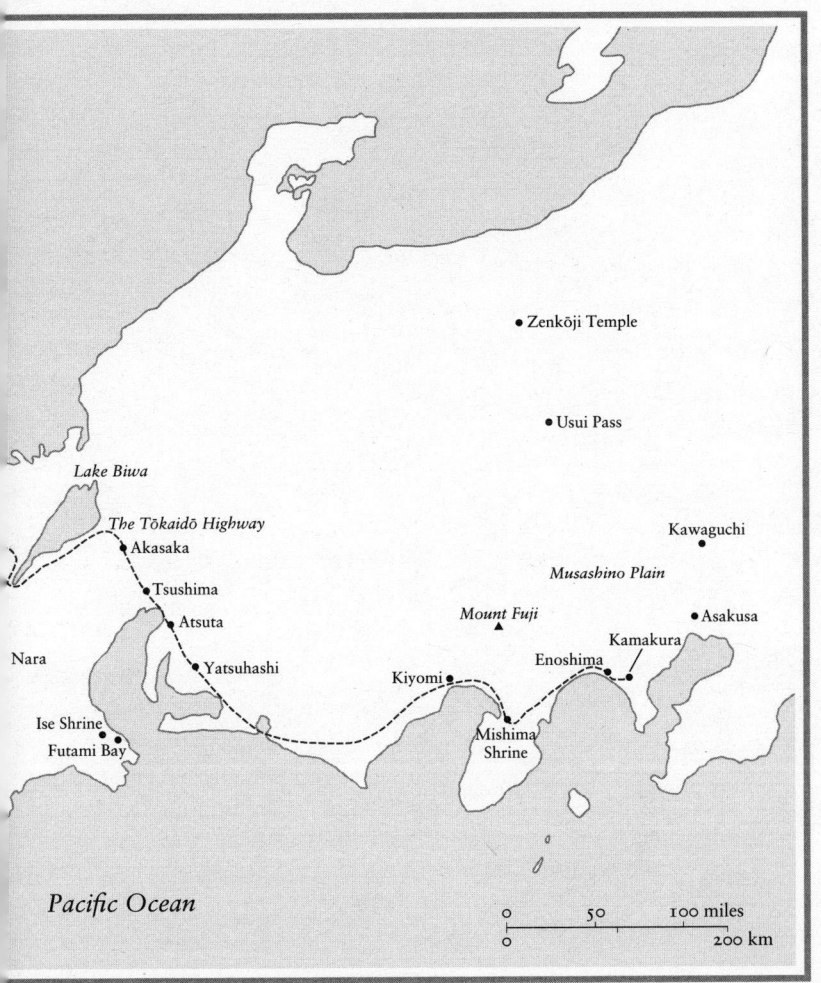

Zenkōji Temple

Usui Pass

Lake Biwa

The Tōkaidō Highway

Akasaka

Tsushima

Atsuta

Nara

Yatsuhashi

Ise Shrine

Futami Bay

Kiyomi

Mishima
Shrine

Mount Fuji

Musashino Plain

Kawaguchi

Asakusa

Kamakura

Enoshima

Pacific Ocean

0   50   100 miles
0   200 km

A Tale Unasked

BOOK 1

(1270–1274)

Night lifted with the rising mists of spring, and this New Year's morning in impatient excitement, the Palace ladies sat formally gathered, bedecked as blossoms and each vying in beauty, myself not least among them. I was, I think, in seven-layered budding plum-pink combination colours, with glossed silk over-robe of scarlet, outer robe of spring-shoot green and Chinese jacket in the special red;[1] beneath this I wore a double inner gown with a raised brocade pattern of plum blossom and twining grasses on an embroidered ground depicting Chinese-style woven fences and plum trees.

My father the Major Counsellor was the server of the New Year's Day ritual herbs for His Highness.[2] After the public ceremony was over, my father was invited within, the ladies-in-waiting were summoned, and there was some wholesale carousing with the Exchange of Cups.[3]

Three sets of exchanges had already taken place at the public ceremony, and my father suggested that they drink the same number here, but His Highness declared that they would now perform not three but nine sets of exchanges. All present were thoroughly drunk by the time His Highness presented his cup to my father with the words, 'This spring I want the "little wild goose"[4] to come to me.' My father bowed deeply, and when he had performed the nine exchanges he rose to leave – but as he did so it seemed to me that His Highness said something to him very quietly, though I had no way of guessing what it was.

Once all the formalities were over I slipped back to my room, where I found a letter from a certain man.[5] 'Today this letter seeks to make its mark on the pristine snows of yesterday, in hopes of perpetuity . . .',[6] it said. With it was a set of eight gowns in graded shades of plum, together with a deep scarlet unlined gown, a spring-shoot green outer robe, Chinese jacket, *hakama* trousers, a set of three *kosode* gowns and another set of two, all parcelled up together in a cloth wrapping.

This was most unexpected and disconcerting, but when I went to return them I discovered a piece of thin paper attached to one of the sleeves, where I read this:

Though our two wings	*tsubasa koso*
may never fold together	*kasanuru koto no*
in married love	*kanawazu to*
wear close and cherished	*kite dani nare yo*
these crane's-down clothes I send	*tsuru no kegoromo*

It was cruel of me to return what had been given with such feeling, I thought, so to accompany the package I wrote in response to his poem:

Separate as we are	*yosonagara*
would it be right	*narete wa yoshi ya*
to wear so close these night robes	*sayogoromo*
since their sleeves must moulder	*itodo tamoto no*
from the lonely tears I weep?	*kuchi mo koso sure*

'Perhaps if love were to remain unchanged . . .', I added.

Late that night, while I was absent on night duty, someone knocked at the back door. Without a thought the little maid opened it, but she reported that the messenger simply handed over a package and disappeared again without waiting for a reply. It was the same one that I had sent back:

If your loving heart	*chigiri okishi*
that swore devotion	*kokoro no sue no*
remains indeed unchanged	*kawarazu wa*
spread these beneath you	*hitori kata-shike*
for your lonely nights	*yowa no sagoromo*

This time I had no way of returning the gift, and so I kept it.

I wore these robes on the third, on the occasion of His Highness's father His Cloistered Excellency Go-Saga's visit to the Palace. 'What particularly lovely colours and lustre!' my father remarked when he saw me. 'Did you receive those robes from His Highness?'

'Oh no,' I answered nonchalantly, my heart beating fast. 'They came from Her Excellency Lady Kitayama.'[7]

On the evening of the fifteenth, someone from my father's home at Kawasaki arrived to fetch me back from the Palace. Unhappy though I was at such an abrupt summons, I couldn't very well refuse, so back I went. I was surprised to find the house unusually finely decked out, with particular care taken over the folding screens, tatami mats, standing curtains and drapes, but I assumed it was for the New Year festivities and thought no more of it, and so the day ended.

The next morning there was a great fuss about preparations for some special guest's food, and talk of 'the senior courtiers' horses' and 'the nobles' carriage oxen'. My tonsured grandmother also arrived and joined in the general buzz of excitement. I asked what was going on, at which my father grinned. 'Oh, His Highness has said he will be paying us a visit this evening because of a directional taboo,[8] and since it's around New Year we are making the place particularly splendid. I've brought you home expressly to serve his meal.'

'But this isn't the *setsubun* evening[9] or anything,' I said. 'What directional taboo is this?'

'Oh dear, you're hopeless!' he declared, amid general chuckles.

But for some reason I had no way of knowing, my own room too was being decked out with particularly splendid folding screens and small standing curtains. 'What's all this finery?' I wanted to know. 'Is this room going to be used for some special occasion as well?' This caused further laughter, but no explanations were forthcoming.

That evening, a white three-layered unlined gown and deep scarlet *hakama* trousers were provided for me to wear. Incense was burned to unobtrusively scent the room, with a great deal more care and solemnity than usual. Once the lamps were lit, my father's wife[10] brought in a colourful *kosode* gown and instructed me to put it on. A little later, my father appeared with a special robe hanger.[11]

'You must stay awake until His Highness arrives, and be prepared to serve him,' he told me. 'Remember, a palace lady should always be unresisting and do as she's told,' he added. With no way of knowing what these instructions might be about, and feeling rather put out by all the fuss, I settled down by the brazier and fell asleep.

And after that? Well, without my knowing it His Highness arrived. My father ushered in the carriage and bustled about giving orders; then it was time to produce the meal. There were cries of 'That ridiculous girl has gone and fallen asleep! Quick, wake her up!'

Overhearing the fuss, His Highness insisted, 'No no, just let her sleep', and so I was left in peace. Meanwhile, having snuggled up beside the brazier near the entrance to my room and pulled my gown over me, I had dozed off and was quite unaware of all this.

Sometime later I started awake to find that the lamp was almost out, someone had lowered the room drapes, and beside me where I slept beyond the screen another person was companionably lying.

I leapt up in amazement and tried to flee. He held me back. He had loved me since I was a little child, he said, had waited down the years until I was fourteen, and so on and so forth, more than I have words to describe here. I did not listen but only wept, so much indeed that I drenched his sleeves as well as my own. Vainly though he tried to comfort me, he did not force himself on me. 'After all these years of unfulfilled longing, I decided this was the moment. Everyone already knows I am here with you tonight; surely there's no point now in continuing to refuse me,' he pleaded.

It was true, I thought, this was no secret dream, people knew of it, and no sooner would this night's dream be over than it would come to weigh on me . . . strange that I should have been so aware of all this at such a moment.

If this had been his plan why hadn't he explained? Why hadn't

I been allowed to talk things over with my father? 'Oh how can I show my face to people now?' I sobbed. This made him laugh. Clearly he thought me hopelessly naive, and this threw me into fresh misery. All night I lay there, refusing to respond with so much as a single word, until at dawn the household began to stir around us.

'I believe His Highness will be departing today, won't he?' I heard someone say.

'"Leaving the next morning looking smug"',[12] he quoted softly to himself.

As he set about preparing to go, he continued to protest and placate me by turns. 'I must say, your extraordinary behaviour last night has left me feeling that the bond we've had since you were little was all for nothing. Now you must be careful not to raise people's suspicions. What will they think if you lie here refusing to come out?' But I still remained stubbornly silent.

'Oh, you're hopeless!' he declared, and with this he finally rose, put on his robes, and ordered his carriage to be brought round.

I heard my father inquiring if His Highness would take breakfast, and it seemed to me I could never face him again. If only I were still that innocent girl I had been yesterday!

I was told that His Highness had left, but still I lay there huddled under the night robe, until before I knew it there came an announcement that a letter[13] from His Highness had arrived for me. Oh woe is me! I thought. My father's wife and grandmother now came to inquire what the matter was and why I still lay there. Hating the thought that others must assume I was suffering the after-effects of a first night of love, I miserably replied that I had been feeling bad since the night before.

People kept fussing about this letter that had arrived, but I had no intention of reading it. 'Come come, His Highness's messenger is being kept waiting. Where is your reply?' they urged, and then someone said, 'Go and tell her father.' It was all too much to bear.

'I hear you're feeling bad,' he said as he arrived, and then, when he was told about the problem of His Highness's letter, 'This is ridiculous! You mean to say you're not going to respond to it?' I heard him opening it.

On thin scarlet-purple paper was written the poem:

After long years	*amata toshi*
that robe grown so familiar –	*sasuga ni nareshi*
though our sleeves	*sayogoromo*
last night remained unjoined	*kasanenu sode ni*
its lingering scent still haunts me	*nokoru utsurika*

Everyone read the poem and proceeded to discuss it, remarking that I was certainly unlike other young girls these days. I simply continued to lie there, feeling more and more wretched.

At a loss, my father declared that it would be impolite to send back something written in another hand,[14] and he simply gave the messenger a reward for his services, apparently adding some message to the effect that his impossible daughter was still lying in bed and so had not yet seen His Highness's letter.

Around noon came a letter from an unexpected quarter.[15] Reading it, I found the following:

Henceforth I would die	*ima yori ya*
for love of you	*omoi-kienan*
were your affections	*hitokata ni*
to drift a different way	*keburi no sue no*
trailing like smoke and gone	*nabiki-hatenaba*

'I have managed to survive until this moment thanks to my trust in you,' he wrote. 'But what now?' It was written on pale blue paper with a coloured design of the poem 'Gone like the clouds / that hide Mount Yearning'.[16] Tearing off the part that said 'Mount Yearning', I simply wrote on it in reply:

You cannot know	*shirareji ya*
these tangled feelings	*omoi-midarete*
deep within my heart –	*yū-keburi*
no mere evening smoke	*nabiki mo yaranu*
that drifts a different way	*shita no kokoro wa*

I sent it off, but found myself wondering what I was doing.

And so the day passed. That evening I couldn't even face a warm medicinal drink, and everyone was by now wondering whether I might have some other illness after all.

It had grown dark when there came an announcement that His Highness was here again. Before I had time to wonder what would happen this time, he drew open the door and in he came, very casual. 'I hear you're not well,' he said. 'What's the matter?' Question though he may, I hadn't the heart to respond but simply lay there.

He settled down beside me then and continued with all kinds of importunings. By now it was becoming hard to refuse him, and I was on the verge of softening a little by quoting the old poem 'If only words were never false'[17] – but I thought of how wrong it would be to that other man who would learn that the smoke had indeed drifted as he feared, and so I was torn and continued to remain stubbornly silent, and this evening he dealt with me quite mercilessly, so that lying there, knowing my thin gown ripped and all now surely lost, the very thought of my own existence and of the coming dawn filled me with bitterness:

Despite my heart	*kokoro yori*
these secret strings	*hoka ni tokenuru*
undone now –	*shita-hibo no*
surely my name too	*ika naru fushi ni*
must soon be sullied	*ukina nagasan*

Such thoughts filled my mind – and it is strange that even at such a moment I could be so aware.

'Though we may be reborn in different forms, our bond will never cease. Though we spend nights apart, no distance will ever lie between our hearts.' So said His Highness, and much else besides, while the brief night drew to a dreamless close and the bells began to toll the dawning day.

'It would make things uncomfortable if everyone were to be thrown into a flurry by my presence once day has come,' he declared, rising to go. 'You may not be longing for me to stay, but at least come out to bid me farewell', and he was so

persistent that I felt I could not remain heartless enough to
refuse. Slipping a light unlined gown over the gown soaked by
my night of tears, I emerged to stand at the doorway.

The moon, two nights past the full, was sinking in the west,
while in the east floated a low bank of clouds, and seeing him
there clad in hunting costume of spring-shoot green on saffron
red with pale mauve robe over heavy brocade *hakama* trousers,
why was it, how had I come to learn, this feeling I now felt –
that he looked suddenly splendid?

My uncle the Zenshōji Counsellor,[18] in pale blue hunting
costume, drew up the imperial carriage. Count Tamekata, who
was at the time Deputy Chief of the Appointment's Office, was
the sole senior courtier in attendance, along with several lower
palace guardsmen and other servants. As His Highness's carriage was being drawn up, a knowing cock was crowing its
heart out as if to wake the world, while the mournful dawn
tolling of the nearby Kannon Temple bell seemed to be giving
voice to my own sorrows. 'Left and right each sleeve / soaked
with differing tears', to borrow Prince Genji's words[19] – and
indeed he may have felt just as I now did, I thought.

Still His Highness did not leave, but lingered urging me to go on
with him along his lonely homeward road. It felt wrong to doubt
him as I did, yet I remained standing there in a tumult of conflict-
ing emotions as the clear moon of dawn slowly paled in the sky.

'Oh dear, you look so miserable!' he declared, and with that
he gathered me up and put me in his carriage and off we set,
before I could so much as tell my father what was happening.
It was like a scene out of some old tale, and I simply sat there
wondering what the future held for me:

Despite the tolling bell	*kane no oto ni*
there is no waking	*odoroku to shi mo*
from what seemed a dream –	*naki yume no*
its lingering taste	*nagori mo kanashi*
sad beneath dawn's sky	*ariake no sora*

On we went, and his continuing vows of love might have lent
the scene the charming air of some romantic tale of abduction,

but my distress only grew as we travelled on, my own tears all I could turn to in my wretchedness, and so we reached the Palace.

The carriage was drawn in through the middle gate to the corner palace building,[20] and His Highness descended. Turning to my uncle the Zenshōji Counsellor, he said, 'She's still such a baby, I just couldn't abandon her there. Keep this quiet for now, and look after her', and with that he retired to his own quarters.

It felt a very different Palace from the place I had known so well since childhood. Suddenly fearful and constrained, wretched at having come away so precipitately and deeply anxious about what might befall me, I wept ceaselessly. Then I heard my father arriving, and it moved me to think that he must be worrying over me.

The Zenshōji Counsellor informed him of His Highness's instructions. 'It won't do at all to keep her hidden away unacknowledged like this at this point,' I heard my father declare. 'His Highness should restore her to the usual position.[21] Keeping it all secret will only make things worse when the story gets out', and with that he left again.

Truly, I thought, what will come of this? I was feeling even more miserably awkward and out of place when His Highness appeared again, but he proceeded to shower me with such endearments that I gradually grew comforted, and found myself thinking that after all this was meant to be, and our previous lives had ordained this bond.

So things continued for ten days, with His Highness never failing to come to me each night; yet my heart was still troubled over that other man who had been so fearful of where that 'smoke' would drift.

Meanwhile, my father continued to insist that it wasn't right for me to be kept there in this manner, and so ten days later I returned home. I hid away unhappily in my room, finding it unbearable to be seen by others, and everyone assumed I must still be feeling indisposed. Then a heartfelt letter from His Highness arrived, declaring that after our recent time together his feelings had grown all the stronger, that the days without me were weighing on him and I must hurry back. With it was this poem:

You may not feel	kaku made wa
such love as I for you	omoi-okoseji
but I would show you	hito shirezu
secretly these sleeves	misebaya sode ni
soaked with my tears	kakaru namida wo

Although I had found his earlier letter thoroughly irritating, this one I was eager to read, and perhaps my reply was a little over-expressive:

I cannot think	ware yue no
your love is meant for me	omoi naranedo
yet hearing of those tears	sayogoromo
my sleeve too	namida no kikeba
grows soaked	nururu sode kana

Before many days had passed I returned to the Palace, this time in the accepted role, but I was still somehow ill at ease there; slanderous rumours had sprung up already, it seemed, such as the story that my father pampered me and had me set up at the Palace like an official consort. Her Highness Higashi Nijō'in was by now looking distinctly displeased, and I felt increasingly dejected and insecure. His Highness didn't exactly stay away, but as the nights went by when he did not come, I was left more and more forlorn. I was also in no position to grumble, as my fellow ladies-in-waiting did, about escorting the other ladies who came and went to him, but I found it a miserable business to have to bow to the ways of the world like this. One way and another, my days were passed in wondering if 'one day I would recall / with longing fondness'[22] this present unhappiness – and so autumn arrived.

Around the eighth month I think it was, Her Highness Higashi Nijō'in was due to give birth in the corner palace building; since she was somewhat older[23] than is usual and her previous births had been difficult, everyone was very anxious, and all the ritual prayers and incantations were performed for her safety – the Shichibutsu Yakushi for salvation, the Godan no Mishiho for protection from calamity, the Fugen Enmei for long life, the Kongō Dōji for prosperity and protection, the great Nyohō Aizen'ō ritual and so on. The Godan Gundari ritual is always paid for by Owari, a province in my father's charge, but this time he announced that he felt particularly strongly about it and would therefore personally make the arrangements for both this and the Kongō Dōji rites. The officiating priest was the abbot of Jōjū Temple.

Soon after the twentieth, Her Highness's pains began, and there was much excitement. Everyone held their breath, expecting the birth from moment to moment, but several days passed and our anxiety grew. Then word arrived that there was some kind of change in Her Highness, and hearing this His Highness went to her side and found her looking very weak. The ritual priest was promptly summoned there, and proceeded to pray just beyond the standing curtain.

His Highness now called over the officiating high priest for the Nyohō Aizen'ō ceremony, the Omuro abbot, and told him that Her Highness seemed beyond saving. 'What can be done?' he asked.

'The buddhas and bodhisattvas have vowed that though our karmic fate is fixed, strength of faith can overcome it,' he replied. 'Have no fear.'

He then added to the ritual priests' chanting a scroll depicting Fudō Myōō, perhaps the very one that had come to the aid of Shōkū,[24] hanging it before Her Highness, rubbing his beads vigorously and chanting a powerful mantra.

'As a child I chanted prayers and sutras ceaselessly through the night,' he assured them, 'and now as a man my days are spent in fierce austerities, so I am assured of the favour and protection of the gods and buddhas.' He swished his beads with renewed vigour to expel the evil spirits,[25] and as the birth progressed his power grew, until smoke virtually rose from him.

Each of the ladies in attendance then presented from behind the blinds a double *kosode* gown or one of gossamer silk by way of gifts to celebrate the occasion, which the superintendent took and passed to a senior courtier, and the upper and lower palace guards gave them to each of the presiding priests. Seated outside at the foot of the stairs, the nobles were waiting with visible anticipation to welcome the birth of a prince.

The Yin-Yang Master[26] now set up his eight-legged altar table in the garden and proceeded to perform the one thousand purifications, and the ladies extended their sleeves from beneath the blinds to receive the purified objects delivered by a senior courtier. Next, the imperial attendants and lesser palace guards led in sacred white horses, which His Highness viewed before they were presented as an offering to the twenty-one great shrines.[27] It all struck me as very splendid,[28] and I felt that if one is to be given human life and be born a woman, this is the kind of treatment one should receive.

Next the great Tendai high priest was summoned, and the three attendant monks did a splendid job of chanting the Yakushi Sutra. Just as they reached the words *kenja kangi*, 'those who saw the child were filled with joy', Her Highness's child was born. Everyone both inside and outside the birthing room pronounced their congratulations, and the ritual steamer was rolled to the north[29] to signify the birth of a girl. It was a great shame. Nevertheless, gifts were presented to the priests just as usual.

Although the child turned out to be a princess, her grandfather His Cloistered Excellency Go-Saga doted on her, and particular care was taken over the fifth and seventh night ceremonies.[30]

One day after the celebrations were over, at around two in the morning, His Highness was chatting in his quarters when there was a great crashing sound in the Orange Garden, as of wild waves smashing onto rocks in a fierce gale.

'What ever was that?' he said to me. 'Go and see.'

I went, and there I witnessed ten or so creatures, bluish-white in colour and shining with astonishing brightness. Their egg-like heads varied from cup size to the size of a vinegar jar, and they went swirling up and up one after another, trailing long thin tails.

I shrieked and fled inside.

Some nobles who were on the veranda asked what all the commotion was about, and gave the opinion that they were departing souls. Then there was a great fuss when someone found some strange stuff like fragments of boiled seaweed lying strewn about under the big willow.

A divination was hastily performed, and it was announced that the cause was the wandering spirit of His Cloistered Excellency Go-Saga, so that evening a ritual was performed to recall the soul to the body and propitiations were offered to Taizan Buku, the god of longevity.[31]

And so it was that around the ninth month, Go-Saga was reported to be ill. His body became swollen, and though there was much bustling about applying moxibustion[32] and so forth it had no real effect. His condition worsened from day to day, and so the year drew to a close.

The new year came but still His Cloistered Excellency remained ill, and there were none of the usual celebrations. Around the end of the first month, when it seemed he was beyond help, he removed to his Saga Palace[33] in a palanquin. His Highness very soon followed, with myself in attendance behind him in the carriage. Her Highness Higashi Nijō'in and the empress dowager Lady Ōmiya'in, Go-Saga's consort, rode together, attended by Lady Mikushige[34] sitting behind.

The medicinal tea that His Cloistered Excellency was to take along the way was placed in two flasks in his presence by the court physicians Tanenari and Moronari, and Tsunetō[35] ordered the lower guardsman Nobutomo to carry them, but when they reached Uchino and he went to drink the tea it was discovered that there was not a drop in either flask. It was very strange. Thereafter this inexplicable event must have weighed heavily on his spirits, for rumour had it that he seemed to be growing worse and worse.

During his visit, His Highness stayed at the Ōidono residence, the home of his mother the empress dowager, in the grounds of the Saga Palace. Day and night he ceaselessly sent messengers, sometimes a man and sometimes one of us ladies or a senior or junior servant, to enquire how his father was. I remember walking along the passage connecting the two buildings, hearing the Ōi River flowing close by and feeling quite desolate at the sound.

The second month began, and now His Cloistered Excellency seemed to be awaiting the moment of death. On the ninth the two Rokuhara constables[36] arrived to pay their respects. Each offered his condolences, which were duly announced by the Saionji Counsellor Sanekane.[37]

His Majesty Kameyama travelled in state to visit his father on the eleventh, and remained there during the twelfth. On the thirteenth there was much bustling about for his departure, but the imperial palace itself remained hushed, and loud sounds were suppressed. His Highness had an audience with His Majesty Kameyama, and the sight of both brothers reduced to floods of tears was enough to 'moisten every eye with dew'.

At around six on the evening of the fifteenth, a great column of smoke rose in the direction of the capital. Whose home can be going up in flames? we all wondered. Then came the news that the fire was at the residence of the Rokuhara Constable Hokujō no Tokisuke, who had just been attacked and killed.[38] How swiftly fortunes turn! He had called on His Cloistered Excellency only a few days earlier to express his condolences, and now he himself had preceded the already perilously frail sovereign into death. Late and soon, death haunts our every moment, yet though there is nothing new in this, how very sad. His Cloistered Excellency never learned of this untimely death, having lost all power of speech since the evening of the thirteenth.

Then, on the morning of the seventeenth, there was a great stir at the news that his condition had taken a turn for the worse. Abbot Keikai and the head of nearby Ōjōin Temple arrived and set about praying and chanting.

'Past virtue brought you into this life as emperor, with a hundred officials at your beck and call. Salvation from hell must be assured. Rise now without delay to the lotus seat of the highest realm of Paradise, and turn to lead thence the masses whom you leave behind in this world below.' So they addressed him, now cajoling, now exhorting, but his heart remained in the grip of the Three Attachments,[39] he spoke no word of repentance, and to the end there was no sign that the words of the teachings had turned his heart – and thus on the seventeenth of the

second month of Bun'ei 9 (1272) at around six in the morning
he died at the age of fifty-three. The heavens darkened, all were
sunk in grief, and everywhere the gaily coloured sleeves were
changed to the black of mourning robes.

On the eighteenth day, the bier was carried to the nearby
Yakusō Temple.[40] Middle Captain Sanefuyu arrived as a representative from the Imperial Palace, together with the princely
abbots[41] of Omuro, Enman-In, Shōgo-In, Bodai-In and Shōren-
In temples. The sorrow of that night passes description. Tsunetō
had been a particular favourite of His Cloistered Excellency,
and everyone was speculating that he would no doubt take holy
orders now;[42] but to the great surprise of all, when he bore the
cinerary urn to interment he was dressed not in Buddhist robes
but in a courtly hunting costume of soft crepe silk.

His Highness was more overcome with sorrow than any,
and wept ceaselessly day and night; we bystanders were moved
to tears to witness it. The world was plunged into imperial
mourning. The everyday cries announcing the time, heralding
comings and goings and so on, all ceased. One could almost
think that here 'even the flowers must bloom in mourning
black'.[43] My father was permitted to wear a blacker shade of
mourning robes than others and requested that I be allowed to
do the same, but His Highness declared that since I was still so
young, I should dress in the usual mourning colour and not dye
my robe a deeper shade.

My father begged both the empress dowager and His
Highness for permission to take holy orders, but after some
prevarication this was refused. He was exceptionally grief-
stricken and visited the grave daily, and he continued to plead
with His Highness, using the good offices of his cousin, Major
Counsellor Sadazane, to send the following petition:

'From the moment I first bowed in humble service to your
father the emperor at the age of nine, I was continually blessed
by his favour. After my father's death and the disinheritance
problems with my mother[44] my debt to him was particularly
heavy, and I served him all the more devotedly. Thus my progress up the ranks surpassed all reason, honours were heaped on
me, and smiles wreathed my face when I read the honours list

for each round of promotions; I have had no grounds for resentment either professionally or privately, and public office never weighed on my spirits. After His Highness left the throne I continued to be bathed in the light of his favour: night after night at the high banquets following the great festivals, for many a year I joined the later drinking party and its entertainments, while in the rehearsals for the supplementary Kamo Festival I was accustomed to wear the ritual purifying robe, and was honoured to see my reflection in the waters of the shrine's sacred stream.

'I rose to the upper second rank, became Major Counsellor, and am the head of my clan. I was granted the position of Chief Minister, but the General of the Right, Tsunetada, presented a petition arguing that this role should be granted only to one who had served as Imperial Guards General, and I was in the process of begging leave to resign the post when His Cloistered Excellency passed away.

'Though I live on, he who has been my support has faded and gone, leaving me bereft of any to turn to. Whatever my official position, I could find no worth in it. I have passed the age of fifty.[45] Who knows how many years are left to me? It is said that to sever all ties and relinquish one's fate to the Buddhist Way is the truest form of gratitude. I beg to be granted leave to fulfil my sincere desire to take holy orders, and to perform services for the soul of the departed.'

For all these heartfelt pleas, however, His Highness again responded that he was unable to grant his wish, and also spoke to him directly at length about it. And so one day passed and then another. It was not that grief was forgotten, but with the natural passage of time, taken up as it was day and night with attending memorial services for the dead, in no time the forty-nine days of mourning[46] were over, the ceremonies were at an end, and everyone returned to the capital. Then messages had to be sent to Kamakura on imperial business, various difficulties ensued,[47] and all too soon the month had ended and the general grief had lessened.

The fifth month is always a season to drench the sleeves with its rains, and the dew of my father's sorrowing tears lay thicker than the dews of autumn. He who never spent the night without a woman now altogether ceased this practice, and he gave up all drinking and partying as well. Perhaps this lay behind it, people said, but all agreed he seemed terribly thin and weak.

On the night of the fourteenth he went to a temple in Ōtani to hear the Nenbutsu service, and the carriage escorts for his return trip spoke worriedly of how yellow he looked. Concerned, we called a physician to examine him, who announced that he had jaundice. Too much was weighing on his mind, he said. Moxa[48] was copiously applied and we all waited anxiously to see how things would go, but he grew steadily worse. I was beside myself with anxiety, and to make matters worse I began to have morning sickness from around the sixth month as well. Awful though I felt, given the situation I couldn't bring myself to mention it.

Since he evidently had no hope of a return to health, my father announced, he wished only to join the late emperor in death as soon as possible, so there must be no prayers for recovery. He stayed for a while in his stepmother's residence, then in the seventh month on the night of the fourteenth he moved to his own house in Kawasaki. The smaller children were left behind while he calmly prepared himself for his end, but I was adult enough by now, I felt, so I alone returned home with him.

Noticing that I wasn't well, he was concerned at first that I had lost my appetite through worrying about him, and tried various ways of comforting me, until he suddenly understood.

'I believe you're pregnant!' he declared. This immediately restored his desire to live, and he set about ordering all manner of invocations to be made for his recovery, starting with a full seven-day Taizan Buku ceremony held in the great hall in Enryakuji Temple, then an outdoor *dengaku* performance at the seven altars of Hie Shrine, a day-long chanting of the Great Wisdom Sutra at Hachiman Shrine,[49] and the dedication of a stone pagoda on the riverbank.

Knowing that this was prompted not by any urge to cling to life but by the desire to live to see the child I would bear, I felt deeply sinful to be the cause of his sudden attachment to this world.

Since he seemed in no imminent danger, around the twentieth I returned to His Highness's Palace. Ever since His Highness had learned of my pregnancy he had been very solicitous and attentive, and I could only hope that things would continue thus 'eternal as the vine upon the wall'. Only recently in the sixth month, Lady Mikushige had died in childbirth, and I was fearful that I might share her fate; it also seemed more than likely that my father too would die, and I was filled with trepidation about what might become of me without his protection. And so the seventh month ended.

On the night of the twenty-seventh I believe it was, fewer people were about than usual when word came from His Highness asking me to come to his quarters. Alone together, we sat quietly talking of things past and present. He spoke of the tragic nature of life's transiency. 'I fear your father too is not long for this world,' he said, 'and when the worst happens you will have no one left to depend on. Who besides myself will be here to take pity on you?' He wept as he spoke, and his solicitude only increased my own sorrow. The night was moonless, and the lantern's faint glow barely lit the room where we sat in secret conversation. The evening drew on, and it had grown late when we heard sudden cries of someone who had come in search of me.

'Who is it?' I asked, and learned that word had arrived from home to tell me that it seemed the hour had come.

Without pausing to prepare, I immediately set off in all haste, dreading that I would arrive to hear he had already breathed his last. Hurry though I may, the road seemed so long that I could have been making my way on some endless journey through the far wilds of the East.

I arrived to find with joy that he still lived.

'The passing dew of my life now awaits the merest breeze to carry it off,' he wept tremulously. 'It weighs on me terribly to think that I go into death leaving you in your condition.'

As the temple bell rang out the lateness of the hour, there was a sudden announcement that His Highness had arrived. This was completely unexpected, and it flustered my ailing father. Hearing the carriage being drawn up, I hurried out to find that

His Highness was arriving accompanied only by two lower guardsmen and a senior courtier. A thin sliver of moon was just then lifting over the mountain rim, casting a wan and desolate light; His Highness's simple patterned imperial cloak of pale mauve spoke gratifyingly of the impulsiveness of his visit.

My father sent to him apologizing that he lacked even strength enough to slip on his court robe, so he could not contemplate an audience with His Highness. 'Yet simply to hear that you have graced me with a visit leaves me with a last precious memory for this life,' he ended – but no sooner was this message delivered than His Highness opened the door and came straight in.

Seeing my father struggling unsuccessfully to rise, His Highness said gently, 'No, stay as you are', put down a cushion and settled himself at the bedside. His tears flowed unstoppably. 'You have been so close beside me down the years since I was a child, and I felt such sorrow learning that your end is near, that I have come to see you one last time.'

'Your Highness, the joy of your visit overwhelms me,' replied my father, weeping too. 'All my fears are now for this poor daughter of mine. Her mother died when she was still an infant, and I was well aware as I raised her that I was all she had to turn to. And now to add to these woes I am leaving her when she is with child. My sorrow and pity for her are beyond words.'

'Inadequate though I am, be assured I will take all care of her,' His Highness promised. 'You mustn't let this attachment stand in the way of your path to Paradise.' He went on speaking tenderly until it was suggested that he should let my father rest awhile, and he left him in peace.

It was past daybreak when His Highness hastily departed, saying that it would be most unfortunate if he was observed being out in such a casual fashion. As he was leaving, my father had a servant deliver to his carriage a special *biwa*[50] that had belonged to his own father the Koga Chancellor, together with a sword given to his father by Emperor Go-Toba at the time of his exile.[51] Attached to its cord was a slip of thin pale blue paper on which he had written:

Though we part here	*wakarete mo*
knowing this bond lasts[52]	*miyo no chigiri no*
through three lifetimes	*ari to kikeba*
I yearn the more	*nao iku sue wo*
for the world to come	*tanomi bakari zo*

His Highness read this with deep emotion. He replied with assurances to my father that he must set his heart at rest, and other messages besides, and he had hardly left before a response poem written in his own hand arrived for my father.

Next time	*kono tabi wa*
we will meet again	*ukiyo no hoka ni*
beyond this sad world	*meguri-awamu*
in the awaited dawn	*matsu akatsuki no*
of that new day	*ariake no sora*

It moved and saddened me to see my father's pleasure in the thought that his poem had so touched His Highness.

On the second day of the eighth month, somewhat earlier than is usual, my uncle the Zenshōji Counsellor delivered the childbirth band[53] from His Highness for me to wear. 'His Highness kindly instructed me not to wear mourning clothes for this occasion,' he explained. He was indeed dressed in an everyday court cloak while his accompanying outriders and guards looked very proper, and it seemed to me that His Highness had hastened this happy event to ensure that my father was still here to witness it.[54] He delightedly ordered that sake be brought in for my uncle, and it smote my heart to think that this was perhaps his final joyful occasion. As a gift to him my father presented a splendid ox named Shiogama, which he had originally received from the Ninnaji abbot.

That day my father seemed somewhat improved, and I dared to hope that he was perhaps recovering. Night came, and I settled down beside him to rest a little and was soon fast asleep.

He shook me awake. 'Oh dear oh dear, whatever will become of you?' he began. 'I should be preparing myself for that path into death that I may be taking at any moment, and instead

I find myself wracked with anxiety over you. The mere sight of you sleeping there so innocently fills me with distress. Ever since your mother died when you were two I have worried over you alone. You among all my children have been the focus of all this devotion and love. Your least smile delighted me with your charms; I sorrowed with you when I saw you sad. Fifteen springs and autumns we have seen together, you and I, and now the time has come for us to part.

'As long as you serve His Highness and all goes well for you,' he went on, 'you must behave with due deference and never neglect your duties. And if things go awry, as can always happen, if His Highness and the world ever turn against you and you find yourself without the means to support yourself, then you must not hesitate to dedicate yourself to the Buddhist Way and ensure your salvation in the world to come, repaying your parents by praying for them and ensuring your rebirth on the same lotus. But if in your abandonment and need you choose to remain in the world, giving yourself to other men or even offering yourself from house to house for a living, understand that I will disown you from beyond the grave. Remember that the bond of man and woman lasts indissolubly through future rebirths. If you should choose not to become a nun but instead make yourself a name among the brothels it would be beyond bearing. But once you take religious vows and leave the world, you are free to do as you will.'

Listening to these heartfelt admonitions, I was miserably aware that these were surely his dying injunctions to me.

Dawn's temple bell began to toll, and Nakamitsu came in bearing the steamed plantain to spread under the invalid.[55] 'Let me just put some fresh leaves down,' he said, but my father stopped him.

'There's no point. My end feels very near now. Give this girl here something to eat, I don't care what.'

How could I eat anything just now? I thought, but he was urging me on – 'Quick. While I can still watch you. Come on!' Choked with sorrow at the knowledge that this was the last time I would ever eat before his eyes, I did my best to obey.

I was given an earthenware plate of yam balls,[56] but this only made him angry. 'This is a forbidden food for someone in her condition!' he declared. It was all very upsetting, and in the end I simply toyed with the food and pushed it away.

As dawn was breaking, it was decided to send for a priest. Back in the seventh month he had called in the elder from Yasaka Temple,[57] who had shaved his head and administered the Five Buddhist Vows, giving him the Buddhist name Renshō. We had assumed he would be the one to come now to help my father to salvation, but for some reason my grandmother had stepped in and insisted that we should instead contact Jōkō, the elderly priest from Kawara Temple,[58] so that is what happened.

We sent word that my father's condition was worsening, but Jōkō was apparently in no hurry to arrive.

Suddenly, my father said, 'The end is at hand. Sit me up!' Calling over Nakamitsu, Nakatsuna's eldest son[59] whom he had looked after since he was a child and who had served at his side all his life, he told him to prop him up, and he sat there leaning back on the young man for support with only a single lady-in-waiting by his elbow rest. I was beside him, and he told me to hold him by the wrist.

'Bring me the surplice that the priest gave me,' he said, and I draped it over the short *hitatare* robe of thick silk that was all he wore. 'Nakamitsu, you must chant the *nenbutsu* invocation[60] with me,' he then instructed, and the two of them proceeded to chant together for close on an hour.

He dozed a little as the sun was emerging, and began to tilt to the left as he sat. Seeing this I shook his knee to rouse him and help him continue to chant, whereupon he started awake, and his steady gaze met mine. 'Oh what will become of . . .' he said, and even as he spoke, at around seven on the third of the eighth month in the ninth year of Bun'ei,[61] at the age of fifty, he passed away.

If only his life had ended while chanting he would have been assured of future salvation, and I desperately regretted having needlessly wakened him so that with his last breath he had uttered those unfortunate words. My head swam. It seemed that the sun and moon above me had tumbled to earth and all light was gone; prostrate with grief, my tears flowed like a river.

Although my mother had died when I was two, that far-off time was gone leaving no trace in my innocent heart. Since that time forty-one days after my birth when I was first placed on my father's lap, fifteen springs and autumns had passed. Looking in my mirror each morning, I was filled with joy that what I saw there was thanks to him; dressing myself each evening, gratitude filled me at the debt I owed him. Thanks to him I had been granted life and limb, and that debt was higher than the heights of towering Mount Sumeru; he had taken on my mother's role in his devoted care for my upbringing, and for this too my gratitude was deeper than the world's oceans. It felt impossible ever to repay or to requite such debts. Words he had spoken rose unforgettably in my mind, and it seemed that all I felt now that he was no more would stay with me forever.

I longed for some way to stay with him and watch his body through to its end, but this I could not do, and so on the night of the fourth he was taken to the burning grounds of Mount Kagura. Watching the smoke rise from the funeral pyre, I yearned to be able to rise with it and follow him, but to no avail, and bitter tears were all the keepsake that I carried home. At the sight of this house now so empty without him, I was overwhelmed with the memory of that dear face I had seen so recently, and wept to think that now I would 'see him but in dreams'. Even the memory of his final injunctions to me filled me with inexpressible emotion:

May this sea of tears	*waga sode no*
that my sleeves hold	*namida no umi yo*
flow to death's river crossing	*mitsusegawa ni*
where I might glimpse	*nagarete kayoe*
at least his dear reflection	*kage wo dani mimu*

On the evening of the fifth, Nakatsuna arrived in monk's robes.[62] He had been assured of rising to the fourth rank if my father had become Chief Minister. How must he be feeling now? I wondered, and I felt a fresh wave of sorrow at the unforeseen sight of him dressed instead in these sombre robes.

'I am about to visit the grave,' he announced. 'What message might I carry from you?' The sight of those dark sleeves soaked with weeping brought tears to every eye.

On the ninth, which marked the first seven days since my father's death, my stepmother took religious orders, along with two ladies-in-waiting and two retainers. The priest from Yasaka Temple was called in to ritually shave their heads while intoning the ordination verses, and I watched with a mixture of envy and inexpressible sorrow. I longed to do as they did, but given my condition it was out of the question, and I wept inconsolably.

The thirty-seventh day ceremonies[63] were especially grand, and a number of heartfelt messages of condolence arrived from His Highness. Indeed barely a day passed without some message from him, and I did wish sadly that my father could still be here to witness these attentions.

Empress Kyōgoku, daughter of Chief Minister Tōin Saneo, was Emperor Kameyama's primary consort and so had his most particular affections, and as she was the mother of the Crown Prince,[64] she was most enviable in both rank and seniority, but she was constantly tormented by spirit possession.[65] Now she fell ill, and her sufferings were assumed by everyone to be from the usual cause, but then came the shocking news that she had suddenly died. I felt her father's sorrow and His Majesty's anguish as if they were my own, and the news caused fresh waves of grief.

For the thirty-fifth day ceremonies after my father's death, His Highness sent an offering for the dead in the form of two circlets of crystal prayer beads, together with a sprig of dew-spangled valerian in beaten gold and silver. With it was this poem:

Even in other years	*sarade dani*
the autumn dews	*aki wa tsuyukeki*
would soak the sleeves	*sode no ue ni*
but now your tears are added	*mukashi wo kouru*
in longing for the past	*namida souran*

This would have delighted my father and he would have made a great fuss over how to respond, so I replied with 'Even in his grave my father must be feeling overwhelmed at this honour', adding this poem:

Think of me now –	*omoe tada*
fresh tears of parting	*sarademo nururu*
added to the dew	*sode no ue ni*
that wets my sleeves	*kakaru wakare no*
already soaked with autumn	*aki no shiratsuyu*

It was indeed autumn, when the long sleepless nights are tinged with all-pervading sorrow, and lying there hearing the 'multitudinous voices' of the fulling blocks beating out their mournful song, head pillowed on a sleeve that glinted with 'the dew of my tears' shattered pearls', that dear face I would see no more was all that filled my yearning heart.[66]

On the morning after the dew of my father's life had faded, there had been an endless flow of messages from the imperial palaces and men of the highest ranks, all calling in person or sending to present their condolences, but among them only Major Counsellor Mototomo failed to appear.[67] It was most untoward.

Ever since that dawn when my father died, a certain man[68] had sent daily to ask after my well-being, and now, by the light of the ninth month's waxing moon, he came to visit. At this time everyone still wore black for His Cloistered Highness's death, and the figure he cut in his plain mourning robe felt of a piece with the colour of my own sorrow. Since I could hardly simply converse with him through a messenger, I arranged to see him in the southern guest room.

'This year has added such sorrow to the many past and present sorrows that we already bear,' he said, 'that our sleeves are never dry. One snowy night at a drinking party last year your father asked me to watch over you, you know. I felt it was an expression of his great love for you.'

Between tears and laughter we talked the night away until we heard the temple bells tolling the dawn. Truly, 'even the long autumn night seemed short when I was with him' and 'the dawn birds sang before our words were done', as the old poems put it.

'This will look suspiciously like a lovers' tryst if I'm seen,'[69] he said as he prepared to leave:

The sadness of death's parting	*wakareshi mo*
now freshly overlaid	*kesa no nagori wo*
to part from you, our sleeves	*tori-soete*
together wet with tears	*oki-kasanenuru*
in the morning dew	*sode no tsuyu kana*

Sorry to see him go, I sent a maid out to his carriage with this poem, and in response came this:

Can it be true	*nagori to wa*
your sadness is for me	*ikaga omowan*
when your parting sleeves	*wakarenishi*
are forever soaked	*sode no tsuyu koso*
in that past parting's sorrow	*hima nakarurame*

Still haunted by the feelings of the night, I recalled it all now in bewilderment, like one recalling some strange 'dream of passing love'. Then I noticed lingering by the middle gate a retainer dressed in hunting costume of dark plum red, who held a letter box – a message from him. It was very tender:

Unable to forebear	*shinobi-amari*
we spent one night of dream	*tada utatane no*
head pillowed on sleeve	*tamakura ni*
and now that night's brief dew	*tsuyu kakariki to*
may draw the blame of others	*hito ya togamuru*

At such a sad time, even a passing diversion such as this exchange lingered in my heart, and I too responded tenderly:

The dews of autumn	*aki no tsuyu wa*
lie on every leaf	*nabete kusaki ni*
of grass and tree	*oku mono wo*
so who could frown	*sode ni nomi to wa*
seeing our sleeves so wet?	*dare ga togamen*

On the forty-ninth day, my half-brother Captain Masaaki was in charge of the final memorial ceremony for our father, officiated by the priest from Kawara Temple, who rolled out the tired old 'loving pairs torn from each other's sheltering wings' cliché that even I recognized all too well. After this was over the high prelate Kenjichi presented as a memorial offering some pages of my father's handwriting on the back of which I had copied sections of the Lotus Sutra. The Sanjō Bōmon Counsellor, the Made no Kōji Counsellor, the Zenshōji Counsellor[70] and others came to attend the service and express their condolences, and it was sad to see each one go their various ways. Alone and in tears, I went to my old nurse's home at Shijō Ōmiya, bereft to have parted at last from everyone who had gathered to share the grief, and words cannot describe all that was in my lonely heart.

Even during these miserable days His Highness had been quietly calling on me, and urging me to present myself back at the Palace once the forty-nine days of mourning had passed, since the world was still dressed in mourning for His Cloistered Highness and my own sombre robes would be quite in keeping. I felt so low, however, that I remained in seclusion. The forty-ninth day fell on the twenty-third of the ninth month, when beneath a waning moon autumn's frail insect song added melancholy to my deep sorrow. 'Still shut away at home? Come, hurry and present yourself', came the message from the Palace, but I could not bring myself to move or imagine when I might do so, and thus the ninth month became the tenth.

Sometime soon after the tenth day a message from a different source[71] arrived: 'I've longed to contact you every day, but then I come face to face with messengers coming and going from the Palace and fear that His Highness may wonder if "unbeknownst you wait for another", and so reluctantly I have kept my silence through the passing days', and so on.

My old nurse's house was on the corner of Shijō and Ōmiya Streets, and on the corner facing Shijō Street the earth wall was badly broken, with a thorny bramble growing over it. Noticing that it branched in two to form just two thick stems, the messenger who brought this message inquired whether the place

was guarded and was told that it wasn't. 'Then it would make
a perfect place to come in and out,' he declared, and slashing
back the bramble with his sword he went on his way. When
I learned of this I was puzzled, but I really never anticipated
anything.

Then, at around midnight, someone knocked softly on the
side door in the moonlight.

'Would that be a water rail knocking? What an odd noise,'
said the young maid Chūjō wonderingly. I heard her open the
door, then cry out in alarm, 'There's a gentleman who says he
wants to stand there and have a word with you!' I remained
rooted to the spot, simply astonished at this unforeseen development and at a loss how to respond, whereupon he came
straight in, no doubt guided by the direction of the maid's cry.

He was dressed in a hunting costume with a raised design
of autumn leaves, and gathered trousers of I think aster-violet,
both of exceptionally soft silk, and it was clear that he had
indeed made his way here in secret.[72]

Heavy with child as I was, I did my best to evade him that
evening. 'If you truly love me please postpone this meeting to
"what lies beyond",' I begged.

'Of course, knowing your condition I wouldn't dream of
behaving in any inappropriate fashion,' he assured me. 'I only
came to talk quietly of my long-held love for you. Spending
the night here in separate sleep would surely be forgiven by the
great god of Ise.'

At such chaste promises, my weak will could find no way to
deny him, and in the end he made his way into my bedroom.

Those many words of love he spoke through the long night
would move even the fiercest tigers of China to tears, and my
heart was anything but made of stone. Little though I thought
to give myself, before I knew it we had shared a first night of
love together, and I trembled to think that His Highness might
know of it in his dreams.

Woken by the cock's crow, I watched him leave in the darkness with reluctant heart. I had no thought of drifting back
to sleep alone, and I was still lying there as dawn's first light
tinged the eastern clouds, when a message arrived:

Making my sad way home	*kaerusa wa*
eyes dimmed with tears	*namida ni kurete*
even the moon of daybreak	*ariake no*
is bitter to me	*tsuki sae tsuraki*
in the pale dawn sky	*shinonome no sora*

'When did my feelings for you grow so strong?' his message went on. 'I feel I might die with misery to have to wait until the night comes round again. And then there is the wretchedness of having to keep this hidden from the world.'

My reply:

Your feelings as you went	*kaerusa no*
unguessable, but I	*tamoto wa shirazu*
saw in my own sleeve's tears	*omokage wa*
your dear face reflected	*sode no namida ni*
beneath the daybreak sky	*ariake no sora*

Meanwhile, I wept in secret to think of what had come about despite all my efforts to avoid it, anticipating the difficulties that surely lay ahead now, but with no one to tell my troubles to. Later that day came another message from His Highness: 'What can be distracting your heart to make you stay at home so long? I am quite lost for what to do at the Palace without you, and there are so few others around . . .' Even more tenderly written than usual, his letter filled me with alarm.

Evening came, and this time he arrived before it was fully dark, filling me with further trepidation. I felt somehow as shy and tongue-tied as at a first meeting. At this point my old nurse's husband Nakatsuna[73] suddenly arrived, 'to mark the occasion of your rare visit to your old home,' as he put it. He now lived at the temple of the Senbon priest, having taken religious vows at my father's death. The sons too only rarely came and went now, but they also arrived for the reunion and the house was suddenly full of activity. This made things very awkward for us.

Far from being the refined lady one would assume from her upbringing in the old palace, my former nurse was actually quite vulgar, much like the boorish foster mother in the old tale,[74] and she now added to my distress and anxiety by joining in the uproar. I could hardly let them know about the hidden presence in the house, or even light so much as a lamp, so I left him in my bedroom and emerged to sit leaning casually against the brazier at the entrance to my quarters under the pretence of enjoying the moonlight. At this point who should show up but my old nurse. Oh no! I thought in consternation.

'Daddy suggests we should help pass the long autumn evening with some games of flip-stones,'[75] she said. 'Come on, in you come now.' The veiled insolence of this exasperated me further.

She then began on the details of what we were to play, listed off the names of everyone who had turned up, all the sons and stepsons, declared that we must all have a drinking party, and went on and on until I was quite beside myself.

'I'm feeling unwell,' I said to fend her off.

'This is just like you, you won't listen to a word I say!' she declared and flounced off. You'd think she was surrounded by young girls who did her bidding, impertinent woman that she was. The main living room shared a courtyard garden with my own room, and the various noises that carried across brought to mind that scene in *The Tale of Genji* in which the prince suffers the uncouth thudding of the mortar being pounded next door when he spends the night with the lovely Yūgao. Oh dear, he's bound to be hearing all this, I thought miserably.

To my chagrin, all those things I had planned to say to him had to remain unspoken; the situation was so difficult that we could only lie there hoping that things would soon quieten down. Then suddenly there was a fierce knocking at the front gate. Someone had arrived. Who could it be? It was the youngest son Nakayori.

'I was held up serving His Majesty's dinner,' I heard him explain. 'By the way, there was an impressive basketwork carriage parked out there on the corner of Ōmiya Street. I went over to see whose it might be and found it was crammed full of sleeping retainers. The ox was tied up some distance away. Where can the owner have gone?'

I listened horrified as my silly old nurse replied, 'Who can it be? Send someone to look.'

'Why go looking?' I heard my 'Daddy' say. 'What's the point, when it's none of our business? Of course I suppose it could be someone who knows she's back home at the moment and has crept in to visit through the broken wall, assuming everyone was asleep. High-born or low-born, girls are always such a worry while ever you have them under your wing', and so on.

Then came my old nurse's voice again, this time from quite close by. 'Oh dear, how alarming! Who could it be? If it's His Highness, why would he be creeping in like this?' Then to my mortification she added, right where he could hear it, 'I'll be the one who's blamed if it's some low-ranking nobody.'

Another son had now joined the general hubbub and there could be no thought of sleep. I could tell that the food and drink had arrived. 'Tell that girl to come out and join us!' shouted my nurse. Someone came and passed on the message, and beside me my maid replied, 'She says she's unwell.' Then there was a rough banging on the door to my quarters and in came the old nurse herself.

I was as shocked as if some stranger had suddenly walked in, and my heart beat loud with terror.

'What's all this about feeling unwell?' she demanded. 'Come and see what they've brought. Come on, out you come', and she knocked on the bedroom door.

I couldn't very well simply ignore her. 'I'm not well!' I replied.

'Listen, we've got some of that "white stuff" that you like so much. You're always demanding it when there isn't any, but now when I tell you there is you turn up your nose. Isn't it just like you! Very well, suit yourself then,' she muttered, and off she went.

I would normally have come back with something snide and clever, but now I was so embarrassed I could have died.

'So what's this "white stuff" you're always demanding?' my lover enquired.

I was tempted to make out that it was something elegant and poetic, such as frost or snow or hail, but I knew he wouldn't have been fooled, so instead I told him the truth. 'I have this funny habit of sometimes asking for some special white sake – but she's blowing it out of all proportion.'

I'll always remember how he laughed and said, 'Well I'm glad I came when I did to learn that! When you visit my house I'll be sure to send all the way to China for the best "white stuff" there is.' There never was or will be such a delightful memory, and it still comes back to comfort me in hard times.

Night after night he came, all the little things about him grew dearer to me with each passing night, and I felt less and less inclined to return to the Palace. Then, around the twentieth of the tenth month, I learned that my mother's old nurse, Gon-dainagon, was ill. It never occurred to me that she might be close to death, but within a few days of hearing the news, word came that she had died. She had lived these many years in the Ayato area of the Zenrinji Temple complex in the eastern hills. Hearing that she was so suddenly gone, I was filled with fresh melancholy at the thought that this tenuous connection to my late mother had now faded too:

Autumn's sad dews	*aki no tsuyu*
and now this wintry rain	*fuyu no shigure ni*
lie on my sleeve	*uchi-soete*
tears upon tears	*shiori kasanuru*
freighting it deep with woe	*waga tamoto ka na*

Meanwhile, I worried that the recent lack of any message from His Highness meant that he had somehow sensed my wrongdoing.

Then word came from him, full of tenderness, asking how things had been with me since our last communication, and announcing that he was ordering a carriage to come and fetch me that evening.

'I fear my mother's old nurse passed away a day or so ago, so we must postpone our meeting to avoid the ritual pollution,'[76] I replied, adding:

Think of me now   *omoiyare*
the dews of this past autumn   *suginishi aki no*
overlaid with wintry tears   *tsuyu ni mata*
my sleeves   *namida shigurete*
soaked deep with sorrow   *nururu tamoto wo*

In response, His Highness wrote:

Little did I know   *kasanekeru*
that this fresh sorrow   *tsuyu no aware mo*
was added to those dews   *mata shirade*
but from afar I too   *ima koso yoso no*
weep to think of it   *sode mo shiorure*

At the beginning of the eleventh month I presented myself back at the Palace at last, but everything felt different now. I was forever recalling my father's face wherever I looked, and I found myself feeling awkward and unsure. Her Highness Higashi Nijō'in too seemed upset and out of sorts for some reason. His Highness very kindly instructed my grandfather Count Takachika and my uncle the Zenshōji Counsellor to look to my needs just as when my father was alive, and ordered that my court robes should be chosen from among the gifts he received. This was all very gratifying, but as for me, I simply longed for my pregnancy to be over so that I could be free again as soon as possible to retire to a life of quiet retreat, to pray for the souls of my parents and escape the karmic bonds that tied me to rebirth in the six realms, and in this state of mind I left the Palace again at the end of the month.

This time I made my way to Shōkutei-In in Daigo to visit Abbess Shingan,[77] with whom I had a connection, hoping to hear her teachings on the Buddhist texts. There I joined the convent life, breaking up firewood 'to keep a tiny thread of smoke alive' in this winter dwelling, where even the thin trickle in the waterpipe 'froze sometimes in its flow', and the end-of-year preparations were 'all to higher ends'.[78]

As the waning moon rose on the twenty-second, His Highness paid me a very stealthy visit. He sat hidden from sight

deep within the basketwork carriage, with behind him the
Zenshōji Counsellor. He had been staying nearby at his Fushimi Palace, he said, when he suddenly took it into his head to
pay me a visit. I did wonder how he could have heard of my
whereabouts. That night he was full of most tender affection,
lingering until the dawn bell sounded before departing.

Dawn's moon still hung in the western sky, soft clouds trailed
above the eastern ridge, and over the mountains' dappling of
snow, white snowflakes drifted like scattering petals, a scene
that might have been made to suit the moment. His Highness's
unfigured cloak over silk *hakama* trousers in the same colour
of mourning likewise matched my own sombre robes, and lent
him an air of touching sorrow. Unaware of His Highness's
presence among them, the nuns had emerged for their dawn
service, clad only in homespun robes beneath rustic surplices,
and I watched with envy as they walked past, announcing the
hour and calling to each other. They apparently only realized
who was among them when the lower guardsmen, all clothed
likewise in sombre hunting costumes, were discovered drawing
up His Highness's carriage, at which some of the nuns fled and
hid in consternation.

He left, promising to come again, and the sorrow of our parting lingered in my tears, the mingled scent of our two sleeves
imbuing my heart with love's deep fragrance as I listened with
emotion to the nuns' voices now raised in prayer. 'Even the
most powerful king is bound in the end to karmic fate,' came
the chant. The dedication that marked the end of the service
left me yearning for more.

As the sky brightened a letter arrived: 'I feel I have never
before tasted such parting sorrow as I have felt this daybreak.'

In reply I sent:

Feelings unfelt till now	*kimi dani mo*
you say. Could I but show you	*narawazarikeru*
how your face	*ariake no*
at daybreak lingers still	*omokage nokoru*
on my tear-soaked sleeve	*sode wo miseba ya*

Perhaps about three days before the year's end, feeling
particularly forlorn, I was seated one evening before Abbess
Shingan, who was doing her best to offer me a little comfort in
my melancholy. 'Remember that you may well not have another
opportunity to live such a peaceful life as this,' she counselled.
We spoke of this and that, and she called in some other elderly
nuns who sat reminiscing about the old days. The melancholy
sight of the water pipe's trickle of water hanging frozen above
the stone basin outside, the echo of a woodsman's axe from
the mountain beyond – all evoked the poignant atmosphere of
some old tale. As night thickened around us, the darkness was
lit with the scattered lights of glowing votive lamps.

The evening service was over and the nuns had declared we
should all sleep early, when I heard a surreptitious knocking
at the side door. 'How strange. Who can it be?' I wondered. It
was he.

'Oh no!' I exclaimed. 'Just think how embarrassing it would
be if anyone catches wind of this dreadful behaviour of yours!
Besides, I'm here in retreat to mourn and pray for my father
and this requires a pure heart. If His Highness chooses to come
calling of course it can't be helped, but how could I possibly
sully myself with a frivolous visit like this? Go home!' I was
quite rude to him.

A thick snow had begun to swirl down, the wind was fierce,
and a snowstorm threatened. 'Oh dear, this is too much!' he
protested. 'Do at least let me come in and shelter. I promise I'll
be off again as soon as the snow stops.'

The nuns nearby apparently overheard our exchange. 'Good
gracious, don't be so heartless and ill-mannered!' someone
exclaimed. 'Whoever it may be, he's surely come especially to
see you. What a way to treat him, on such a cold and stormy
night!' The side door was opened, a fire was lit, and in he came,
complaining bitterly.

The snow conspired to keep falling, piling high on mountain
ridge and low eaves alike. The wind howled all night. He could
hardly leave, he claimed, and even when the sky grew light he
simply slept on, perfectly at home. The whole situation filled

me with deep unease. I lay there worrying but couldn't think what to do.

The sun was well up when two of his retainers appeared with various things they had prepared by way of gifts. 'Oh dear, how difficult,' I thought, watching as the items were distributed to my hosts.

'Oh good, now we'll be able to forget about the end-of-year cold!' they exclaimed to each other. 'How thoughtful to provide surplices and robes like this, not to mention offerings for the altar. We poor mountain folk have been absolutely showered with blessings!' Short of the arrival of the heavenly hosts in person, there could surely be no greater occasion than His Highness's visit. Yet they had barely turned out to see His Highness off, and no one had exclaimed over the privilege of having him there – and now, when you would think they should disapprove and rebuke, all these nuns could think of was the marvellous gifts they'd received. Witnessing their delight, I couldn't help wondering at the ways of this world of ours.

His gift for me was a rather subdued set of formal robes to welcome in the new year, consisting of layerings of, I think, pale blue over three white *kosode* robes and so forth. I was rather worried that people might get wind of it, but we spent the day drinking sake together. The following morning, feeling he really could stay no longer, he reluctantly left.

'Come out just to see me off,' he pleaded, so I rose and stepped outside. In the faint light of dawn, the white snow on the ridges all around shone with astonishing beauty. Two or three retainers in sombre white hunting costumes arrived to accompany him on his way, and when he had gone I was quite perturbed by the unquenchable longing that filled me.

On the last night of the year my old nurse and her family sent to bring me back, on the grounds that I really shouldn't be here in the depths of the mountains in my condition, so I reluctantly returned to the capital and there saw out the year.

The new year was a gloomy affair everywhere owing to the continued general mourning. The first three days, normally so full of auspicious ritual at the Palace, were very dreary, and a fresh wave

of sorrow at my father's death added to my woes. My condition
also forbade my visiting the usual family shrine[79] for the beginning
of spring's traditional prayers, but I went and stood before the
shrine gate to pay my respects. I have written elsewhere[80] of seeing
my father in a dream there, so I will say nothing of that here.

Towards evening on the tenth of the second month, my birth
pangs began. His Highness was not in a happy frame of mind[81]
and I was of course still in mourning, so the time was anything
but auspicious, but my uncle the Zenshōji Counsellor took
charge and organized everything for me. His Highness sent to
Ninnaji Temple[82] for a performance of the Aizen Myōō rituals
and to Narutaki for prayers for long life, and asked the abbot
of Bishamon Temple to conduct the Seven Buddhas Yakushi
ritual on my behalf, all at their various temple headquarters. In
my own quarters, it was arranged that the high prelate Shingen
would perform the Shō Kannon salvation rites. It also happened that my uncle the Nanajō Abbot Michichō was down
from his austerities on Mount Ōmine at the time and paid
a visit, saying he was very conscious of my father's anxious
injunctions to him concerning my welfare.

Towards the middle of the night my pains became intense.
There was now a little more commotion, and my aunt Lady
Kyōgoku arrived from the Palace on behalf of His Highness.
My grandfather Count Takachika was also on hand, but I wept
to think that my father should have been here too. Feeling a
little faint, I was leaning against someone when I thought I saw
my father, just as he had been in life, his face full of concern. He
came and stood behind me, and the child, a prince, was born.
Wonderful though it was that the birth had been so smooth,
it only prompted me to worry with fresh keenness about my
secret shameful behaviour and what it might lead to now.

The Zenshōji Counsellor unobtrusively presented His Highness's formal gift of the traditional ceremonial sword on the
birth of a prince, and quietly organized the payment of the exorcist priest[83] and so on. My mind was crowded with thoughts of
how I would have been in my father's Kawasaki house if this
had been the old days, while my grandfather Count Takaaki
was already calling for the robes for the wetnurse and setting in

motion the various auspicious ceremonies, beginning with the
bow-twanging exorcism. Yet I was filled with a sense of unreal-
ity, imagining how this year might develop before its close.
Festive though the occasion of the birth was, yet my private
misery made all this feel a dream . . .[84]

The final month of the year is always a busy time for Shinto
ceremonies and so forth at the Palace. For my own part, I felt
the urge to spend my time in Buddhist practice, and had retired
to my old nurse's house, but now my lover took it into his head
to visit by the light of the 'dreary' year's end moon, and we
spent the night lovingly together.

'I took the dawn cock's crow for that widowed crow that
disturbs the night,'[85] he said, 'and now daylight is upon us
and I've left it too late to depart unnoticed', and on he stayed.
Apprehensive though I felt, I kept him company. Then a letter
from His Highness arrived.

It was full of most tender words, and ended with this poem:

In the dark night	*mubatama no*
I dreamed and saw	*yume ni zo mitsuru*
your night-time robe	*sayogoromo*
its sleeve spread	*aranu tamoto wo*
upon another's	*kasanekeru to wa*

'It was so vivid that I pray it was truly a dream,' he added.
I was appalled. Just what could be this dream he had seen?
I wondered. I knew I must feign a puzzled innocence in my
response:

Alone and sad	*hitori nomi*
I spread this lonely sleeve	*kata-shikikanuru*
without you	*tamoto ni wa*
where only moonlight lies	*tsuki no hikari zo*
reflected in my tears	*yadori-kasanuru*

I wrote, though I was painfully aware of how deceitful I was
being.

We spent that day peacefully together. It was inevitable that those at home knew of it, or the women at least, but there was no one I could talk to about the situation so I kept my worries to myself. That night I dreamed that my lover gave me a fan with lacquered ribs and a gold-dust design of pines, together with a little silver oil bottle, which I hid from others in the bosom of my robe. I woke in surprise to hear the dawn bell ringing. It seemed such a strange dream, but the man who lay beside me told me he had dreamed the same thing. How extraordinary!

In the new year, His Highness ordered twelve scribes at the Rokujō Palace to make sutra copies on his behalf.[86] Mindful of the dream-like events of the previous year, he chose to avoid causing trouble to others by using things from his own storehouse to pay the expenses. He also undertook to draw blood from his own finger to write out a portion of the Lotus Sutra on the back of the deceased emperor's own handwritten document, and to prepare himself for this sacred task he entered a period of abstinence from New Year's Day until the seventeenth of the second month, including abstinence from all relations with women.

Meanwhile, around the end of the second month I noticed that I didn't feel normal and had lost my appetite. For a while I put it down to an illness of some sort, but then I connected it back to the dream that my lover and I had shared. There was no denying the condition I was in. I understood that this was the reward for my own sinfulness, and I was secretly filled with unassuageable gloom, though I could confess the situation to no one.

I had largely excused myself from the Palace owing to the purification rituals then taking place, and had been spending most of my time back home. My lover came calling constantly and it wasn't long before my condition became evident to him; he declared that he was sure I was pregnant, and from then on he was particularly assiduous in his care and attention. 'If only there was some way to avoid His Highness learning of this!' he lamented. His fervent prayers for a safe childbirth made it hard for me to resent him as its cause.

From the end of the second month I began returning to the

Palace from time to time and normal relations with His Highness resumed. At around the fifth month His Highness was led
to believe that I was in the fourth month of my pregnancy,
though in fact it was by then the sixth month, and I was filled
with anxiety that this discrepancy would soon become obvious.

On the seventh of the sixth month, my lover sent word insisting that I return home. I did as he asked, wondering what this
could be about, whereupon he personally gave me a ritual
childbirth band.[87] 'I did hope to present this with a special ceremony back in the fourth month,' he said, 'but I waited out of
fear that the world would learn of it. Then I heard from the
Palace that their childbirth band ceremony would be held on
the twelfth, so I came up with this solution.' I was moved by
this evidence of his deep care for me, but with this came fresh
fear at my likely fate.

He carefully spent the usual three days there with me, then
on the evening of the tenth, just when I was due to return to
the Palace, I suddenly became ill. Unable to go as planned, on
the evening of the twelfth my uncle the Zenshōji Counsellor
brought the official childbirth band from His Highness, as he
had done before. Seeing it brought back to me the scene of the
previous occasion,[88] when my father had been on his deathbed
and so filled with anxiety.

Autumn is the season of sorrow, but I knew only too well that
these endless tears of mine were more than simply autumnal. I
could come up with no way to plausibly explain the difference
of more than a month between my expected birth date and
the time His Highness was anticipating. Yet I could not summon
the courage to simply end it all and drown myself, and so I let the
days pass as I agonized fruitlessly over what to do, and in this
way the ninth month arrived.

Fearful of possible rumours, on I think the second day I
produced some hasty excuse and went back home. My lover
promptly came that night. He settled down beside me and we
discussed what to do. 'First, you must announce that you are
gravely ill,' he advised me. 'Then let it be known that the Yin-
Yang Masters[89] have advised that this illness requires no one
should come near you.'

I did as instructed, lying low all day and letting no one approach except for two whom I knew well and trusted, and declaring that I would not so much as take a drink of water. Yet with no one to visit me there, I did think sadly how different this would have been had my father still been alive. I sent word to His Highness explaining that I was not in a position to receive messengers from the Palace, so he communicated only rarely. How much longer would this deception work? I wondered desperately.

For now at least, everyone still believed that I was ill. My uncle called around and sent in worried messages from time to time, concerned that I was being left to languish like this. 'What do the doctors say?' he asked.

'They tell me it's contagious so I'm being careful to stay secluded,' I sent in reply, and refused to allow him in.

'I'm terribly worried about you,' he insisted, so finally I darkened the room and lay huddled under a robe while I reluctantly received him, but I barely spoke, and he left believing that all I had said was true. Yet as I watched him go, I was filled with fear.

No one else approached me; my lover alone stayed constantly at my side. At one point I was distressed to overhear him softly instructing a retainer to spread the word that he had gone on pilgrimage to Kasuga Shrine. 'Send someone there in my place,' he added, 'and if any message arrives for me, they should respond as they believe I would.'

Soon after the twentieth at around dawn I felt the birth pangs beginning. I had told no one beyond the bare one or two whom I trusted to know the situation, so there was only a minimal fuss now to prepare for the event. Just what would be said of me if I were to die in childbirth in such circumstances? I wondered miserably, and witnessing my lover's tender care and concern served only to deepen my gloom. There was not much progress until darkness set in; then, once the lamp was lit, I felt the birth rapidly approaching, but despite the dangers of this time no one was there to twang the bow and keep the evil spirits at bay,[90] and I lay there huddled under the night robe, suffering alone.

Around the time when the late temple bell tolled, my agony was so great that impulsively I struggled to raise myself. 'Oh dear!' my lover exclaimed. 'Someone should be holding you from behind I think. That must be why the birth is being so difficult. How should I do it?' He propped me up, I clung to his sleeve, and the child emerged without further problem.

His first reaction was to exclaim in delight; then he busied himself ordering the maids to be quick and bring me some rice broth and so forth, impressing those in the know with his unexpected grasp of such matters. He brought the lamp close to examine the child properly, and we saw thick black hair and eyes already wide open. This first glimpse of my child provoked a surge of love that couldn't help but move me. He wrapped her in the white robe that lay ready beside him and cut the umbilical cord with the knife by my pillow. Then he took the child in his arms as I lay watching and went out without a word, and I never saw her again.[91]

I longed to beg for one more glimpse, but after all it would only have made me sadder. Instead, I simply lay there without a word, though there was no hiding my tears. They were enough to tell him how I felt, however, and he said comfortingly, 'There there, this surely won't be the last time. If she survives you will certainly meet again.' But that single glance when our eyes met was enough to make my child's face unforgettable to me. It broke my heart just to know that it was a girl, and not to know where she had been taken. But it was useless to wonder, and all I could do was stifle my sobs in my sleeve to keep others from hearing.

When daylight came, a message was sent to His Highness to say that my condition had considerably worsened, that at dawn I had miscarried, and that the child had been seen to be a girl. His reply came together with copious medicines. 'The doctors tell me that this can happen to anyone if they have a high fever,' he wrote. 'Do take good care and recover well.' I was filled with fresh trepidation at his tenderness.

When no problems occurred in the days after the birth, my companion felt he could safely go home. I was instructed to present myself at the Palace again after the hundred days[92] were over, so I stayed on there, idle and confined. Not a night passed when my lover did not visit, but we were both in a constant state of anxiety that word of our relationship might somehow spread.

Word now came that my little boy, who had been born the year before and was being raised in private under my uncle's care, was ill. Surely my own wrongdoing had brought this about, I thought, and forebodings filled me. Sure enough, on the eighth of the tenth month, as a wintry rain dripped from the eaves, I learned that his life had faded like the passing dew. Although I had prepared myself long since, you can imagine my wretchedness at the news. My son dead before his mother; torn from the child I loved – the pain and sorrow of both these were the double burden I bore. Those tears I wept as a child to lose my mother, then once grown to lose my father, now became fresh tears at the loss of my own children, and there was no one to turn to in my misery.

As my intimacy with my lover grew deeper with the passing days, I would return to bed each morning after he left to weep at the memory of our reluctant parting, and as I waited each evening my sighs mingled with the temple bell that tolled the hour's lateness. Then when he finally arrived, I was filled with agony lest the world learn of it. In the meantime, while I was home I longed to see His Highness's dear face, and when at the Palace I begrudged the many nights he now spent with others, and grieved over this new distance between us. It seemed to me that within my own self were gathered the myriad sufferings that Buddhism teaches us are the lot of humans, those countless delusions that torment us day and night, until I was filled with the urge to leave this illusory realm of love and commit myself to the Buddhist Way.

When I was perhaps around nine, I remember seeing an illustrated scroll depicting the poet-monk Saigyō's ascetic wanderings,[93] which showed steep mountains on one side and a stream flowing in the foreground, where Saigyō sat gazing at the cherry blossoms scattering around him. The poem he was composing was:

When the wind blows	*kaze fukeba*
white waves of blossom	*hana no shiranami*
surge over rocks –	*iwa koete*
so hard it is to cross	*watari-wazurau*
this mountain stream	*yamakawa no mizu*

It filled me with envy, and even though his rigorous austerities were beyond me, a longing grew in me to cast off the world and wander wherever I wished, as he did, sighing beneath the blossoms, lamenting the passing dew, grieving over autumn's falling leaves, and writing just such a record of my own wanderings to leave in my memory when I was gone. But being born a woman, inescapably bound to submit myself to the cares and sorrows of submission to men, I had bowed to the will of my father as a child, and devoted myself to His Highness through this sorry life. Yet my true impulses had always lain elsewhere, and now such thoughts as these filled me with a deepening urge to put this unhappy life behind me and take religious vows.

That autumn, distressing events were afoot.[94] Humiliated by the appointment of a superintendent tasked with setting up a formal retirement palace for Emperor Kameyama's future use, His Highness returned his own official title of Retired Emperor to the imperial court and prepared to take holy orders. He summoned all his retainers, paid them off and released them, stating that only Hisanori should remain in his service, and all wept as they left the Palace. He chose the various people who should continue to serve him in his new cloistered role, and for the ladies in his service he named Lady Genkimon'in and myself, which felt to me like 'joy hid within sorrow'.[95]

Then, at the eleventh hour, the military government in Kamakura managed to soothe His Highness by declaring his young son by Lady Genkimon'in to be the future Crown Prince, and the Palace was instantly transformed into a place of excited celebration. The image of Go-Saga that had pride of place in the corner palace building was transferred to his Ōgimachi Palace, and the corner palace building now became the new Crown Prince's quarters. Lady Kyōgoku, who was in His Highness's service with me and had also served him during his reign as emperor, was now freshly instated with the new name of Dainagon no Suke and placed in the service of the Crown Prince. Although we were never close, she was a relative of my dear father, and her move added to my sorrows. But though my heart yearned only to leave all this behind and 'go to the mountains', my fate seemed to be binding me inexorably to this life. Another unhappy year was drawing to a close and His Highness was insistent that I come to him, so I resigned myself to remaining in the secular world, and returned to the Palace.

My grandfather Count Takachika saw to the provisioning of my formal robes and so forth, though as always in a rather perfunctory way, and I suppose I should say I was grateful for the way he looked after my interests. But since my little son the prince had died my conscience was haunted by my lover's guilt and my own misdeeds. That innocently smiling little face had been so like His Highness's. 'It's just like seeing my own reflection in a mirror!' he had exclaimed on a private visit to see him, and thinking of this now filled my days with inconsolable sorrow.

Then, to add still further to my unhappiness, I found myself suddenly barred from Her Highness's presence and my name struck from the list of those who served her, though I had done nothing wrong that I could put my finger on. His Highness protested that this did not mean that he too was rejecting me, but it was all very difficult and dreary, and I was more and more inclined to withdraw into myself, while at the same time clinging desperately to the proof of His Highness's tender pity for me.

The Imperial Priestess,[96] Go-Saga's daughter, had retired from shrine duties when she went into mourning for her father, but had been required to stay on at Ise until her allotted three years were over. Around this autumn, she at last returned to the capital and took up residence in the Kinugasa area near Ninnaji Temple. As she was related to my father, he had frequently placed himself at her disposal, and had gone to particular trouble for her when she travelled to the shrine to take up her position. I had fond memories of all this, and felt sorry for her now in her lonely and secluded life, so I called in there often to provide some comfort and distraction for her.

Towards the middle of the eleventh month, arrangements were made for her to go to the Saga Palace on a formal visit to the empress dowager, and the old lady sent to His Highness saying that it would feel rather awkward with just the two of them and asking him to come too. She had remained firmly opposed to His Highness in the recent difficult political situation and the problems over the appointment of the new Crown Prince,[97] but of late she had been more friendly towards him, and he felt he was in no position to refuse so he made preparations to present himself. Since I was a frequent visitor to the Imperial Priestess, he suggested that I accompany him.

I sat alone in the rear of his carriage on the way there. I wore triple robes in the withered field combination of yellow over pale green, beneath a fine silk robe of plum red. Since the installation of His Highness's young son as Crown Prince, everyone at the Palace had worn the formal Chinese jacket over their robes, so I added a Chinese jacket in the special red.[98] I was all by myself, without even a lady-in-waiting to accompany me.

We arrived at the Palace, and a peaceful conversation ensued during which His Highness sought to explain my presence by saying, 'I raised this girl from infancy so she is thoroughly used to palace service, and this is why she accompanies me here and there. But Her Highness misinterprets this and has barred her from entering her quarters. I personally have no cause to reject her, however. After all, her late mother and father both begged me to look after her in memory of them.'

'Yes indeed, how could you dispense with her service? It is so unsettling not to have someone familiar with palace service on hand to see to one's needs,' replied Her Cloistered Highness. Then, turning to me, she continued with warm affection, 'Do feel free to call on me at any time.' I could only wonder how long such kindness toward me would last.

Their peaceful talk continued that evening. His Highness took his meal with her, and when the evening grew late he retired to sleep in the room that looked out over the court football grounds. I was the only one with him, although the Saionji Counsellor[99] and the Zenshōji Counsellor had also accompanied him, together with his aides Nagasuke, Tamekata, Kaneyuki and Sukeyuki.

The following morning, Her Cloistered Highness sent a deputation of an ox carriage driver, a palace servant and one of the lower guardsmen to fetch the Imperial Priestess. His Highness went to great pains over his formal robes for the occasion of this meeting with the priestess, choosing a formal cloak in the withered field combination with a woven design over a pale mauve under-robe brocaded with gentians, and aster-violet trousers, all richly imbued with incense.

The arrival of the Imperial Priestess was announced as evening drew in. Partitions had been removed from the southern apartment of the main building to make it more spacious, with charcoal-grey standing curtains and smaller curtain stands set up. Soon after hearing that the Imperial Priestess's audience with Her Cloistered Highness had begun, a lady-in-waiting arrived bearing a message for His Highness: 'She has arrived, but things are feeling rather dismal. Do come and join the conversation.'

He duly presented himself, with myself in attendance as usual, bearing his ceremonial sword for him. Her Cloistered Highness was clothed in a heavily patterned thin charcoal-grey robe beneath a draped pale grey cloak, and was seated behind a low standing curtain of the same colour. The Imperial Priestess was in triple robes in the plum-red combination over a blue unlined gown, which gave a rather odd and unfortunate impression. Her lady-in-waiting, a relative of hers, was in five-layered robes of graded purple rather than in full formal wear.

The Imperial Priestess was past twenty, and seeing her maturity of beauty one could well understand why the gods of Ise had been reluctant to let her leave. In terms of flowers, one might compare her to the cherry blossom, though this might not be apparent to the casual glance; even glimpsed through the layered mist of a shielding sleeve, this beauty would surely bewilder and arouse the viewer. I could all too easily imagine what thoughts it was prompting in His Highness's heart, knowing him as I did, and I pitied her as I watched.

The conversation proceeded, with the priestess speaking falteringly of Ise and its sacred mountain, until finally His Highness remarked, 'It really is very late. You must spend a quiet day here tomorrow viewing the bare winter trees on Mount Arashi before you go home.'

As soon as he returned to his room, he turned to me saying, 'What shall I do? Whatever shall I do?'

Sure enough, I thought wryly.

'You've served me well ever since your infancy,' he went on. 'If you could do this for me now I will take it as a token of your sincere devotion.'

So off I went as his emissary.

'His Highness was delighted to see you today,' I reported to her, 'and feels you may be lonely in your strange bed tonight', and I quietly handed her a letter with the following poem, written on thin ice-white paper:

You cannot know	shirareji na
that having seen just now	ima shi mo mitsuru
your lovely face	omokage no
it straight away	yagate kokoro ni
entered my heart	kakarikeri to wa

It was late, and all her ladies-in-waiting had settled down to sleep in a huddle nearby, while she had retired to her bed behind a low standing curtain. I approached and gave her His Highness's message. She blushed and said not a word, nor did she so much as glance at the letter but simply put it down.

'How should I reply?' I asked.

'There is no way to respond to such an unexpected message,' she replied simply, and turned back to sleep.

I didn't feel I could press the point, so I returned to His Highness and told him what had happened.

'Well then, take me to where she's sleeping. Come on, come on!' he demanded. He was so maddeningly insistent that in the end it was easiest just to do as told.

Formal robes would have been too pretentious under the circumstances, so he stealthily made his way to her rooms dressed in no more than a single robe and wide-bottomed trousers. I went ahead, and quietly slid open the door. There she lay, just as before.

Everyone around her was apparently fast asleep, for no one raised the alarm. Crouching low, he scuttled in.

Who knows what happened after that. I couldn't very well go off and leave him, so I lay down beside a nearby lady-in-waiting. This woke her. 'Who's this?' she demanded.

'I thought it was a shame that Her Ladyship came with so few of you,' I replied, 'so I decided to come and join you.' She seemed to take me at my word, for she began to chat. This seemed rather imprudent, and I felt so awkward that I excused myself by saying it was late and I was tired, and pretended to sleep.

Her Ladyship was not far away behind her curtains, and I was aware that His Highness didn't have to try very hard before she gave in to him. This was a great shame, I thought.[100] He would have found her so much more interesting if she had resisted him until dawn.

Before first light His Highness emerged and returned to his own quarters. 'The blossom is lovely to behold,' he remarked, 'but the branch proved frail and gave way all too easily.'

So it's just as I thought, I said to myself.

His Highness slept until the sun was high, finally waking around noon. 'Oh dear, this is a bad morning to have slept in so horribly!' he exclaimed, and hastily set about writing her a next-morning message.

Her only reply was along the conventional lines of 'your face still haunts me after last night's dream'.

'How will you be entertaining your special guest today?' His Highness inquired of his mother, and when she replied that she had no particular plans, he instructed the Zenshōji Counsellor to prepare a drinking party. That evening the message arrived that all was ready, and he then sent word to Her Cloistered Highness informing her and inviting her to attend. Being in a position to serve both Her Cloistered Highness and the Imperial Priestess, I was in attendance to pour the sake.

For the first three rounds the sake cups remained empty,[101] but then Her Cloistered Highness declared that this was rather a shame and instructed the Imperial Priestess to proffer her cup and pour for His Highness. The Saionji Counsellor Sanekane and my uncle the Zenshōji Counsellor were then summoned to sit beyond a standing curtain at a lower level, and I took His Highness's cup and offered it to Sanekane. He deferred to the Zenshōji Counsellor on the grounds that he was in charge of today's event, but he demurred. 'You're the one she chose,' he insisted, so I first served Sanekane and then my uncle.

Her Cloistered Highness now declared that since she had had no real entertainment since her husband's death, this evening they should enjoy themselves to their heart's content, and she summoned one of her ladies to play the *koto*. His Highness was provided with a *biwa*, as was Sanekane, His Highness's Aide Kaneyuki performed on the *hichiriki* flute, and things grew increasingly lively as the night progressed. The two Counsellors sang some sacred Kagura songs, then the Zenshōji Counsellor sang that old favourite, 'The Village Where the Parsley Grows'.

His Highness pressed me to pour for the Imperial Priestess, but she stubbornly refused to accept it. When I told him, he picked up the sake bottle and declared he would pour for her himself. At this point Her Cloistered Highness said, 'Since you are doing the pouring, let us have a little something to go with it.'

His Highness then sang the popular song that goes:

> The poor charcoal seller
> his coat is thin and old
> yet he gathers wood for others' fires
> against the coming cold
> this sad old man.

Her Cloistered Highness enjoyed this immensely, and she now asked that the sake cup be passed to her. She proceeded to drink three cups, then offered it to the Imperial Priestess. His Highness took it and once more went in behind the Imperial Priestess's curtain.

'They say the Son of Heaven has no parentage,' Her Cloistered Highness remarked loftily, 'but it is surely owing to my humble self that you attained that heavenly realm and became an emperor', and she proceeded to demand more entertainment.

'Everything from the gift of life itself has indeed been thanks to none other than your esteemed self – the imperial realms I inhabited, and the honoured name of Emperor with which I was endowed,' responded His Highness graciously. 'How could I ignore a command from you?' and he sang this popular song:

Before you
there on turtle hill
auspicious cranes
gather to dance.
Such fortune and longevity
is all your own
and beneath heaven all the world
lies tranquil now.

He sang this three times, and three times Her Cloistered Highness offered him the sake cup.

He accepted and drank, then turning to my uncle the Zenshōji Counsellor he offered the cup to him with the words, 'The Saionji Counsellor was offered his own personal cup from the lovely lady here.[102] You must have been quite envious.' Then he gave sake to the other senior courtiers, and with that the gathering came to an end.

I was sure he would visit the Imperial Priestess again tonight, but he declared he had drunk too much and was feeling unwell, and after asking me to massage his back he went to bed and slept till morning.

The next day the Imperial Priestess returned home, and His Highness went on to call at the nearby Imabayashi Mansion, the home of his grandmother, Her Excellency Lady Kitayama, who was ill with a cold. He stayed there that night, and on the following day he returned to his own Palace.

That evening, Her Highness Higashi Nijō'in sent Chūnagon, one of her ladies-in-waiting, with a message for His Highness. What can this be about? I wondered.

Here is what she said: 'Given Nijō's astonishing behaviour, I have denied her access to my quarters, yet I now find that she has been granted special favours by Your Highness, riding in your carriage with you wearing the triple robes,[103] so that everyone assumed she was your primary consort. I simply cannot tolerate it. I have been thoroughly humiliated, and I beg leave to retire to the Fushimi Palace and take religious vows forthwith.'

This was His Highness's reply: 'I have received your message, and I assure you that there is not and never has been any need to be concerned over Nijō. Recall that her late mother when she was her age served me with great dedication day and night. She meant a great deal to me and I hoped to promote her interests in every way possible, but alas death took her from me. She begged me before she died to protect this child in memory of her, and I have been at pains to fulfil this vow. Recall her late father the Major Counsellor, who on his deathbed gave me instructions for her care. It is said that a ruler owes his position to the loyal service of his subjects, as subjects owe their situation to the beneficence of the ruler. I was only too happy to accept the late Major Counsellor's request, and he died at peace knowing that he would not be troubled beyond the grave with concern over his daughter's welfare. A ruler's promise once made cannot be revoked. Her parents will be watching from the shadows. How could I send this blameless girl from the Palace to an uncertain fate?

'Furthermore, this is hardly the first time she has worn the triple robes. When she was first presented at the Palace at the age of four, her father asked that she officially enter the court as the adoptive daughter of her grandfather, the Koga Chancellor, since his own status was too low, and as such she was permitted the use of a five-corded ox carriage,[104] as well as the special layered *akome* gown and double brocade. Also, her mother being the adoptive daughter of the former Kitayama Chancellor Saionji Saneuji, by extension Nijō too has assumed the name of adoptive daughter of his wife Lady Kitayama. When she ceremonially donned *hakama* trousers as a child it was Lady Kitayama herself who tied the strings, thus announcing to the world that she was permitted to wear the layered robes and special white *hakama*. Nijō has also for many years been permitted to use a mounting platform for her carriage. I can see no reason why you should suddenly question her rights in such matters.

'Perhaps some worthless lower guardsman or some such has put it about that Nijō has been behaving like an empress. If such is indeed the case, please inform me of the details and I will deal with her accordingly. Even so, it would hardly do to banish her from the court to an uncertain fate, so I would simply demote her to the rank of lesser lady-in-waiting in my service.

'It is no secret that her father declined to accept it when she was given the high-ranking name of Nijō, which is why no one is required to use it and people seldom do. Despite her official status at court as adoptive daughter of her grandfather, he declared that this did not mean she should be granted such a name. "For now she should be simply known by her personal name of Akako," he said. "When in due course I rise to the rank of Chief Minister, that is the time to afford her an appropriate name."

'As the daughter of the Chancellor, she has naturally been entitled to wear a fine silk robe. The various houses all press their various claims – the Kazan and Kan'in branches trace themselves back to the eighth-century chancellor Fuhito, of course, but the Koga branch to which Nijō belongs is a relatively recent line, only going back to the tenth-century Prince Tomohira, the seventh son of Emperor Murakami and brother to two others, which is why the daughters of the Koga branch generally do not seek to go into palace service. But her mother was an exception, and at her insistence I have kept her daughter in my service since she was a child.

'I believed you understood all this, and I must say your words come as a great surprise to me. As to your proposal to take religious vows, such an urge must spring from an inner karmic impulse and find its natural moment to be fulfilled; it is not a matter on which I as an outsider can pass judgement.'

Such was the substance of His Highness's reply.

The situation only deteriorated further after this, leaving me in a very difficult position, but it was a great comfort at least to know that he felt for me so deeply.

As for the Imperial Priestess, His Highness had not visited her since that night in Saga, and I could well imagine how miserable she must be feeling. It weighed on me that the way I had paved for them was left untrodden. 'Surely you should send word to her before the year has ended,' I suggested. He agreed, and wrote proposing that he send for her when she had the time and inclination.

Her foster mother the nun had very soon learned what had happened, and when I called there I found her indignant and weeping. 'The poor girl long believed that her only relationship was to be with the gods,' she said, 'and ever since that foolish night she has been sunk in gloom.'

On she went until, tired of being berated, I cut in. 'I was actually sent to ask if she might have the time for a visit,' I said.

'As to that, there is never a time when "the reeds would stand to bar the way", as the old poem says,' she replied.

I duly reported this to His Highness.

'Well, if it were a matter of having to "force my way through forests and o'er steep mountain paths" to attain her, the challenge might make me feel more eager,' he responded, 'but I'm afraid the way has been too easily breached already.' Nevertheless, around the middle of the twelfth month he ordered up a nobleman's carriage and sent it off to bring her to him in secret.

It was a long way from her residence to the Palace, and she arrived late at night. The corner palace building was now being used as the residence of the Crown Prince, so the carriage was drawn up at the roofed corridor leading to the Willow Pavilion and she was conducted into the small room next to the day room. I was, as usual, on duty behind a nearby screen, and I could only agree as I overheard her protesting to him about his long neglect of her since their night together. The tolling of the dawn bell mingled with her sighs as she departed next morning, and her tear-soaked sleeves at parting could not but provoke tears of sympathy.

The year drew to an end and troubles crowded my mind, but comfortless as I was, I could not even soothe myself with a visit home.[105]

One evening, when it was clear that Lady Genkimon'in was to spend the night with His Highness, I excused myself from night duty after dinner by claiming that I had a stomach ache, and retired to my room. Suddenly there was my lover, standing in the upper doorway. 'It's very late,' he said. Fear of possible discovery made me nervous, but it was true that for various reasons we had not met for quite some time recently, so I quietly let him in. He left before dawn, and I was dismayed to find that this parting was more painful to me than the farewelling of the old year. I find myself weeping again to remember it now.

BOOK 2

(1275–1277)

'Like the white colt that flashes past', the passing years rolled on, 'waves on swift water never to return', and I had now reached the age of eighteen. Even as I gazed on the new year's tranquil spring days with their flocks of twittering birds, uneasy thoughts were never far from my mind, and I could take no real pleasure in the new season's splendid ceremonials.

This year the Kazan'in Chancellor, the new superintendent, attended the New Year's Day ritual herbs ceremony.[106] He had been appointed by the recently retired emperor Kameyama the previous year under circumstances that had considerably upset His Highness,[107] but since His Highness's own son had now been appointed Crown Prince his resentments were somewhat soothed, and no doubt he had decided that he should not prolong his bitterness, which was why the superintendent had been invited.

The palace ladies were all dressed in particularly impressive finery for the occasion, and their attendants had also clearly put much thought into their various colour combinations. New year though it was, my own thoughts were of the past, recalling my father at the New Year celebrations of another year, and I wept afresh at memories of old times.

The Crown Prince announced that we should be divided into two teams for the New Year's gruel-stick games,[108] and there was a flurry of hasty preparation on the fifteenth. As usual, the two sides belonged to His Highness and the Crown Prince, the men and women each being chosen by drawing lots, with a lady assigned to each of the men. On the Crown Prince's side the team consisted of men, starting with the Custodian Chief Minister,[109] whereas on His Highness's side it comprised women, aside from His Highness himself. Everyone drew lots for their partner, and I was partnered with the Custodian Chief Minister. We were told to each come up with an imaginative idea for a gift that the loser must provide.

The worst of it for us ladies was that His Highness wasn't content to pursue us himself but enlisted some of his courtiers to help him run us down and strike us. This so annoyed me that I later consulted the Crown Prince's mother Lady Genkimon'in, and we decided to turn the tables on him on the eighteenth and strike him in return.

That morning after breakfast the ladies gathered in their apartment and were assigned various places to wait – Shindainagon and Gonchūnagon by the upper entrance to the Yudono apartment, with Bettō waiting outside, Chūnagon placed in His Highness's quarters, and Mashimizu and others along the corridor. Meanwhile, Lady Genkimon'in and I were in a nearby room, casually chatting. We were certain that His Highness would come along, and were ready to pounce.

In he came, dressed very informally. Sure enough, he suspected nothing. 'Why is no one about in my quarters?' he demanded plaintively. 'Is there anyone around here?'

Lady Genkimon'in seized him. 'Oh! Oh! Quick someone!' he cried, but no one ran to help. Counsellor Morochika did try to approach from the veranda room along the corridor where Mashimizu was lurking, but she intercepted him. 'I'm afraid there are reasons you can't pass, sir,' she said, and when his eyes fell on the gruel stick she was holding he turned and fled. Meanwhile, I managed to land some satisfying blows on His Highness, who was full of apologies and promised never to enlist others to beat us like that again.

We felt very pleased with how well this had gone, but when dinner was served in his quarters that evening His Highness complained bitterly to the assembled nobles: 'This year I am thirty-three, which is deemed an unlucky year, and sure enough I have met with misfortune. Just look what has happened. To have achieved the exalted realm of emperor, only to find myself beaten like this – it's unprecedented! Why did none of you realize what was happening? Or were you all party to it as well?' He berated each in turn, and each hastened to vindicate himself.

Among those present were the Nijō Minister of the Left, the Sanjō Bōmon Counsellor Michiyori, the Zenshōji Counsellor Takaaki, the new Saionji Counsellor Sanekane, and the Madenokōji Counsellor Morochika. They all added their condemnations to his in various ways: 'The perpetrator may be a Palace lady, but that does not lessen her crime. Even the enemies of the long-ago imperial court never behaved so outrageously! Heaven knows, no one dares to so much as step on the shadow of one such as yourself! It is a most grave offence to actually strike Your Highness like this', and so forth.

In typical fashion, my uncle Takaaki put himself forward and demanded to know the name of this wicked lady. 'Tell us quickly, and let us all discuss the best punishment for her crime!' he cried.

'Shouldn't the punishment for such a crime go beyond the perpetrator to include her relatives as well?' asked His Highness.

'But of course,' everyone agreed. 'Relatives of the six closest degrees would all be implicated.'

'Well,' said His Highness, 'the person who struck me is in fact the daughter of former Counsellor Masatada, granddaughter of the Shijō Counsellor Takachika, and, er, the niece I believe of the Zenshōji Counsellor Takaaki, your good self, indeed one could even say your surrogate daughter – Lady Nijō. So this in fact concerns you most directly.'

At this all the gathered nobles burst into peals of laughter. 'It would be terribly inconvenient to have to exile a lady at New Year,' they exclaimed, 'and even more so if her relatives had to be dealt with as well. There are precedents for this. Reparations must be made immediately!'

At this point I spoke up. 'I could never have anticipated this,' I declared. 'Not only did His Highness give us such a beating on the fifteenth, he summoned his nobles and courtiers to beat us too. This made me quite aggrieved—but who am I to complain? I held my peace, until Lady Genkimon'in suggested that we take our revenge and asked me to be her accomplice. I only struck you, Your Highness, in compliance with her wishes. It is not just I who should take the blame.'

Nevertheless, it was decided that the worst crime was actually striking His Highness, and reparations were to be made.

My uncle the Zenshōji Counsellor carried the message to my grandfather. 'Deplorable behaviour!' he exclaimed. 'Quick, we must make amends!' He made a great fuss about the need for haste, so everything was quickly assembled and on the twentieth he duly presented it all with great ostentation. His Highness received a set of cloaks, ten gowns, and a sword. There was a sword each for the Nijō Minister of the Left and six other nobles, and the ladies were given a hundred bundles of fine thick Michinoku paper. He immediately followed this up on the twenty-first in the same way by presenting to His Highness a miniature *koto* and *biwa* made of damask cloth and glossed silk with strings of scarlet-purple thread, together with a basket woven in silver thread that held a lapis lazuli sake cup; a horse and an ox each for the nobles; and for the ladies he ordered up ten little lidded picnic baskets made of dyed cloth containing gourds done in wrapped thread.

The remediation party was a very grand affair, and when Abbot Ryūben happened to arrive he was immediately invited to join the party.

A large carp was now produced to be carved up. Turning to the abbot, His Highness said, 'We have the precedent of the Uji abbot.[110] Come on, do dismember this carp for us, Your Reverence. You can't deny that you come from a family famed for its skill with the carving knife.'[111]

The abbot resolutely refused, since it contravened his Buddhist vows, but His Highness continued to insist. Finally, my uncle produced a cutting board and placed it before the abbot, then took a knife and a pair of special fish-handling chopsticks from the folds of his robe and laid them beside it.

'There, now come on,' urged His Highness. His sake cup was before him. The abbot was eventually forced to comply, and it was a sight rarely witnessed to see him in his brown clove-dyed Buddhist robes cutting into the carp. He only made a small incision, then declared that it was quite impossible for him to sever the head.

But His Highness wouldn't hear of it, so the poor abbot

finally sliced off the head with impressive skill, then hastily excused himself and left. His Highness was full of praise for him, and sent after him as a gift the lapis lazuli sake cup in its silver basket that he himself had just received.

My uncle then returned to the subject of the reparations, pointing out that he and my grandfather had been deemed guilty and paid their dues, but this only covered the maternal side of the family. 'I understand that there is also a grandmother on her father's side, and an aunt,' he said. 'What is Your Highness's pronouncement on them?'

'You have a point,' His Highness replied, 'but since they aren't really blood relations, it's carrying it too far to extend the blame to them. That would be quite excessive.'

'Surely not, Your Highness. Do appoint me as messenger to them with the news. Then there is her great-aunt Lady Kitayama, who has been involved in Nijō's upbringing since infancy, not to mention her mother's.'

His Highness turned to Counsellor Sanekane. 'What about you then? You're surely implicated as Lady Kitayama's grandson and family representative,' he said.

Sanekane argued strenuously that the connection was altogether too distant, but His Highness would not accept this reasoning, and Sanekane was forced to make reparations too. He duly presented His Highness with a boat made of aloeswood incense in which sat a tiny boatman fashioned from three pieces of musk, together with a robe. To the Nijō Minister of the Left he gave an ox and a sword, and to the other nobles an ox each, while the ladies received a hundred bundles of thick Michinoku paper with designs in gold leaf, ripple pattern, plum and so forth.

Matters could not be left there. Uncle Takaaki sent word to my tonsured grandmother, telling her of these untoward events. 'Others have offered reparations. What will you do?' he asked.

'As to that,' she wrote in reply, 'this child lost her mother at an early age and her father was full of such tender concern for her that he sent her to be cared for at court from infancy on. I would have thought that she would therefore have been given a finer upbringing than if she were at home. I cannot bring myself to believe that with all her advantages, brought up before His Highness as she was, she could have grown to misbehave in such a fashion. This failure can only be blamed on His Highness himself, it seems to me. Perhaps her lack of judgement where rank and status are concerned derives from having been thoroughly spoiled by His Highness. I cannot judge.

'I would be obliged if His Highness would send a message setting out precisely what crime I may be accused of, for this is most certainly no concern of mine. If her father were alive, he would no doubt have felt obliged to offer reparations out of his love for her. As for myself, I feel no such compulsion. If ordered to disown her by His Highness, I am quite prepared to do so.'

This letter was brought to His Highness and read out before the assembly.

'She does have a point,' the nobles agreed. 'It's true that since Nijō was brought up in the court, the origin of the problem lies here. And of course, as the saying goes, a woman's first lover must see her through this life into the next.'

'What's this?' cried His Highness. 'I'm the one demanding reparations! Are you saying I should also be the one to pay them?' But a number of people asserted that if His Highness could pronounce on the guilt of others, it was not unreasonable that others might also pronounce on His Highness's guilt, and so it was decided that he in turn should offer reparations all round. Tsunetō was put in charge of the retributions ceremony, at which each noble received one of His Highness's swords and the ladies a gown each. It was all hugely entertaining.

In the third month, the time came to hold the Lotus Ceremonies[112] for the departed spirit of the former emperor. The great hall at the Rokujō Palace had burned down, so it was held at the great hall at His Highness's Palace at Ōgimachi. While His Highness was attending the final day of the ceremony, a certain exalted person[113] paid a visit to the Palace. Announcing that he would settle down to await His Highness's return, he made his way to a spot between the two roofed corridors.

I went there to greet him, and having assured him that His Highness would be back soon I was turning to leave when he asked me to stay a little longer. I had no idea what this might be about, but as he was not someone to fob off with some vague excuse, I did as I was told.

He went on to talk casually about the past, saying how often he recalled things that my father used to say, and it made me wistful to hear him speak like this. Then, as we sat there peacefully chatting, for some reason he suddenly blurted out the following extraordinary confession.

'I fear the Buddha must find my priestly devotions impure, knowing my secret thoughts.'

I was completely taken aback, and was about to rise to my feet to cover my confusion, but he seized my sleeve.

'Promise me that you will at least find time for us to meet,' he pleaded. His tears bespoke his unmistakable sincerity. This was all very difficult, but now there was a sudden bustle at His Highness's return, and I pulled myself free and made my escape.

I was still reeling as I watched them meet, and the episode just passed felt like some extraordinary dream. 'It's been a long time since your last visit,' His Highness declared, and he pressed the abbot to have some sake. Bending to pour for them, I thought with a private thrill of excitement that none could know the secret that my heart held.

In due course, word came that the military government in Kamakura was displeased by the continuing bad relations between His Highness and the newly retired emperor Kameyama, and that His New Highness Kameyama was to pay a visit to our Palace. He let it be known that he wished to view the court football ground[114] and requested that a game should be arranged.

At a loss how best to proceed, His Highness consulted the Konoe Minister Kanehira.

'It is customary to provide sake before such a visit is too far advanced, and to have sweet persimmon wine at half time when His Highness changes into formal robes', came the reply. 'One of your ladies should serve.'

As to the question of who should be selected, it was decided that I was of an appropriate age and birth for the role, so the choice landed on me.

My clothes for the occasion were seven layers of robe in soft plum red over rouge red, with a cloak of kerria yellow over spring-shoot green, blue-green Chinese jacket and glossed silk over-robe, with gossamer silk *hakama* trousers. Under this were three raised weave *kosode* gowns in graded shades of plum, and two of Chinese weave damask.

His Highness Kameyama arrived, and when he found that the two brothers' seats had been placed on the same level he complained that the arrangement was wrong. 'The proper seating placement was ordained in our father's reign,' he declared, and he ordered his seat to be moved to a lower level.

His Highness the host now entered. 'Well well,' he said. 'In *The Tale of Genji* when Emperor Suzaku visits Prince Genji, His Majesty orders that the host's seat should be raised to an equal height, but I see you have done the opposite, Your Highness. Very odd.' Everyone was impressed by the elegance of this remark.

When the formal meal had been served and three rounds of sake exchanged, the Crown Prince arrived and the games commenced. At half time, when Kameyama withdrew through the eastern corner side door, Lady Bettō – dressed in a five-robe combination of blue-green over scarlet-purple, with scarlet middle robe, willow green outer coat and kerria yellow over spring-shoot green Chinese jacket – carried in an earthenware sake cup in a woven basket and a gold decanter containing sweet persimmon wine, which I took and offered him. He pressed me to drink first. The games went on until dusk, when torches were lit and His Highness Kameyama departed.

The following day came a message from him, delivered by his retainer Nakayori:

What's to be done?	*ika ni sen*
I thought that face	*utsutsu to mo naki*
unreal, and yet	*omokage wo*
I find I cannot waken	*yume to omoeba*
from this dream	*samuru ma mo nashi*

It was written on thin crimson paper and tied to a sprig of willow.

Feeling it would be impolite not to send some reply, I wrote on thin pale blue paper attached to a sprig of cherry:

Be it real or be it dream	*utsutsu to mo*
it matters not	*yume to mo yoshi ya*
since in this world	*sakurabana*
the cherry blooms	*saki-chiru hodo to*
only to scatter	*tsune naranu yo ni*

More messages from him followed thick and fast . . . ,[115] but I asked Counsellor Morochika to send a carriage and returned home.

In due course a new worship hall was built for the Rokujō Palace, and in the fourth month when His Highness moved there the dedication ceremony was held. It was a Mandala Service[116] presided over by Abbot Kōgō with the support of twenty monks, after which the Kenjichi Grand Abbot performed another dedicatory service for the adjacent Jōchō Hall.

The imperial procession to the event consisted of five carriages. I was seated on the left in the first carriage, and to my right sat Lady Kyōgoku. I wore a seven-layered robe set in the carnation pink combination of shaded soft plum red over white, under a coat in the young iris combination of blue on pale plum. Lady Kyōgoku was dressed in a five-layered robe set in the wisteria combination of pale scarlet-purple over spring-shoot green. For the three days of the ceremony I wore white robes with formal train and Chinese jacket of deep scarlet, and *hakama* trousers.

A garden competition[117] was proposed, and a tiny garden plot was assigned to each of the nobles, senior courtiers, and court ladies of the top two ranks. I was given a little east-facing plot beside His Highness's quarters, a connecting section in front of the new Jōchō Hall, where I set up a lovely little arched bridge over an artificial stream, but late in the night the Zenshōji Counsellor crept in and stole it to put in his own garden plot. It was very entertaining.

The eighth month arrived, and now His Highness began to feel far from well, although he had no particular illness. He refused food, he was bathed in sweat, and with each passing day our anxiety mounted. A doctor was called and set about applying moxa to about ten places, but his condition remained unchanged. On perhaps the eighth of the ninth month, ceremonies to prolong life were begun, but seven days later there was still no change in his condition and everyone was deeply apprehensive.

It so happened that the cleric who came to the Palace to perform these ceremonies was the same man who had tearfully confessed his feelings for me back in spring. He now beseeched me whenever I arrived with messages from His Highness, but I managed to go on evading him until at length an adoring letter arrived that spelled out his feelings and ended by demanding a reply. This was all very difficult. Tearing off the edge of a paper hair-binding cord, I wrote the single word 'dream', and rather than deliver it I simply left it there for him to find.

When I next arrived, he casually tossed me a sprig of scented anise such as is offered in Buddhist ceremonies. Catching it, I retired to a corner to look at it, and discovered that something was written on one of the leaves:

Rising at daybreak	*shikimi tsumu*
to pluck the sweet anise	*akatsuki oki ni*
with tear-wet sleeves I yearn	*sode nurete*
for revelation of that moment	*mi-hatenu yume no*
when this dream's fulfilled	*sue zo yukashiki*

This was so elegant and delightful that I began to love him just a little. I started looking forward to bearing messages to him, and I now responded with pleasure to the things he said.

One day he visited His Highness and lamented that the illness still seemed to be showing no improvement. He then gave instructions that when the ceremony was about to begin later that day, someone should be sent to the adjacent audience room with a suitable transference object.[118]

His Highness passed on these instructions, indicating that I should take one of his robes, but when I duly arrived with it all the attendant priests had apparently retired to their various rooms to put on their ceremonial robes, and no one else was there.

I found myself alone with His Holy Eminence. 'Where should I put the transference object?' I inquired, and he told me to take it to the small anteroom next to the ceremonial altar room. I did as I was told, and found it solemnly lit. Then, before I knew it, he was suddenly there with me, now wearing soft silk[119] rather than his priestly robes.

'The Buddha leads us even through dark delusion,' he murmured, sobbing as he seized me in his arms.

Horrified though I was, I was in no position to protest against someone so exalted. 'The Buddha himself would surely tremble . . . ,' I whispered, but to no effect.

What followed seemed a fleeting dream, scarcely to be believed as real. In no time the priests were announcing that the ceremonial preparations were ready, and he hastily made his escape through the back door. 'We must meet again after the pre-dawn service,' he said as he left.

Very soon the evening ceremony was smoothly under way, exactly as usual, and I was chilled at how calmly he proceeded to offer up his prayers so brazenly after what had just occurred. Seeing him there, illuminated by the all-pervading light of the holy lamps, I was filled with misery at thoughts of the darkness to come in the next world – but although no great passion drove me, I chose a moment after the pre-dawn service had ended when no one was about, and went to him again.

This time the ceremony was behind him so we could go about our assignation a little more calmly. His tearfulness was painful to witness. At length came sounds of movement portending the break of day. Before we parted he insisted that we each put on the gown that the other wore next to their skin, by way of a keepsake.

Afterwards, wrong though it somehow felt, my heart could not rid itself of touching memories of him. I slipped quietly back to my room to lie down for a while, and there I came upon something tucked into the hem of the gown he had given me, and taking it out I found a rather torn sheet of Michinoku paper on which was written:

Unable yet	*utsutsu to mo*
to disentangle dream	*yume to mo imada*
from what is real	*waki-kanete*
a lingering sorrow haunts	*kanashisa nokoru*
this moonlit night of autumn	*aki no yo no tsuki*

I imagined the hasty moment he had somehow found to
write this, and it brought home to me the strength of his feelings for me. Now we seized an opportunity every evening to
meet, and it shamed me to imagine how the Buddha must feel
about the impure invocations addressed to him in those nightly
services before the altar.

By the twenty-seventh, as the services were drawing to an
end, His Highness was greatly improved, and on the following
day His Holy Eminence was set to depart at their conclusion.

'What chance can we hope for to meet again?' he lamented
on our final evening. 'I will let dust gather in the worship hall
and neglect the sacred fire ceremonies in pining for you. If you
feel as I do, perhaps you too should don Buddhist robes and
retreat with me to the mountains rather than cling to life in this
difficult world, sunk in unhappiness.'

His words filled me with alarm.

As the dawn bell tolled the break of day, he rose and tore
himself away. How had he come by the loving words he spoke
as we parted? I wondered, deeply touched. It worried me to
think that those secret tears his sleeves held might somehow
come to alert others to our wrongdoing.

And so it was that after the final ceremony he departed, leaving me with yet another foolish burden to weigh on my heart.

In the ninth month a magnificent Flower Service[120] was held
at the newly rebuilt Rokujō Palace, and even His Highness
Kameyama attended. We court ladies were each to offer flowers, so everyone took considerable care over their robes and so
forth and there was a great fuss, but my low spirits made me
reluctant to join in the excitement. After the service was over
both retired emperors proceeded to the Fushimi Palace to select
pines.[121] The Konoe Minister Lord Kanehira was to take part

as well, but something prevented him and he sent a message
instead with this poem:

Surely Fushimi's mountain	*fushimiyama*
will from this day	*iku-yorozuyo ka*
prosper through generations	*sakau-beki*
like the ageless green	*midori no komatsu*
of the pines you gather	*kyō wo hajime ni*

His Highness's response:

Like the green pines	*sakau-beki*
added with each new year	*hodo zo hisashiki*
to grow through the ages	*fushimiyama*
Fushimi's mountain too	*oi-sou matsu no*
will prosper long	*chiyo wo kasanete*

They stayed there two days, with excursions to the southern
palace and delightful drinking parties, before returning.

Two years earlier in the seventh month, when I returned to
the Palace after some time at home, I took with me a certain fan
whose story was as follows: I had had a piece of fan paper,[122]
the top and bottom edges decorated in a tiny ripple pattern,
with nothing else except a design of water drawn on its pale
blue paper, over which was written with silver paste the words
'love like the curling smoke',[123] and had sent it with some fine
wooden ribs to someone to have it made into a fan. The daughter, herself an excellent painter, exchanged it for a fan on which
she had painted a scene of water and autumn fields, adding the
words 'though I see the bright moon over other bays'.[124]
    This I took with me to the Palace, and His Highness, noticing
that it was by a different hand than usual, pestered me to know
what man had given it to me, so I told him the whole story.
Inspired by the beauty of the picture, he now lost himself in a
fantasy of love for this girl he had never seen, and for nearly
three years kept endlessly importuning me to arrange a meeting.
    Finally, on the evening of the tenth of the tenth month, it was

somehow organized that she was to come to the Palace. His
Highness was on tenterhooks, and dressed with particular care
for the occasion. At this point Sukeyuki, one of his aides, arrived
to announce that he had brought 'the beautiful young lady you
asked for'. This was unexpected, and His Highness instructed
that this other lady be taken to wait in her carriage by the Pond
Pavilion at the Palace's southern edge facing Kyōgoku Street.

When the first bell of evening struck, the long-awaited daughter arrived. I was wearing a double-layered blue-chequered
robe with a design of vines stitched in scarlet-purple, and over
it a fine silk robe of soft plum red and a red-weave Chinese
jacket. Receiving the usual order to bring the lady to him, I
went to meet her at the carriage, and I was struck by the enor-
mous amount of noise she made as she descended, far louder
than the usual decorous swish of silk.

I took her along to the smaller room that had been specially
prepared beside the day room, imbued with the carefully chosen
scent of fine incense. She was dressed in a double-layered robe
with a blue inner layer and a raised brocade design of a large
slatted fan about a foot across, over scarlet *hakama* trousers,
both very stiff and awkwardly worn, and at the back her collar
stood up like something high priests might wear. Her face with its
impressive nose and eyes was most alluring, and at first sight she
seemed quite splendid, though in no way did she strike one as a
well-born young lady. She was plump, tall and solidly built with a
pale complexion, the sort who would look good in the role of primary palace lady at some grand event in the Ceremonies Hall, her
hair all formally done up, tasked with bearing the ritual sword.

I announced her arrival and His Highness entered, dressed
in a pale mauve cloak with woven chrysanthemum design
and wide-bottomed trousers. The scent of his heavily incensed
clothing could be smelt at a hundred paces, and hung thick
in the air even with a screen between us. They talked, and I
winced for her as I heard the forthright way she answered, and
smiled to myself at the thought that this would not be likely to
please him. Before long they retired.

As always, I remained nearby in attendance, with the Saionji
Counsellor Sanekane also on duty outside the papered door

beyond the threshold. It was all over before the night was at all far advanced, indeed so quickly that it seemed nothing could have had time to happen. His Highness emerged without further ado and summoned me. 'Tamagawa Village,'[125] he said curtly. I did feel sorry for her. She was sent home even before the pre-dawn bell had tolled.

He gloomily changed robes, refused food, and instead instructed me to massage him here and there before he went off to sleep. I imagined how the pouring rain must be adding further misery to the poor girl's tear-soaked sleeves as she made her way home.

When morning came I remembered the lady whom Sukeyuki had brought, and reminded His Highness.

'Oh yes,' he said, 'I'd completely forgotten her', and he told me to go and see her. I rose and went out, to find the sun already well up. There outside the Pond Pavilion stood a bedraggled carriage, quite drenched and clearly the worse for wear for being rained on all night.

Horrified, I ordered that the carriage be brought over. The retainers hastily emerged from sheltering under the roof of the gatehouse and did as they were instructed.

I saw that she wore a double-layered robe in the willow combination of white on green, with a pattern of what appeared to be a scattering of flowers, though it was completely soaked through from the leaks in the carriage roof so that the flowers of her under-robe showed through the two glossed silk *kosode* gowns in a most unfortunate way. Her sleeves showed the effects of a long night spent weeping, while her hair was so wet, either from tears or from the leaks, that it looked newly washed.

'I can't present myself in this dreadful state,' she wept, refusing to leave the carriage.

Indeed she did look terrible, I thought. 'I have some fresh clothes in my room that you can put on before you go in,' I said, and explained that there had been a sudden emergency the night before. The poor girl simply continued to cry, however, wringing her hands pitifully and begging to go home, and since it was by now broad daylight I decided the situation was past saving and sent her back.

I reported all this to His Highness. 'How awful!' he exclaimed and hastily sent a letter after her, but all that came in response was an inkstone lid engraved with the words 'like a spider seeking / lost on the grassy moor',[126] which held something wrapped in thin pale blue paper. His Highness opened it and found a small lock of hair,[127] and written on thin multi-coloured paper the words 'it is for you I sought'. With it was this poem:

Worthless as I am	*kazu naranu*
knowing I will be	*mi no yo-gatari wo*
a butt of the world's gossip	*omou ni mo*
fills me with still greater pain	*nao kuyashiki wa*
at love's fruitless dream	*yume no kayoiji*

This was all there was to it. It was all a great shame, and though His Highness sent in search of her a number of times he could never learn where she had gone, though we guessed she had taken religious orders. Many years later, in fact, I heard that she had joined a strict nunnery in a certain Saraji Temple in Kawachi, and it seemed to me that this was an instance of 'joy hid within sorrow', since that sad experience must have set her on the joyous path towards the Buddhist truth.

An unexpected letter now arrived from His Holy Eminence 'Ariake'[128] through a connection of one of the young lads in his service. Clearly his genuine feelings for me continued, which made things rather difficult. I replied to his messages from time to time but there was absolutely no way we could meet, which I was not entirely unhappy about.

And so the year ended. In the new year the two retired emperors held a Flower Competition,[129] and we were so taken up with going off into the far hills in search of blossoms that I had not a moment to spare. There was no time for secret comings and goings with 'Akebono',[130] and all I could do was send uneasy letters. I remained at the Palace without going home right through that year until autumn arrived.

Somewhere towards the middle of the ninth month, I think it was, a long letter arrived from my uncle the Zenshōji Counsellor. 'Please come. I have something I want to discuss with you,' he wrote. 'I am presently in the Izumoji area[131] and there are some ladies here who wish to see you. Could you find a way to come here please? I am personally undertaking this introduction, and as you know I would do whatever I could for you.'

He was in earnest, and he clearly believed I felt the same.[132] On Ariake's side, there had been a close connection with my uncle since childhood, and since we were related he had come up with this plan as a way to meet me. This was evidence enough that his feelings for me were genuine. For my part, though, in typically perverse fashion I felt resentful and alienated, and considerably alarmed. I refused to respond to him, and sitting there self-protectively in the bed I was amused to think that I probably looked as if 'ambushed by love / before, behind'.[133] I felt quite detached as he wept and swore his love for me the long night through, and secretly promised myself this night must be our last.

Dawn approached while he poured out his misery to its bitter end, but the rooster's crow urging his departure only filled me with heartless pleasure. The Counsellor discreetly cleared his throat and murmured something nearby and Ariake rose to leave, but then back he came again to beseech me one more time.

'Do at least come out to say goodbye,' he begged, but I excused myself by saying I felt unwell and continued to sit there. Watching him go off weeping like this, I was guiltily aware of how his yearning heart still lingered there beside me.

I was none too happy with my uncle either, and before the dawn was far advanced I claimed I was needed at the Palace and hurried back. I lay down in my room, but I was unnerved by a vision of Ariake's face still there beside me as it had so recently been.

His letter arrived around noon. It was long and thoroughly sincere, and with it I found this poem:

How could I speak again	kanashi to mo
of sorrow	ushi to mo iwamu
or of unhappiness	kata zo naki
having seen your face	ka bakari mitsuru
for that brief time?	hito no omokage

My feelings were still unchanged, but he seemed so miserable and tormented that it felt wrong to fail to respond this time at least:

What of this heart	*kawaruran*
you feel has changed?	*kokoro wa isa ya*
In other hearts	*shiragiku no*
the white chrysanthemum	*utsurou iro wa*
may lose its pure colour	*yoso ni koso mire*

I could find nothing to say in response to his long and rambling letter, so I sent only this.

He continued to send all manner of messages after this, but I never replied, let alone initiated anything myself, and found various ways to avoid ever seeing him. Then, perhaps prompted by how quickly the year was drawing to an end, a long missive suddenly arrived with a covering letter from my uncle.

'I enclose a document,' it began. 'This is all most unfortunate. You must not spurn His Holy Eminence like this. His powerful feelings for you surely spring from some deep karmic connection, and it pains me that you have treated him so unfeelingly and brought things to such a pass. I very much fear what will happen if you fail to respond appropriately to what he has sent this time.'

Ariake had sent an official-looking folded document, ostentatiously sealed with paste at top and bottom. I opened it to find that it was written in the form of an oath bearing on one side the talismanic mark of some main temple somewhere in Kumano,[134] and on the reverse side commencing with an invocation to all the nation's sixty deities, beginning with Bonten and Taishaku. It continued:

Since joining the priesthood at the age of seven in humble aspiration to attain the spiritual status of the enlightened, I have devoted my days to invocations before the altar and to rigorous ascetic practices, praying first for the perpetuity and prosperity of the imperial line and more generally for the extinction of sin and attainment of ultimate rewards for all humanity, full of

hope that the great gods and buddhas would someday vouchsafe
a revelation to me. But such was not to be, and through some
cursed fate I have spent these past two years night after night
soaking my sleeves with tears of misery for love of your dear
face. When I perform the sutras before the altar's holy image, it is
your words that rise up in my mind; it is your letters that I place
on the altar as holy texts, and those letters that I open to read by
the altar's sacred lamp to comfort my heart.

Tormented by these feelings, I decided to seek the help of your
uncle, assuming he could easily oblige me. But I was deceived in
my belief that you felt as I did, and all came to naught. I therefore
hereby renounce all thought of communicating with you further
by letter or by speech in this lifetime. Yet, since my heart will
never be able to forget you through future realms and incarna-
tions, I am condemned to hell. Never will I forgive this. All the
rituals and ascetic devotions dedicated to the Two Worlds, from
first to last, every accumulated merit I have achieved, I hereby
dedicate to rebirth in the three lower realms. Denied all hope in
this lifetime, may the power of these prayers ensure that we meet
again in hell.

As a little child I was innocent and unknowing, and since the
day when at seven I shaved my head and took Buddhist robes I
never once shared a woman's bed nor felt desire for a woman,
nor will I ever again. Perhaps it seems to you that those words
of love I spoke may well have been spoken to other women too?
The very idea fills my heart with bitterness against your uncle,
who helped to place me in this position.

When I saw that this missive invoked Amaterasu, Hachiman
and many other great deities my hair rose in horror and I felt
sick with fear. But what could I do? I wrapped it all up and
returned it, writing on the covering page only this:

Believing that	*ima yori wa*
these words you write	*taenu to miyuru*
will be the last	*mizuguki wa*
tears soak my sleeve	*ato wo miru ni wa*
to see their traces	*sode zo shioruru*

I sealed it as before and sent it on its way, and that was the last I saw of him. There was nothing more I could say to him, and thus the sad year ended.

In the New Year it was the custom for His Holy Eminence to pay an early visit to His Highness. He duly came, and there was the usual drinking party.

Since he was in no way a stranger at the Palace and this was a small family affair held in His Highness's own apartments, it was impossible to avoid being on hand to serve him, but when His Highness ordered me to pour the sake for His Holy Eminence and I rose to do so, my nose began to bleed and dizziness overcame me. I withdrew, and for the next ten days I was very ill. What could have brought this on? I wondered in terror.

In around the second month, His Highness Kameyama paid an informal visit to His Highness, and an archery competition was proposed. Kameyama suggested that should His Highness's side lose he must be shown a parade of all the Palace ladies, high and low, and if his own side lost he would do the same with his own entourage.

His Highness's side lost, and he assured his half-brother before he left that he would arrange a showing of his ladies for him. He then called in the tonsured Major Counsellor Sukesue for a consultation about how best to go about it. 'What would be some unusual way to present them?' he asked the assembled company.

His nobles each gave their opinion. 'It would be boring simply to line them up in the ladies' quarters as is done for the New Year ceremonies,' said one, while another gave the opinion that it would also be rather eccentric to have each present herself for inspection one by one, like someone having a private audience with a fortune teller. His Highness was inclined to the idea of constructing a pair of elegant dragon- and swan-headed boats and recreating the scene from *The Tale of Genji*[135] by filling them with ladies holding water pitchers, but it was pointed out that it would be a great deal of trouble to make the boats so the idea was abandoned.

Sukesue then suggested a game of court football with groups of eight ladies each from the three different ranks as the players, dressed up as youths of various ranks. The four marking posts[136] would be set up in the corners of the Orange Garden. It would make wonderful entertainment, he said, and everyone agreed.

The high-ranking ladies were allotted nobles to be their aides, while the next in rank had courtiers and those of lower middle rank were assigned upper palace guards, and we were all told to present ourselves dressed for our parts. This involved donning hunting trousers and sword, lacquered clogs with toed socks, and so on. What an idea! What's more, this wasn't planned to take place at night but in broad daylight. How could anyone feel comfortable with that? But there was no help for it, so we all prepared ourselves as instructed.

Sanekane was tasked with being my aide for the occasion. He dressed me up in hunting costume lined in pale blue and with a scarlet-layered undergown. The motif of a waterfall, intended to allude to *The Tale of Genji* poem 'the roar of the waterfall / provokes my tears', was created by depicting rocks with balls of aloeswood sewn onto the left sleeve with an embroidery in white thread of water pouring onto them, while on the right sleeve was sewn an artificial spray of cherry blossom with a great scattering of embroidered petals down the sleeve. The trousers depicted a scene of rocks and weirs with another scattering of petals.

Lady Gondainagon's aide was Sukesue, who clothed her in hunting costume lined in spring-shoot green. On the left sleeve was the design of a watchtower and on the right a cherry tree, while a sprig of bamboo was attached to the left leg and on the right a little lamp holder, and it was all worn with layers of scarlet unlined gowns. The others all wore similarly creative outfits; the big room in the middle building was divided up with folding screens into dressing rooms and we twenty-four ladies had fun getting rigged up in our various inventions.

The original idea was that we make a decorative imitation of a football which was simply to be presented to His Highness Kameyama, but then it was decided that the opening ritual of the game should be acted out by kicking the ball up, with someone catching it in her sleeve as it fell, then removing her clogs and carrying it over to place before him. Everyone miserably

excused themselves from being the one to perform this difficult first kick, so a particularly skilled lady in Her Highness's
retinue, Shin'emon no Kami, was recruited to be among the
'nobles' and play this role. This was certainly a wonderful
honour for her, but even so I didn't envy her. As head of the
team of eight 'nobles', I was the one designated to catch the
ball in my sleeve, remove my shoes, and present it to His Highness Kameyama. It was all very festive and splendid.

The reed blinds along the south side of the room had been
raised for viewing, and the two retired emperors and the Crown
Prince were seated there with the nobles ensconced below them
on either side. The courtiers stood about here and there nearby.

We duly filed in along the hedge and crossed the garden,
attended by our various aides clad in hunting costumes of
various colours. Kameyama announced that he wished to
hear the names of all the ladies. He had arrived around noon
and the drinking had long since begun. Tamekata, who was in
charge of the event, conveyed that Kameyama was impatient
to see the game and kept urging us to be quick, but though
everyone cried 'Yes yes, we're almost ready!' we continued to
dawdle until darkness drew on and the torches were lit.

Finally our various aides, bearing lights, one by one announced
our names, and in turn we faced Kameyama, pressed our sleeves
together, greeted him and moved on past. I was so embarrassed
I could barely produce a word. Even I found it delightful to
watch everyone, starting with the eight middle-ranking ladies,
move off to take up their places at the marker posts, and need-
less to say all the men of various ranks were simply entranced.

I duly caught the ball in my sleeve, placed it before Kameyama, and hastily attempted to retire, but to my great distress
he detained me and insisted that I serve him sake dressed in my
costume.

I will leave to your imagination the various scenes that had
taken place over the two or three days leading up to this event,
with the male assistants each attending to his assigned lady in
her room, helping to tie up her hair in the appropriate fashion,
training her to wear the lacquered clogs, and generally fussing
and flirting.

Not long after this there was a second archery competition, and this time His Highness won.

As a result, he was invited to Kameyama's Saga Palace, where his thirteen-year-old daughter Togosho, who was raised by her nurse Lady Azechi, was presented as a Gosechi Dancer[137] performing the first night rehearsal, with the higher-ranking ladies playing the supporting roles that were performed by the children and lesser attendants in the event itself. There was a parade past the northern guardhouse by nobles in the special robes with padded hems and senior courtiers and sixth-rankers with one shoulder bared, in imitation of the real event. All the Gosechi details were reproduced, including the outfitting of the lesser ladies, and words cannot describe how entertaining it was to see the men's Gosechi dance on the roofless stage and the special performance before the imperial presence.

The competition continued with a further archery contest, which His Highness lost again. This meant that it was again his turn to entertain his half-brother with an event at his Fushimi Palace, where he reproduced the scene from *The Tale of Genji* at the Rokujō Mansion where the ladies play music together.[138] Lady Genkimon'in took the part of Genji's favourite Lady Murasaki. The seven-stringed *kin* played by Onna Sannomiya in the story was represented by a thirteen-stringed *shō no koto*,[139] and my grandfather Count Takachika specifically requested that this important role should be given to his young daughter, a recent arrival at court. This upset me for some reason, and I was inclined to withdraw altogether, but it was decided that since His Highness Kameyama had singled me out at the court football event he would look for me again, so I was assigned the role of Lady Akashi on the *biwa*.

I had first learned the *biwa* from my uncle, Middle Counsellor Masamitsu, when I was seven, beginning with two or three pieces, but I didn't put in much dedicated practice. Then when I was nine His Highness took up the task of teaching me. I didn't progress to learning the three secret pieces, but I played all the usual ones such as 'Sogō' and 'Manjuraku', and at the age of ten I performed in concert with His Highness at the Shirakawa Palace on the occasion of Go-Saga's fiftieth birthday celebration. His Cloistered Excellency praised me for playing so sweetly, and presented me with the gift of a *biwa* made from a single piece of flowering pear wood with rosewood pegs, in a cloth case of red embroidered silk. I continued to play from time to time but never progressed very far with it, so I wasn't very happy to be given this role now and took part rather sulkily.

For this occasion I was instructed to follow the description in *The Tale of Genji* by wearing a willow combination of white over blue robes and a scarlet glossed silk over-robe, with a spring-shoot green outer robe and kerria yellow over a spring-shoot green top layer. It was galling to have been singled out to play the lowly role of Lady Akashi.

Lady Genkimon'in was also far from accustomed to playing the Japanese *koto*, having only recently begun to learn. In fact the only one among us who was an accomplished player would have been the recent arrival on her substitute *shō no koto*. Genji's daughter Lady Nyōgo was performed by the Kazan'in Chancellor's daughter, the Lady of the West Wing, who was therefore entitled to sit beside the main role, Lady Murasaki. I was to sit to the right of the tatami platform opposite Lady Murasaki. The instructions were that the seating should follow the same order as for the court football event, but this didn't feel right somehow. The recent arrival was playing the role of Onna Sannomiya, after all, so I felt she should be the one given the upper place, but these were His Highness's orders so I made no objection.

I arrived at the Fushimi Palace together with His Highness. Witnessing the recent arrival turn up on the day in a carriage bearing her family crest and formally accompanied by retainers brought back moving memories of my own earlier self. Then His Highness Kameyama arrived, and the drinking began.

For our part, we ladies seated ourselves in the prescribed order and placed our various instruments before us with the cushions all arranged just as described in the 'Spring Shoots' chapter of *Genji*. When the time came, His Highness played the role of the host, Prince Genji, while Kameyama took the part of

Genji's son Yūgiri. Kanetada and Saneyasu were ordered to stand at the foot of the stairs and play the flute and the *hichiriki* flute while the ladies settled into their places. The drinking party was conducted in the adjoining room, and halfway through the proceedings Their Highnesses were to join us.

At this point, however, my grandfather Count Takachika arrived. He took one look at the ladies' seating and began to expostulate. 'No no, this is all wrong! Onna Sannomiya's position must be up there in front of the host's table! She is the aunt, after all, while Nijō is only the niece.[140] This lady should be in the higher place. I was placed higher than her father in my day. Why should my daughter be seated lower? Change this seating!'

My uncle and Sanekane came over and explained that this seating had been specified by His Highness, but his response was, 'Be that as it may, this is all wrong!' and in the end no one was willing to stand up to him. His Highness was still in the adjoining room and there was no point hoping that someone was going to go in there and report all this, so I was demoted to the lower seat as he insisted.

I suddenly thought of that carriage ride when this principle of seating was reversed,[141] and emotion overcame me. Why should it matter if one was 'aunt' and the other was 'niece'? How many fine people are born from humble mothers? Should they all be spoken of in terms of their relationships like this? Just what was this anyway? It was all quite ridiculous. I could see no point in being part of such a humiliating situation, so I rose to my feet and left.

I retired to my room, left a message for His Highness if he should come asking for me, and set off for Kobayashi, near the graveyard of Sokujōin, where my nurse's mother, Lady Iyo in her former life when she served Princess Senyōmon'in, had gone to live when she became a nun on the princess's death.

The message I left was written on a sheet of thin white paper and tied with the severed top string of a *biwa*:

Knowing now   *kazu naranu*
the sorrow of my worthlessness   *ukimi wo shireba*

> I break the *biwa*'s strings   *yotsu no wo mo*
> vowing never in this world   *kono yo no hoka ni*
> to play again   *omoikiritsutsu*

I left this with the instruction to tell His Highness, if he should come, that I had gone back to the capital.

Meanwhile, the drinking party had reached the midway point and Their Highnesses emerged for the performance as arranged, to find that no one was there in the role of Lady Akashi with her *biwa*. His Highness demanded to know what had happened, so Lady Genkimon'in told him the whole story.

'That's perfectly understandable,' he said when he heard it. 'She had every reason to leave.' When he inquired at my room he learned that I had already left the Palace, and was given the message I had departed knowing that he would come to fetch me. It was all so sudden and unexpected that apparently the whole mood of the event was spoiled.

He showed my poem to his half-brother, who declared that I had behaved with admirable refinement. 'What pleasure can we have in this performance by the ladies now?' he said. 'I'll be on my way. You won't mind if I take this with me?' and off he went with my poem.

The recent arrival was thus deprived of the chance to play her *shō no koto*. Everyone declared that Count Takachika had behaved outrageously. 'You can put it down to the perversity of old age,' they agreed. 'Nijō's response was in fine taste', and so forth. And thus it ended.

Early the next morning His Highness sent to look for me at my old nurse's house in Shijō Ōmiya and my grandmother's place at Rokujō Kushige, but neither could give any report of my whereabouts. He went on to search high and low, but naturally enough no one could tell him where I was.

This seemed a golden opportunity for me to leave the world and take religious orders, but unfortunately it was impossible because I had been aware since the twelfth month that I was pregnant. Instead, I decided to stay hidden away until the birth was over and make the move then.

Having sworn never to play the *biwa* again, I sent the

instrument that His Cloistered Excellency Go-Saga had given me as an offering to Hachiman Shrine, along with a portion of the Lotus Sutra which I copied onto the back of a letter my father had written.[142] This I wrapped in a sheet of paper on which I wrote:

I hereby offer	*kono yo ni wa*
these severed strings	*omoi-kirinuru*
that I will play no more	*yotsu no o no*
with as a prayer	*katami ya nori no*
my father's treasured writing	*mizuguki no ato*

Thinking back over it all, I recalled how two springs ago, on the thirteenth of the third month, Ariake had first spoken of his love with the words 'I cannot leave this branch unplucked',[143] and then in the twelfth month I had received that letter with its terrible curse. Then not many months later, this year on the same thirteenth of the third month, came the event that so disgusted me with life at the Palace where I had served so long, when I renounced the *biwa*. The man who had stood in lieu of parent to me since my own father's death had now turned against me. 'She has dared to question my orders and run off,' he declared, 'and while I live she shall not return.' When this was reported to me I was filled with trepidation. What had brought me to this point where it seemed every possible avenue was now closed to me?

Sure enough, His Highness continued to look for me hither and yon, and Akebono too scoured every temple and mountain retreat he could think of in search of me. News of this only served to keep me firmly in hiding, but I did make my way stealthily to visit Abbess Shingan[144] in her retreat, feeling that this was a fine opportunity to deepen my connection to the Buddhist Law.

There word reached me from afar about all the goings-on at the Palace, where Count Takachika was in charge of organizing the imperial seating for the fourth month's Kamo Festival,[145] which both Their Highnesses attended. The Coming of Age Ceremonies for both the Crown Prince and the young Emperor

Go-Uda were also held that month. The event required a Counsellor of advanced years to officiate, and since my grandfather Count Takachika was a former Counsellor he was deemed unsuitable, so, with what seemed an excessive desire to display his loyalty, he announced that he would borrow the title from his son the Zenshōji Counsellor for the day. This gesture was much admired, and my grandfather did indeed officiate at the ceremony. The title was to have been returned once this was over, but instead my grandfather turned around and conferred it on his favourite, Tsunetō. The upshot of this was that my uncle had been inexplicably stripped of his title, and he was extremely bitter towards his father for having tricked him like this. This was around the time when my grandfather was doing his best to attain the post of Counsellor for Takayoshi, his son by his present wife, and it seemed to my uncle that he was conferring this title elsewhere to promote his own interests. Feeling that he could no longer remain under his father's roof, my uncle retreated to the house of his father-in-law, the Kujō Middle Counsellor.

This was shocking news and I longed to visit him, but fearing that word of it would get out I wrote to him instead, revealing where I was and urging him to come.

He wrote back saying that he had been terribly anxious since he learned of my disappearance. 'I'm delighted to hear from you,' he wrote. 'I will come this evening, and we can exchange our recent unhappy news.'

He arrived as the darkness drew in. It was near the end of the fourth month, and the late blossoms that still clung here and there looked strikingly white in the midst of all the fresh green leaf. The bright moonlight cast deep shadows among the trees where deer grazed or wandered. The whole scene deserved to be painted. The evening bells of the temples were sounding as he arrived. We met in a corridor connected to the meditation hall, and the chanted evening prayers could be heard nearby. The service ended and the nuns emerged. Seeing the touching poverty of their humble hemp robes, this casually powerful man grew suddenly quiet and wiped away a tear with the sleeve of his stiff silk hunting costume.

'I long to turn from all attachments that tie me to the world and pursue the Buddhist truth,' he told me, 'but the knowledge that I would be betraying your late father's heartfelt request to protect you holds me back.'

Yes, I thought, I long to do the same. What more can I say? And in bitter sorrow I soaked the sleeves of my thin robe with tears.

'After the birth my plan is to retire to a mountain temple,' I told him, 'so we may well be wearing Buddhist robes together.' And so we talked on, speaking together of all the unhappiness that filled our hearts.

In the course of this talk he told me about seeing the terrible document that His Holy Eminence had written. 'Though I was blameless, nevertheless it made my hair stand on end to read it. Both for you and for myself, I truly feel this is a kind of ret-ribution.' He went on to tell me that when everyone had been searching high and low since I disappeared, His Holy Eminence had called at the Palace and on his way out had said to him, 'Can what I have heard about her be true?'

'I told him that I had no idea of your whereabouts to date. I can't say what was in his mind, but he paused and stood silently by the Middle Gate for a while, trying to disguise his tears behind his cypress wood fan, and as he went on his way again he murmured these words from the sutra – "No peace in our world of delusion; we live in the sufferings of the burning house."[146] He was clearly moved by deeper emotions than the usual sorrows of longing, sadness, wretchedness or pain, and I can all too well imagine how he must be suffering as he offers up those prayers before the altar.'

Memories of that 'moonlit night' with its 'lingering sorrow'[147] came back to me, and I found myself tearfully regretting the cruel things I had said to him.

My uncle left as the dawn was breaking, concerned that he might be seen, since 'a dawn departure has a guilty look to it', as he remarked. No sooner was he gone than a message from him arrived. 'When you take that path of Truth, do not forget this moving night and our sorrow at parting this morning':

Foolishly forgetting	*hakanaku mo*
the truth of this brief world's	*yo no kotowari wa*
inconstant ways	*wasurarete*
tears of intolerable pain	*tsurasa ni taenu*
now soak my sleeves	*waga tamoto ka na*

In reply I wrote, 'Indeed it is true, the reality of this world is pain, yet I weep the more to know what grief this is.' I added this:

Yes, true it is	*yoshi saraba*
and the world's pain	*kore mo nabete no*
is made more painful	*narai zo to*
to recognize that our own pain	*omoinasu beki*
is but the way of this sad world	*yo no tsurasa ka wa*

Meanwhile, Akebono had despaired at my disappearance and gone into a twenty-seven-day retreat at Kasuga Shrine. On the eleventh night he dreamed[148] that he saw me there in front of the second shrine building, looking quite unchanged. Reassured, he hurried back to the capital, and when he reached Fujinomori[149] he crossed paths with one of my uncle's retainers who was carrying a thin letter box. On a shrewd impulse and without seeming to pry, he said casually, 'No doubt you're on your way back from Shōkutei Temple. Have you heard when Lady Nijō might be taking religious orders?'

Assuming that he must know all about it, the fellow replied, 'Yes, the former Zenshōji Counsellor called there last night from his father-in-law's mansion where he's staying, and I'm just on my way back from delivering a message to her from him. I've heard nothing about when she may take religious orders. It does look very much as though she will, however.'

Akebono was delighted to have his intuition about my whereabouts confirmed, and there and then he requisitioned the horse that his accompanying retainer rode and sent it back to Kasuga Shrine as a gesture of gratitude to the god. Then, to avoid being seen visiting me in broad daylight, he took himself off instead to the nearby Upper Daigo Temple to call on a monk of his acquaintance.

Unaware of all this, that evening I was sitting looking out at the summer trees while I listened to the abbess expounding the teachings of the great Pure Land monk Zendō when I heard someone step unannounced onto the veranda. At first I assumed it must be one of the nuns, but hearing the swish of silk robes I guessed it was someone wearing court robes, and turning I saw the sliding door beside me open a crack.

'You've been determined to hide yourself away, but the gods have led me to you.' It was Akebono. How can this be? I thought, my heart racing. But there was nothing to be done.

'Everything was so hateful to me that I made the decision to leave and come here,' I told him. 'Under the circumstances you can receive no special treatment from me', and with that I rose to leave.

All the tender words that poured from him as always did touch me, it's true, but I had determined on this path and felt no temptation to go back to the Palace as he kept urging me to do. 'Look, here you are in this delicate state,' he insisted, 'and who else can you rely on for sympathy? It's not as if His Highness's love for you has waned, after all. Is it really right to behave like this just because of that cross-grained old grandfather of yours? Come on, do as His Highness asks, just this once', and so on, and he ended up staying till the following day.

He sent a letter of greeting to my uncle saying that he had unexpectedly discovered me in hiding, and he hoped they could meet. 'Do please come,' he urged warmly. So that evening my uncle arrived, and they spent the night drinking together 'to while away their sorrows'. Before Akebono left they discussed the matter and agreed that he would report to His Highness that he had learned of my whereabouts from my uncle. Sorry to see them both go, I went out to say goodbye. My uncle, dressed as he was in an informal hunting costume of crepe silk with a design of a cypress fence woven through with moon flower vine, chose not to be seen and set off while it was still dark. The bright moon was about to set as Akebono, in a light tan hunting costume, lingered on the veranda while his carriage was brought round.

'It has been delightful to unexpectedly meet like this,' he said to the abbess.

'Here in this humble dwelling where we spend our days in earnest devotions as we await the coming of Amida,' she replied, 'this unexpected guest of ours has had occasion to bring us a magnificent visitor such as yourself, dressed in such finery that it puts our black robes to shame, a veritable light shone on this poor mountain home.'

He then explained how after searching every nook and cranny for me, the Kasuga deity had revealed me to him in a dream. It really was just like the story of the captain in *The Tale of Sumiyoshi*.[150]

The dawn bells seemed to be urging our daybreak parting. As he was about to depart he murmured something I didn't catch. I insisted he repeat it, and he recited:

Knowing all	*yo no usa mo*
the misery of this world	*omoi-tsukinuru*
I lament the tolling bell	*kane no oto wo*
that tells of parting	*tsuki ni kakochite*
beneath the moon of dawn	*ariake no sora*

or so I think it went. Sad to see him go:

This misery and pain	*kane no oto ni*
swells with the sound	*usa mo tsurasa mo*
of the tolling bell	*uchi-soete*
and lingers with me	*nagori wo nokosu*
like dawn's lingering moon	*ariake no tsuki*

Today I felt that fresh obstructions had arisen to hold me back from that path I had determined on.

'I don't think that these gentlemen will spread the word about your whereabouts,' the old nun said to me, 'but my insistence to his messengers that you aren't here weighs on my conscience. I think it's best that you should go to Lady Iyo's retreat in Kobayashi.' I could see her point, so I asked my uncle to send a carriage and returned to Kobayashi in Fushimi.

The day ended without incident. My nurse's mother Lady Iyo exclaimed when she saw me, and said there had been many callers from the Palace asking if I was there, including a number of visits by Kiyonaga.[151] Yet as I listened to her chatter I seemed to see before me Ariake's face, and hear those words of his – *No peace in our world of delusion; we live in the sufferings of the burning house.* How distracted with sorrow I have been! I thought sadly.

Beneath the fourth-month sky with its scudding showers, I heard from its hiding place among the fresh green leaves on Mount Otowa the first early summer call of the *hototogisu.*[152]

Hototogisu	*waga sode no*
comfort these tears	*namida koto toe*
I weep onto my sleeve	*hototogisu*
filled with sad thoughts	*kakaru omoi no*
beneath the sky of dawn	*ariake no sora*

The nuns rose while it was still dark and began the pre-dawn service, the bell of nearby Sokujōin Temple rang to awaken the world, and I too rose and joined them in their chanting.

The sun was well up when a messenger – the man who had once slashed the brambles to give Akebono entry – arrived with a letter from him. He wrote touchingly recalling our night together, then went on to tell me news of our child, the girl who had been whisked away at birth like some passing dream, whose face I had never seen again but whose fate had always haunted me. She had been ill since the spring, he wrote, very ill, and when the Yin-Yang masters were consulted[153] their opinion was that it was due to my longing for her. 'Parental love is indeed an unending bond, so I can well believe it,' he wrote. 'When you come to the capital I must show her to you.'

It wasn't that I actually yearned for her or pined over her, but 'unbidden thoughts will rise', as the saying goes. Whenever I paused to wonder how old she must be now, memories of that face I had seen for a brief moment the night she was born could not but move me with loving thoughts. I could indeed see how the sorrow of our lives' separate threads might blight the future. 'This is very disturbing,' I replied. 'I do hope I can have a chance to see her.' I was left feeling full of concern for the child, and haunted by unhappy fears of what future news of her I might hear.

Evening came and the night service was conducted, whereupon I went to meditate in the private worship hall with the little Buddhist image, and found an ancient nun already seated there chanting. Those sacred words that bring one to the Buddha reached my ears from some distance away, and filled me with faith. Then came the sound of the outer folding door opening and I clearly heard people beyond. Curious about who it might be, I slid open the papered door beside me a little to look, and discovered a portable palanquin with a couple of lower guardsmen and servants in attendance. It was His Highness.

I was utterly astonished, but our eyes had already met and it was impossible to hide. Retaining my composure, I simply sat there while he had the palanquin brought up to the veranda and descended.

'I've had quite a time tracking you down,' he announced. I said nothing.

He then ordered that the palanquin be sent back and a carriage prepared. 'You seemed set on cutting your ties with the world. That's why I've come,' he explained while he waited, and he went on to berate me for including him in my bitterness against my grandfather.

I could see his point, but I replied that the world had become hateful to me, and I had seized this chance to leave it.

He told me that he had been at the Saga Palace when he unexpectedly learned my whereabouts. Deciding that there was little point in sending yet another messenger to urge me to return, he had moved to his nearby Fushimi Palace and come from there in person to talk to me. 'Whatever you may think,' he said, 'I want you to stay calm and hear me out while I explain my unhappiness at your absence.' On he talked until, weak-willed as ever, I ended up joining him in his carriage.

All night we talked. He declared that he had had no idea of what had occurred on the day of the concert, and swore that come what may he would never favour anyone over me, invoking his gods and mine, and he so awed me that I agreed to go back to the Palace, though it filled me with gloom to think that my chance to leave the unhappy world had slipped beyond my grasp again.

The sun had risen by the time we set out for the Palace, and he urged me to make haste and come right away. I could only comply, resigned to the fact that it must be.

All my things had been sent back home, so for now I was settled in Lady Kyōgoku's room, and I found it very tiresome to have to conform to the ways of the world again. Around the end of the fourth month, the childbirth band ceremony[154] took place at the Palace, prompting all sorts of memories for me.

The time now came for me to meet the little girl whose face I had seen for that one dream-like moment. I was called to a completely unknown house for the meeting, as her usual home was deemed to be poorly set up for such an occasion. I had planned to call there on my way back from the annual visit to my mother's grave on the fifth of the fifth month, but Akebono insisted that it was an unpropitious month for the meeting and besides, it would hardly be suitable to combine it with a visit to a grave, so I was taken there on the last day of the fourth month instead.

The little girl was dressed in a plum-red *kosode* robe with raised brocade pattern. Her hair had been left to grow since the second month and hung prettily around her face. She was as dear as I had remembered her from that night's brief glimpse.

His wife had given birth at around the same time, but the child had died and she had taken on my child in its place, so everyone assumed it was her own. Hoping to wed her to the future emperor, they were raising her with great care and planned to introduce her to the court, I learned. It felt strange and difficult knowing that my child was now the darling of another family. His Highness had no idea of this secret of mine, and it terrified me to think he might ever suspect that such a thing had been kept from him.

Around the eighth month I think it was, the Konoe Minister Lord Kanehira paid a visit to the Palace. He came often, having

been asked by Go-Saga on his deathbed to support His Highness in every way possible, he said. His Highness was always
very welcoming, and as usual there was a private drinking
party at the Palace when he arrived, at which I served.

Seeing me, Kanehira said, 'Well well, I heard you'd gone
missing. What mountain fastness were you hiding yourself
away in, eh?'

'It needed little short of a wizard's magic to discover her,'
joked His Highness. 'We tracked her down on Mount Hōrai,[155]
you know,' and so on.

'But seriously, the old Count's senile perversity is simply
beyond words,' Lord Kanehira went on. 'The Zenshōji Counsellor's unfortunate retirement was another shameful case of
it. Just what goes on with all these power struggles, eh? Was
there really such a pressing need for Tsunetō to be given his
title? And have you really given up the *biwa* forever?' he said,
turning to me.

I didn't really respond, so His Highness cut in. 'Yes, she
swore a solemn oath to that effect to the god Hachiman, and
not just for herself but for future descendants.'

'Such a shame to make this decision, and still so young,' said
Kanehira. 'That Koga family of hers is very proud and sensitive.
As for Tsunetō, he probably put himself forward to the Count
for promotion to Counsellor. The Koga are the only family to
have continued a direct descent from Emperor Murakami's line,
of course. The story goes that my brother, the ex-Chancellor
and Regent Okanoya,[156] once took a fancy to the Koga family
retainer Nakatsuna, who came from a long line of loyal retainers to the household, and suggested that he might also serve in
his own family. "I serve the Kogas," he replied proudly. "How
could I do such a thing?", to which my brother replied, in a
letter written in his own hand, "The Kogas are a special case
and the normal rules do not apply to them, so you should feel
quite free to combine positions." Surely the Count was quite
unjustified in claiming seating precedence for his daughter just
because she was Nijō's aunt.

'My son the former Prime Minister told me,' he continued,
'that he called on His Highness Kameyama and in the course

of a long talk His Highness remarked, "Poetry is the highest accomplishment for a woman, you know. The poem Lady Nijō wrote in the midst of that whole painful business impressed me. It's in the old traditional imperial style that's come down through eight generations, and it shows an astonishing sensibility for one so young. A fellow named Nakayori who serves in my palace and is related to the family[157] is apparently searching high and low for her after learning of her disappearance." He said he was quite perturbed about her whereabouts himself when he learned of it, it seems.

'By the way,' he went on, 'my second son, Lieutenant Middle Counsellor Kanetada, has quite a talent for *imayō*.[158] Would you mind inducting him into the secrets of the art, Your Highness?'

'I have no objection,' His Highness replied, 'but it would be rather awkward to do it here in the main Palace, so I suggest we go to Fushimi.'

The event was arranged for two days later, so His Highness's procession there had to be hastily arranged. It was to be all very private, so there were only a few retainers accompanying him and meals were to be strictly informal. Only the Superintendent of the Imperial Kitchen went along, I believe.

I had been quite busy with various outings recently so my robes were looking particularly worn and limp, and now that I was to accompany His Highness on this unexpected excursion, I was at a loss how to lay hands on appropriate clothes to wear. After the *biwa* incident I was no longer on speaking terms with my grandfather the Count, who would normally have supplied such things, so I was even more delighted than usual to receive from Akebono a set of unlined gowns in the yellow and green valerian combination, over which went a red Chinese jacket with an embroidered design of dewy autumn fields on the sleeves, plus a gossamer silk *kosode* gown and *hakama* trousers.

The only people there were Lord Kanehira, his son Morotada and his second son Kanetada, together with Sanekane, Michiyori and Morochika, who accompanied His Highness from the Palace. My uncle's Kujō home was close by, and His Highness sent repeated messages insisting that nothing should prevent him from joining them, but my uncle declined, saying he had retreated from the world. Finally the retainer Kiyonaga was dispatched especially to fetch him, and he relented and came. Quite unexpectedly, with him he brought two *shirabyōshi* performers,[159] though no one had any idea of this at the time.

The two performers remained in their carriage at the upper Fushimi Palace building while the transmission of the teaching took place in the southern building. After the event the drinking party began, and at this point my uncle revealed their presence to His Highness, who was most intrigued and asked that they be brought in.

They were sisters, they said. The older one, in her twenties, wore a set of unlined gowns in the soft plum-red combination with *hakama* trousers, while the younger was in a striped valerian combination unstarched hunting costume with a design of bush clover down the sleeve, over which she wore wide-bottomed trousers. The older one's name was Harugiku and the younger was called Wakagiku.

They sang a few short *shirabyōshi* songs, then His Highness said he wished to see them dance. They had brought no hand-drum, they said, so one was found which my uncle played for them. First Wakagiku danced. Then His Highness wanted to see the older dance. At first she declined, explaining that she had long since given it up, but he pressed her until she finally relented.

She put on her sister's wide-bottomed hunting trousers over her own trousers, and performed a wonderfully unusual little dance. Then His Highness demanded a longer one, so she followed this with some auspicious dances. As the night wore on, His Highness grew extremely drunk, and the two dancers were later taken home without his knowledge, while everyone else agreed to stay there that evening and return the following day.

While His Highness was asleep, a certain private matter[160] took me in the direction of the Tsutsui Pavilion. A chill and stormy wind sang in the pines, and the mournful piping of autumn insects lent its sorrow to autumn's melancholy. A clear moon was rising late, and the whole scene made me ache with unanticipated feeling as I made my way back through the hushed night of this rustic place, draped only in a light bath robe, when suddenly from behind a reed blind at the edge of the Tsutsui Pavilion a hand seized me by the sleeve.

I honestly thought it was a ghost, and I let out a shriek. 'For heaven's sake be quiet,' said a voice. 'If you make all this noise at night you'll attract the tree spirits.'[161] So it was him.[162] My heart froze. I tried to tug myself free and go on my way, but though my robe was torn his grip held. There was not a soul around, and I found myself being dragged in behind the blinds.

The building too was empty. 'What are you doing?' I cried, but there was no resisting him.

'I've loved you so long,' he declared, and so on and so forth, all those things I'd heard so many times before. How tiresome it all was, the same old words of love. I barely listened, and only struggled to break free and get back to His Highness as soon as I could.

'It's late, and His Highness will be awake and looking for me,' I begged, in an effort to convince him to let me get away.

'Promise me you'll somehow find a moment to come back to me!' he pleaded, and since there was no escape I swore on all the gods that I would do so. Finally I managed to leave, but I trembled to think where this promise of mine would lead.

His Highness was now revived enough to call for another round of drinking, so everyone gathered and the rowdy party began again. He was horribly drunk. 'Such a shame you sent that Wakagiku girl away so soon,' he declared. 'We'll stay another day and you must call her back.' Once he was assured this would be done he was satisfied, and after drinking a great deal more he fell asleep again. But there was no sleep for me that night. Unreal though it felt, what had happened stayed with me as no mere memory of a dream.

The next night His Highness was to host the party, with his retainer Suketaka in charge. An extravagant banquet was prepared, the two dancers came again and a vast amount of sake was consumed. Since His Highness was host, the proceedings were particularly elaborate. A silver sake cup holding three pieces of musk was placed on an incense wood tray and presented to the older sister, while the younger was given a silver tray that held a lapis lazuli cup containing a piece of musk.

The party went on until the pre-dawn temple bell. Asked to stand and perform again, Wakagiku sang the song about the split statue of Fudō.[163] When she came to the words 'those lustful dreams still lingered / deep in the abbot's heart', my uncle threw me a meaningful look. The relevance of the words had struck me too, and I sat there frozen with dismay. The party ended in a general uproar of voices and uninhibited dancing.

His Highness finally settled down to sleep, and I was sitting beside him massaging his back when the dreaded figure of the man from the previous night appeared nearby. He called to me, saying he had something to ask me, but what could I do? I couldn't very well just get up and go to him.

'Do come, at least while His Highness is sleeping,' he kept pleading. Then I heard His Highness murmur softly, 'Quick, off you go. No need to worry.'

I wanted to die from misery and mortification. I was kneeling at His Highness's feet. Lord Kanehira reached over, seized me by the hand and dragged me reluctantly up. 'You must stay on night duty near His Highness,' he insisted, pulling me off round the corner. It horrified me to think of His Highness lying there pretending to sleep, hearing it all from the other side of the papered door. I wept and resisted as best I could, but I must have been really quite drunk. Finally, around dawn, he left. I was not to blame for any of this, but I felt utterly miserable as I lay down beside His Highness again. He was extremely cheerful, which I found very hard to bear.

The next day we were due to leave, but Lord Kanehira announced that as the two dancers wanted to stay longer, we were to remain another day, and he would provide the banquet this time. So we stayed on. Dreading what fresh event might occur, I was resting somewhere other than the sleeping quarters when a letter from him arrived:

Still unawakened	*mijikayo no*
from that short night's dream	*yume no omokage*
your face stays in my heart	*sameyarade*
as your lingering scent	*kokoro ni nokoru*
still haunts my sleeve	*sode no utsurika*

'This morning I worried that His Highness may have been awake just on the other side of the door,' he wrote.

My reply:

I cannot even tell	*yume to dani*
if it were dream	*nao waki-kanete*
but how I long to show you	*hito shirezu*
the true colour of this sleeve	*osōru sode no*
that holds my hidden tears	*iro wo misebaya*

His Highness kept insisting I should come to him, so I finally presented myself. Perhaps he was concerned that I might be miserable, for he treated me with a thoroughly cheerful friendliness that only left me feeling worse.

The party began, and before it was fully dark His Highness set out by boat to the upper Fushimi Palace. As the night drew on, he called for cormorant fishing,[164] and had a cormorant boat brought up and attached to his so that he could watch. He then decided to reward the three fishermen with the set of unlined gowns I wore.[165] After he returned, more sake was consumed and His Highness became quite excessively drunk. Very late that night, he finally retired, at which point Lord Kanehira appeared once more.

'How dull it is to spend all these nights away from home!' he began. 'And besides, Fushimi is known from of old to cause sleepless nights.[166] Here, light me a taper. There are sure to be all sorts of unpleasant creatures around.' On and on he went, driving me mad with his pestering.

'Go on, why don't you go to him?' His Highness himself urged. I was truly miserable.

'You must forgive an old man his perversities,' continued Lord Kanehira. 'Our ages may raise eyebrows, but there are plenty of examples from the past where an older man becomes a young girl's protector.' He said all this right beside where His Highness was lying. Words cannot express how wretched I felt.

His Highness was, as usual, in high spirits. 'I'll be lonely sleeping here by myself,' he declared, and insisted we stay close by, so I spent a second night with Lord Kanehira right next door to where he lay.

The following morning there was a great flurry of preparation for departure before dawn. We rose and parted, leaving me feeling 'a mere empty shell'.[167]

On the way back to the capital I sat behind His Highness in his carriage, along with Sanekane. All the carriages travelled together as far as the Kiyomizu bridge, but at Kyōgoku Street His Highness's carriage continued north while Lord Kanehira's and the others turned west, and as I watched them receding into the distance the pang that I felt at parting astonished me to wonder just how I could have learned to feel like this.

BOOK 3

(1281–1285)

With everything becoming ever more difficult and distressing and no obvious way out of this oppressive situation, I longed constantly to leave the world and retreat to some mountain temple, and my failure to be able to fulfil this urge made me despise myself for my weakness and worldly attachment. Haunted by these thoughts, even my dreams portended a growing distance from His Highness. I did everything in my power to avert it, but to no avail.

It was around the middle of the second month.[168] Flowers were budding everywhere and the spring breeze carried the scent of plum blossom, filling my heart with unfulfilled yearning and adding a keener edge to the forlornness and unhappiness that I could share with no one.

Hearing His Highness call for someone, I went to see what he might need and found him standing quite unattended and alone in the room next to the bathing room.

'The ladies-in-waiting are all back at home at present. I'm feeling quite abandoned, and even you are spending all your time in your room. Who are you pining for now?' he said, suspicious as ever.

At that very moment a visit from His Holy Eminence was announced. His Highness immediately returned to his quarters to greet him, with myself in attendance, helplessly doing my best to affect indifference.

Princess Yūgimon'in, who was then still known as Imagosho, was only a young girl at this time. She had been ill for days, and His Highness now asked His Holy Eminence to perform invocations to Nyohō Aizen[169] for her recovery. He also ordered on his own behalf a ceremony dedicated to the Ursa Major deity,[170] to be performed I think by the Narutaki prelate.

The conversation proceeded tranquilly while I waited nearby, wondering anxiously what Ariake must privately be feeling about the situation. Then someone arrived to announce that the little princess's illness was worsening, and His Highness hurried off to her room.

'Please be so kind as to wait until His Highness returns,' I said. We were now alone together, and I found myself sitting face to face with him while he poured out his heart in a litany of all he had felt through the bitter days and months without me until this moment. Ashamed though he was, his tears overcame him. What could I say? I could only sit and hear him out.

Meanwhile, His Highness had quietly returned, and unbeknownst to us had paused behind the door, overhearing all this. Always alert to matters of the heart, unfortunately he very soon grasped what had transpired between us.

When His Highness finally walked in, Ariake did his best to pretend that nothing had occurred, but there was no hiding such tear-sodden sleeves, and I trembled to imagine how His Highness must be judging what he saw.

Around the time the lamps were lit, Ariake took his leave. The evening that followed was hushed and unpeopled. As I sat rubbing His Highness's feet while he settled down to sleep, he said to me, 'You know, I heard some astonishing things earlier. What on earth is all this about? My brother and I have been extremely close since childhood, but I had no idea he was capable of this sort of thing.'

There was no point denying it, so I made a full confession, hiding nothing, from my first meeting with His Holy Eminence to that moonlit night when we parted.

'What an extraordinary relationship,' he exclaimed. 'Still, I tremble to think what such bitterness might lead to, given that he longed for you so desperately that he inveigled your uncle into arranging a meeting only to be coldly rejected. These passions can grip anyone whoever they may be, as we know from past examples. Think of the love-crazed Bishop Kakinomoto, whose spirit possessed the empress and finally killed her despite all the powers of the buddhas and bodhisattvas. Then there was the holy man from Shiga Temple, with his deluded passion for Lady Kyōgoku that was quickly cured when she took pity and responded with a compassionate poem requesting his spiritual help.

'This is no ordinary passion that has gripped my brother,' he continued warmly. 'You must understand this and be kind to him. No one will know that I'm aware of the situation. He will shortly be staying here at the Palace to perform the rites I requested, and you must find an opportunity to help him put all this bitterness and resentment behind him. You may not feel it's appropriate when he is here to perform religious rites, but believe me, I know what I'm doing. You must feel quite free to go to him.

'I say this knowing that you are at one with me in all things. Don't so much as hesitate, just do everything you can to dispel this bitterness and anger,' he continued. Such words could only fill me with misery.

'Remember that I was the first man to love you,' he went on, 'and in all these years since, I have never lost my feeling for you. It's just a shame that I haven't been able to give full expression to my love and act as I wished. After all, it was your mother who first taught me the pleasures of the bed. I loved her in secret, but I was still so young. I had to keep my yearning hidden from the eyes of those around me while she went on to become the lover of Fuyutada and then of your father, while I was reduced to seizing secret moments to go to her. I worried over you while you were still in the womb, and when you were just a babe in arms I watched over you carefully, longing to see you grown.' Such talk of my own past both moved and distressed me.

And so the morning came, and the first day of the ritual service. There was a great bustle to set up the altar and prepare the room, while I was filled with private forebodings, and fearful lest my face betray my feelings to others. His Holy Eminence's arrival was announced, and though I managed to seem nonchalant in his presence, misery filled me at the knowledge of what was in His Highness's mind.

I felt constantly uneasy as I went to and fro all day delivering messages from His Highness to His Holy Eminence; then that evening before the first night's service began, my guilty distress only grew when I found myself instructed to take to him a folded document on which His Highness had written certain questions he had relating to the esoteric teachings. When I arrived to deliver it I found the room for once empty of others. A hazy spring moon shone softly in on Ariake where he sat leaning on an armrest, intoning sutras.

'I swore to the Buddha that I would forget you after our unhappy parting in the autumn moonlight,' he said to me, 'yet I still find being here with you now so hard to bear that come what may I cannot give you up. Despite all my prayers to be spared existence in the same world as you, the gods deny me. What is to be done?' he finished, barring my way.

Fearful though I was that this might somehow become known and my reputation ruined, I stayed – but before that dream of love could be achieved, it was interrupted by a sudden bustle of activity and the announcement that the time for the night service had arrived. I slipped out by the back door, feeling that it closed between us like a barrier gate. 'We must meet again after the late-night service is over,' he insisted, but I returned to my room, feeling that I really could not remain in such an impossible situation.

Yet that night his face stayed with me in the tears I shed, far more than it had done that night of his 'lingering sorrow'.[171] What can have happened in our past lives to create what could only be this karmic bond between us? I wondered. I lay down to sleep, but no dreams came to me, and the morning light found me still wakeful. There was nothing for it but to rise and go to wait on His Highness.

Very few people were about. 'I carefully set things up last night,' he said. 'I trust he didn't realize the situation? Be careful not to make him suspect that I'm in on this, won't you. It would be distressing if he felt awkward with me.' There was no way to reply to this.

It was wretched to imagine Ariake's state of mind as he performed the sacred rites in this state of defilement. On the eighteenth, the sixth night of the ceremonies, His Highness paid a visit to the central hall to view the red plum that was blooming particularly brilliantly and beautifully that year, and I accompanied him until late that evening. Hearing the sounds that indicated the end of the final night's ceremony, he filled me with consternation by saying, 'It's late, and the last night of rituals is over. Take your leave and go to him.'

When the temple bells of midnight had rung, His Highness summoned Lady Genkimon'in to his side and settled down to sleep in the little room beside the Orange Garden. I wasn't simply doing as I was told; I did somehow yearn to see Ariake once more before he left, so I went around to the room where we had met before. He was there, and it was clear that he was indeed waiting in the hope that I might come.

I knew full well that my only salvation lay in breaking these worldly ties, yet here I was, my heart still haunted by His Highness's words of love whispered so recently in my ear, and by the scent of him as we lay close that still permeated my sleeve, and now another lover brought fresh sorrows to that sleeve, and there was no one I could tell my troubles to.

He wept bitterly at the thought that this would surely be our final night together. Bewildered though I felt, I found myself thinking that it would have been better to have ended things with our previous painful parting. Still, it was too late for that. The short night was over with the dawn, the evening's brief time together like a momentary flash of light on passing dew, gone all too soon, and at our parting there could be no knowing on what far-off evening we might ever meet again:

Parting once	*tsurashi tote*
so painfully	*wakareshi mama no*
your face re-met	*omokage wo*
is now reflected	*aranu namida ni*
in fresh tears of sorrow	*mata yadoshitsuru*

Well, it was pointless to let my thoughts linger over it all. The little princess had by now recovered, and Ariake was to leave after the evening ceremony was done. Yet inevitably, the image of him remained to haunt my heart.

I had left him before first light and returned to my room to sleep, but suddenly there was an unexpected summons from His Highness to come immediately, delivered by his retainer Kiyonaga. Lady Genkimon'in had been with him last night, so why should he demand I come so quickly now? My heart beat fast as I went to him.

'It was so late when you went,' he said when I arrived, 'but I sent you because I couldn't help thinking of all he must be feeling as he waited for you. I wouldn't have been so understanding if this had been any ordinary, everyday passion, but knowing him as I do I simply couldn't leave him to languish. That is why I let you go.

'Well, last night I had a strange dream. I dreamed that His Holy Eminence presented you with his sacred five-pronged *vajra*,[172] which you tucked into the bosom of your robe and concealed from me. I took you by the sleeve and asked why you should hide this from me, when we understand each other so well. You looked miserable, wiped away your tears and took it out, and I saw that it was silver. It had belonged to my father Emperor Go-Saga, so I said, "This should be mine", and stood there reaching to take it, at which point I awoke. This is surely a prophecy, and last night's encounter will make it come to pass. If you do indeed prove to be pregnant, it will undoubtedly be by "the seed of another tree",' he finished.

I found this difficult to believe, yet for the rest of that month he did not call me to his bed, for which I could blame no one but myself, I felt. Sure enough, in due course it became clear that the prophecy was true, and I despaired to think what would become of me now.

It would have been around the beginning of the third month. Not many people were about, His Highness had retired to the annex without taking his evening meal, and he called me to keep him company there. I was rather worried about what he might say, but he talked gently on and on, assuring me of his undying love, and I was torn between joy and unhappiness as I listened.

'I made a point of not calling for you after that dream,' he said. 'I chose to wait for a month to pass, but I've been very lonely without you.'

So there had indeed been a plan behind it, I thought in bewilderment. But it was true, from that month it had become clear that I was pregnant, there was no doubting or denying it anymore, and it was pointless to torment myself now over the fruits of that night.

Meanwhile, a coolness had developed between me and Akebono, the man I could in a sense call my first lover, since his bitterness over those events at the Fushimi Palace.[173] Justified though he no doubt was to resent me, this continued to weigh on my mind.

Then one day at the beginning of the fifth month, that time when the water-iris stems are picked for the fifth-month ceremony,[174] a message from him arrived while I was briefly back at home for my mother's annual memorial ceremony:

Deep I reached	*ushi to omou*
to find a stem	*kokoro ni nitaru*
that matched this depth of pain	*ne ya aru to*
and found my sleeve	*tazunuru hodo ni*
was soaked with sorrow	*nururu sode kana*

He added much else besides. 'While you are back at that house where no one's on guard,[175] I hope to call and talk if only briefly,' he added.

I simply wrote in reply:

Pain upon pain	*ukine wo ba*
washes through my life	*kokoro no hoka ni*
despite my heart's deep roots	*kake-soete*
and there is not a day	*itsumo tamoto no*
my sleeves are dry	*kawaku ma zo naki*

'I used to feel that nothing could ever come between us, and yet . . . ,' I added, and indeed it all felt quite hopeless. Then, very late that night, he came.

All our tales of sorrow were not yet shared when we heard a sudden commotion outside, and there were cries that a fire had broken out not far from the Palace. Under the circumstances, Akebono decided he couldn't stay and he hurried away. The short summer night was about to end, and it was too late for him to think of coming back. As the sky grew light, this message arrived: 'Last night's obstacles brought home to me the growing distance that separates us. Sensing how the future will unfold, my heart is heavy.' With it was this poem:

Will the waters of our hearts	*taenuru ka*
flow to forgetting	*hito no kokoro no*
and our love run dry –	*wasure-mizu*
this love we swore together	*ai mo omowanu*
that finds no way to meet?	*naka no chigiri ni*

Indeed I also felt that last night's sudden obstruction to our meeting hinted at a deeper truth.

Though the love we swore	*chigiri koso*
may indeed be over	*sate mo taekeme*
there can be no end	*namidagawa*
to this undrying	*kokoro no sue wa*
flow of tears	*itsumo kawakaji*

If I had remained at home for a while longer our bond would surely not have been broken, but that evening a sudden summons from His Highness arrived saying that something urgent had arisen, and a carriage was sent for me, so back I went.

At the beginning of autumn my morning sickness at last eased.
   'It must be about time to tie the childbirth band,' remarked His Highness. 'Does His Holy Eminence know about it yet?'
   'No, he doesn't. When could I have told him?' I replied.
   'He need feel absolutely no embarrassment with me about all this,' His Highness continued. 'He may feel rather abashed at first, but after all there is no escaping what karma has ordained. I plan to tell him that he has no reason for shame.'

What could I say? I could just imagine how Ariake would feel on hearing this. But if I begged him not to I feared it might be taken as offensive insolence, so all I could reply was, 'As you wish, Your Highness.'

Around that time there was a set of lectures on the esoteric Buddhist teachings at the Palace, during which His Highness questioned the scholars on various points of doctrine. His Holy Eminence came to take part, and stayed four or five nights. After the various events were over, a little sake was provided, which I served.

As they drank, His Highness observed to everyone, 'After wide-ranging inquiry and having studied the matter deeply, I have concluded that relations between the sexes are not considered a sin in Buddhism. One is powerless in the face of inescapable karmic bonds. This is why we see so many examples of it from of old. Take the saintly ascetic Jōzō, for example. Having heard that his karma from a previous life dictated that he would form a relationship with a woman from Michinoku, he attempted to kill her without success, but ended up succumbing to her charms. Then there was the holy man from Shiga Temple and his lust for Lady Kyōgoku, who asked for his spiritual help. Unable to overcome his passionate desires, he turned into a blue demon.[176] Or think of the story of the wife whose desire for her absent husband turned her to stone. All intimate relations with beasts are also the result of karmic destiny. These things are beyond the reach of human power to control.'

I couldn't help feeling that all this was personally directed at me, and I was awash with tears and perspiration as I listened.

Luckily, however, the drinking session ended without mishap and everyone retired.

His Holy Eminence was about to leave too when His Highness held him back. 'The night is late and all is quiet. Stay for a while and let us talk further on the teachings,' he said. Ill at ease, I left and slipped back to my room, and I had no idea what His Highness said after that.

Late that night I was summoned to him. 'I found a fine chance to talk to him as planned,' he announced. 'Even someone driven to sinful folly by the excesses of parental love could not feel as strongly as he does', and he shed a tear. There was nothing I could say in reply, and it was impossible to repress the tears that were already soaking my own sleeve.

He was particularly tender with me that night. 'I assume you were listening back then when I spoke about the inescapable nature of our karmic bonds,' he said to me. 'Later I told him about overhearing those astonishing things that night. "You will no doubt be feeling quite ashamed," I said to him, "but I have made a solemn oath to speak honestly to you, and there must be no rift between us as a result of it all. In your position, it would be terrible if word of this got out. Remember that these irrepressible feelings of yours are simply the result of actions in your previous life, and please don't let it disturb you further. This past spring I could see that she was indeed with child, which confirmed a dream I had had. I kept her from my bed until the third month, just to verify for myself the truth of this bond between you and whether my dream had really proven correct. You can imagine, I'm sure, how sincere my intentions have been. If I speak falsely, may I lose the protection of the deities of Ise, Iwashimizu, Kamo and Kasuga, those divine protectors of the nation. No, you must not feel ashamed with me. After all, this has not changed my feelings for you in the slightest." '

'After I finished,' His Highness continued, 'His Holy Eminence remained silent, surreptitiously wiping away his streaming tears, before he replied, "There is nothing left to say in the face of what you have told me. The karmic consequences of my former life are truly wretched to me. I will remember through countless lives to come the debt I owe you for these kind words of yours. I cursed the bitter fate that led me to this folly, and for three years I strove to free myself of my passion, but even as I prayed and chanted my thoughts were constantly of her. So obsessed was I that I wrote a formal vow to all the gods which I sent to her. Yet still my infatuation continued. Then fate drew me back and I found myself in her arms again, bewailing my powerlessness to despise myself for it. And now you say that it has borne this fruit. Well, one of the young princes must replace me in my role of imperial abbot, and I will take the black robes of a true renunciate and seclude myself deep in the mountains. You have been wonderfully kind to me all these years, but the joy I feel in this one generous act will remain with me through all the lives to come." With that, he rose and left. It was deeply moving to witness his love for you,' His Highness concluded.

The tears of mingled emotions that I wept as I listened surely epitomized Prince Genji's 'left and right each sleeve / soaked with differing tears'.[177]

I was anxious to know how Ariake was feeling about all this, and as he would soon be leaving I called on him late that night with the pretence of bearing a message from His Highness. Other than the young acolyte who was sleeping nearby, he was all alone.

He came to the little side room we always used. 'What "joy hid within sorrow" it all is,' he sighed. 'My heart has been so full to overflowing that I almost pity myself.' The pain of these long months was fresh for me too as I listened. I was determined to avoid further entanglement with him, yet tomorrow would be the final day of the lectures, and the knowledge that this would be our last night inevitably overcame me.

He wept ceaselessly that night, and I found myself wondering where this would all finally lead for me. He told me everything His Highness had said, just as it had been reported to me. 'His understanding gave me hope that I could see you again,' he said, 'and it has brought home to me the full force of my love for you. And now there is this unexpected development, proving that our bond is truly deep and extends beyond this lifetime. I was just so moved and grateful when His Highness insisted that he would love and care for the child, and I await the birth with bated breath,' he finished, smiling through his tears.

We heard the sounds of morning beginning around us, and I rose to leave. 'On what far-off evening can I hope to meet you again?' he sighed as I left, choking with tears, and I felt the same:

If only this 'moon of dawn'[178]   *waga sode no*
reflected now   *namida ni yadoru*

in tears that soak my sleeves	*ariake no*
could stay with me	*akete mo onaji*
after day has come	*omokage mo ga na*

Such thoughts revealed to me that I had surely come to feel as he did.

I lay down to sleep, pondering the inescapable karmic bond between us. Then came a message from His Highness: 'I spent the night alone and waiting for you.'

He was still in bed. 'I imagine you've just come from him, still full of yearning and resenting the dawn that drew him from your side,' he said when I arrived. I did not know how to reply. Others would never find themselves in this position, I thought miserably. Why me?

He clearly misread my tears, for he continued coldly, 'You'll be longing to go back to sleep and dream of him again in peace, I'm sure.' He was in a mood to take things amiss, and continued to make life difficult for me with various ill-tempered accusations.

'Sure enough,' I thought bleakly, 'this will all end badly. Oh what will become of me?'

But the harder I cried the more ruthless he became. 'See? You're simply aching for him, aren't you. You wish I hadn't summoned you to me, it's clear', and with this he rose to his feet. This was all too difficult, and in despair I slipped back to my room.

Feeling very low, I stayed in my room till evening, all the more depressed to imagine what he would say about this. The thought of presenting myself before him filled me once more with an urgent desire to simply leave the world and retreat deep into the mountains.

This was the final day of the lectures, and His Holy Eminence called on His Highness. They chatted easily together, but I felt so awkward that I retreated to the room beyond the bathing room, where I came upon Akebono.

'Here I am on official duty,' he said accusingly when he saw me. 'I would have thought you might take the opportunity to say a few words to me at least.' I felt besieged from all directions.

Then came a summons from His Highness, and on presenting myself I was told to prepare for a drinking party.

Feeling that a private event in some quiet room with just a
couple of palace ladies in attendance would be rather unsoci-
able, when His Highness heard Morochika and Sanekane out
in the central hall he invited them to join him. There followed a
rowdy party, and when it was reluctantly ended His Holy Eminence went off to perform the final evening rituals in the little
princess's apartments, after which he departed, while I was left
with a heart clouded with sorrows I could share with no one.

Later, a quiet ceremony was held at the Palace for the tying
of my childbirth band,[179] and I quailed to imagine how His
Highness might be feeling. I was then required to spend the
night with him, and during the intimate time we spent together
he showed not the slightest reserve or resentment toward me,
which could only provoke me to fresh uneasiness.

Considerable fuss preceded the ninth month's Flower Offering Ceremony,[180] which was to be particularly elaborate.
Owing to my pregnancy I asked leave to return home, but His
Highness declared that my condition was not yet very obvious
so I should attend with the others.

I was on night duty, with a formal costume of pale mauve-
grey robes beneath a red Chinese jacket, along with a set of
unlined gowns of yellow ochre on white under a leaf-green
Chinese jacket, when I heard His Holy Eminence's arrival
announced. I found my heart beating fast.

He entered the worship hall to make a personal presentation of flowers at the altar. He had no way of knowing that I
would be in the adjoining room, but just then one of the attendant monks appeared and told me that His Highness had sent
requesting that I check to see if he had dropped his fan in the
worship hall and bring it to him. This seemed odd to me, but I
opened the sliding door to the worship hall and looked. There
was no fan there. I closed the door again and reported this to
the monk and he returned to His Highness, but now Ariake slid
open the door a crack.

'My heart has been so heavy with thoughts of you,' he said,
'and seeing you here like this brings it all home to me. I hope

to find some reliable person to carry letters to you at home. Others must never get to know of it, you see.'

I couldn't see how that might happen, but out of concern to protect his reputation I felt in no position to say no. 'Well, just so long as no word of it gets out,' was all I replied, and with that I closed the door.

Sometime after His Holy Eminence had left, my time on duty ended and I reported to His Highness. 'Well, how did things go with that message about the dropped fan?' he asked, and laughed. Then I understood that, in typical fashion, he had set the whole thing up.

The tenth month arrived, and in that year when all seemed particularly forlorn, the chill autumn showers that haunted the sky vied with the hopeless tears that soaked my sleeves. I now went into retreat at Hōrinji Temple in Saga, where my stepmother these days lived as a nun.

The coloured leaves on Mount Arashi scattered on a wind that seemed to sweep the sad world away, settling like a brocade on the foaming rapids of the Ōi River, and I was filled with memories of all that had happened both in the public world and in my own life. Vivid among them was the memory of the ceremonies for the dedication of the late emperor's handwritten copy of the Lotus Sutra that were held here,[181] which brought back to me those dear faces of old and even the offerings each had made. In my longing for the past I 'envied the returning waves', and in the cries of the nearby deer I 'felt I heard other sobbing voices raised with mine':[182]

My own sorrows	*waga mi koso*
never cease to flow	*itsumo namida no*
in these endless tears –	*hima naki ni*
but what does the deer	*nani wo shinobite*
sigh for in its crying?	*shika no nakuran*

One evening when I was feeling particularly melancholy I saw an important-looking courtier arrive. It turned out to be the Yamamomo Captain Kaneyuki,[183] who startled me considerably by approaching my room and asking to speak with me.

'Her Cloistered Highness the empress dowager has suddenly become ill and His Highness has been visiting her nearby at her Ōidono residence since this morning. He called at your old home but was told you were here, so he sends to tell you he has arrived. It is a hurried expedition so no ladies have accompanied him. He says to tell you to come right away. If you are in the midst of ful-filling some vow of seclusion, you can resume your retreat later.'

It was the fifth day of my religious retreat and two days still remained, but reluctant though I was to break it, His Highness had gone to the trouble of providing a carriage for me, and when I heard that he had brought no ladies with him on the assumption that I would be here in Saga, I felt in no position to refuse, so I set off immediately for the Ōidono residence. Sure enough, I found that all the palace ladies were away on leave at the time His Highness had set out and no one suitable was left to accompany him, so he and His Highness Kameyama had come to visit their mother with no ladies in attendance, relying on my presence here to see to their needs. They shared a single carriage, with Sanekane seated in the rear.

When I arrived, Her Cloistered Highness had just provided the evening meal. She was suffering from a bout of beri-beri, and since it was nothing serious her sons decided to celebrate the fact with a banquet. His Highness began proceedings, with Sanekane doing the honours. Ten white wood boxes painted with coloured scenes, containing rice and side dishes, were placed first in front of the empress dowager and her two sons, and then similarly for the others present. Everyone drank three rounds of sake, after which the dishes were removed, to be followed by more rice and various dishes with further rounds of sake.

Her Cloistered Highness received a miniature model *biwa* done in plum red and scarlet-purple silk and the plectrum in glossed weave, and a tiny *koto* made of dyed cloth. Kame-yama was given a set of metal gongs whose frame was made of twisted scarlet-purple silk, and the gongs themselves of square pieces of dappled dye cloth hung by amulet cords, together with hammers whose handles were of aloeswood set with crystals.

The empress dowager's ladies were all given a set of a hundred bundles of thick Michinoku paper as well as various objects made of dyed fabric, while the men received great bundles of dyed and undyed leather strapping. It was all very magnificent, and the entertainment went on all night.

I played my usual role of serving the sake. His Highness played the *biwa*, Kameyama the flute, Kinmori the *koto*, likewise the empress dowager and the little princesses,[184] while Sanekane was on the *biwa*, Kinhira the *shō*, and Kaneyuki the *hichiriki*.[185]

As the night deepened, the air was filled with the keening of the stormy wind in the pines of nearby Mount Arashi. Then the bell of nearby Jōkongō Temple echoed in our ears, whereupon His Highness chanted the Chinese poem 'over the citadel's tiled roofs',[186] which was so appropriate and moving that the other entertainments paled in comparison.

'Where has the sake cup got to?' Her Cloistered Highness asked, and when I replied that it was presently with Kameyama, she indicated that His Highness should recite something while she drank from it. Kameyama surrendered the cup to His Highness, who took it with the sake bottle and entered his mother's curtains, where he poured a cup for her. He followed this by chanting the auspicious Chinese poem 'In this glorious time', and his brother joined in.

'Let me speak with the honesty of the old,' Her Cloistered Highness began. 'Sorrow though it is to me to be born into this sullied world in these latter days, still I have been honoured to attain the position of empress and to be parent to two emperors, namely yourselves, and thus the mother of two imperial generations. I am now past sixty, and nothing more remains for me in this world. All I wish for now is to attain the highest realm of paradise. But I must say the music I have heard tonight has sounded to me like the dawn music heard on the supreme lotus of paradise, and I felt those voices might surpass the song of the phoenix of heaven itself. Now I would like to hear an *imayō*[187] and have another cup of sake', whereupon she invited Kameyama to join her behind the curtain. Sanekane was asked to sit by the curtain, which she requested be partly raised with a small standing curtain drawn up to shield her from view.

Both their Highnesses now sang:

Ah I cannot forget
that moving memory,
the secret love that crept to me
unknown to any other,
those evenings waiting patiently,
each promise made forever,
two figures meeting but to part
lit by the dawn's pale moon – ah
now as I remember
my sorrow's never done.

Both voices were unequalled in their beauty.

Finally everyone more or less descended into drunken tears and began to reminisce about old times, until they rose glumly and the party broke up. His Highness returned to the Ōidono residence, his brother beside him to see him on his way. Sanekane declared that he felt unwell and retired, while two or three of the courtiers came away with His Highness.

'There are so few others, why don't I spend the night here to keep you company?' Kameyama suggested to his brother, and they settled down together for the night. I was the only other present, and His Highness demanded I massage his legs. This made me quite uncomfortable, but there was no one else I could delegate the task to so I did as I was told. Kameyama then began to insist that I should be kept there to sleep beside them both.

'But she's pregnant,' His Highness said, 'and has retired for the confinement. It's just that no other ladies could come with me so I asked her to be here instead. She's in no fit state at the moment. Another time perhaps.'

'You'll be right here beside her so surely there's nothing wrong with it,' Kameyama insisted. 'Just think of *The Tale of Genji*, where Emperor Suzaku allowed his brother Genji to spend the night with his beloved Onna Sannomiya. Why should this situation be any different? After all, I've offered you any of my own ladies that you fancy. How could you now turn around and refuse me?' This would have been around the time when His Highness had set his sights on having Kameyama's young princess, who was being brought up by Lady Azechi and was spoken of as the future Imperial Priestess.[188]

His Highness didn't order me to stay, however. He was horribly drunk, and he fell straight to sleep. No one of importance was about, so Kameyama declared that we needn't go elsewhere, and took me off behind the nearby folding screen. His Highness was completely unaware of this, and I was appalled.

Towards dawn he returned to his brother's side and roused him, and His Highness finally awoke for the first time.

'Well, your bedfellow clearly made her escape while I was sleeping like the dead,' he said.

'Oh no, she's been here all along,' Kameyama replied, which made me tremble with fear as I listened. But I pinned my hopes on the fact that I had personally done nothing really wrong, and in fact there were no further questions.

And so another evening came. This time it was Kameyama's turn to play host for the drinking party, which Kagefusa was in charge of. 'Yesterday Sanekane did the honours, but today it's just one of his retainers representing His Highness Kameyama,' some murmured. 'They're not in the same league!' The food was the usual fare, and the sake was nothing special.

Her Cloistered Highness was presented with a rock made of dyed cloth standing on a representation of water, with a little aloeswood boat loaded with clove incense. His Highness received a basket of woven silver which held an aloeswood pillow. The ladies were given representations of mountains with designs of waterfalls and so on, made of thread and cotton wadding, while the men received persimmons made of dyed leather and dyed cloth.

'And specially for Lady Nijō, who is here to serve His Highness,' announced Kameyama, and I was presented with fifty-four little bound books inscribed with the chapter names of *The Tale of Genji*, with covers of Chinese weave damask and ten pages each of dapple-dyed scarlet-purple cloth. Everyone had already drunk and caroused to the full the night before, and the evening was rather lacklustre. Sanekane was absent, having apparently caught a cold. Some said he was just pretending to be ill, whereas others were inclined to believe him.

Their two Highnesses retired again together to the Ōidono residence and took their meal there, both served by me. Then they settled down to sleep in the same room again. I felt very reluctant to stay with them for the night, but there was no way round it so I dutifully stayed, and the woes of this sorry world were yet again brought home to me.

In due course they both returned home, while I remained there on the grounds that I was not only heavily pregnant but still needed to complete my vow of seclusion at Hōrinji. Their two processions left together, with His Highness accompanied by Sanekane and the Tōin Counsellor riding with Kameyama.

Her Cloistered Highness suggested that I should stay with her that day, since life would be lonely now that the lively company had left, and it was while I was there that a letter arrived from Her Highness Higashi Nijō'in. I couldn't guess what it might be about, but when Her Cloistered Highness read it she exclaimed, 'What on earth is this? She must be out of her mind!'

'What is it?' I asked.

'She says it has come to her notice that I have been lavishing attention on you like an empress, and the tales of our recent entertainments here make her envious. She also says with feeling that she may be old, but she doesn't believe she deserves to be treated with such contempt', and she chuckled. I was mortified, however, and I decided to retreat to my nurse's home at Shijō Ōmiya.

No sooner had I arrived than a message came from Ariake. He had installed himself nearby in the home of a favourite young protégé of his, and I now began to quietly come and go from there. Unfriendly tongues will wag, and I soon learned to my horror that rumours were spreading. But he took it calmly. 'If my reputation is ruined then so be it,' he said. 'In that case, we must go off into the mountains together and live in a brushwood hut.' He continued to see me, and I felt utterly helpless.

Late in the tenth month I was feeling particularly ill and forlorn. His Highness had deputed my grandfather Count Takachika to make arrangements for the coming birth, which added to my woes.[189] 'What will become of this dew-brief self?' as the old poem has it; such was my state of mind when, very late one night, I heard the stealthy sound of a carriage arriving and there was a knock on the door.

'Lady Kyōgoku has arrived from the Palace,' came the announcement.

This made no sense to me. The gate opened, and there, deeply hidden inside a simple basketwork carriage, was His Highness. I was flabbergasted.

'There's something I particularly need to discuss,' he said tenderly. 'Your affair with Ariake is being talked of everywhere. I'm even hearing of misconceptions that involve me personally. This is all very upsetting. Now I have learned that the child of another lady who was preparing to give birth has just this evening been stillborn. "Don't spread this around," I said. "Pretend the child hasn't arrived yet." We must take the child you're about to have and send it there, and say that your child was born dead. That should dampen these rumours somewhat at least. I came up with this plan because I so hate to hear the terrible things people have been saying.' At this point a sudden cock's crow alerted him to the dawn, and he departed.

Touched though I was by his solicitude for me, I was filled with sorrow at the thought that my unhappy secret loves condemned me again and again to see my child become the child of another, like the unhappy heroine of some old tale.

In no time a letter from him arrived. 'Last night's strange visit haunts me,' he wrote tenderly:

How close to you	*arenikeru*
I felt still	*mugura no yado no*
beneath the boarded eaves	*ita-bisashi*
of that weed-tangled	*sasuga hanarenu*
ruined hut[190]	*kokochi koso sure*

But for how much longer, I wonder? I thought forlornly:

With love and pity	*aware tote*
you came calling here	*towaruru koto mo*

but for how much longer?   *itsu made to*
Sorrows entangle me   *omoeba kanashi*
in this weed-filled garden   *niwa no yomogifu*

That evening, a message arrived that Ariake was in the neighbourhood, but I had not felt well since around midday, perhaps because the birth was imminent, and I had no inclination to go out and meet him. However, to my consternation he came late that night. Only a few trusted others were with me, so I let him in.

I told him about the previous night and what His Highness had said. 'Well, I could never keep the child myself of course,' he said, 'but it's a terrible shame that you too must be condemned to such an unhappy outcome. There are many instances of this kind of situation that have a happier resolution, after all.' He was very downcast. 'But this is His Highness's plan, so there's nothing we can do about it.'

The child was born that night just as the temple bells announced the coming dawn – a boy. Without even taking the time to look at him closely, Ariake immediately laid the darling child in his lap.

'It can only be a deep karmic connection from a previous life that has brought you into this world,' he said, tears pouring down his cheeks, and he continued talking earnestly to the child as if to an adult until the unfeeling sky grew light, when he reluctantly tore himself away and departed.

I did as instructed and relinquished the baby. Since there was no celebration of his birth, word spread that my child's life had 'faded like the brief morning dew', and all the horrible gossip ceased. His Highness had been very thoughtful and astute, and saved both public and private reputations. But celebratory gifts arrived from someone who understood the situation well, making me worry that it might not be so easy to conceal things after all.

The child was born on the sixth of the eleventh month, and Ariake's visits continued after that with such extreme frequency that it made me quite apprehensive. Late on the night of the thirteenth he came as usual, with news that there was considerable unrest about.

The year before last, the sacred tree of Nara's Kasuga Shrine had been brought to the capital by petitioning monks and shrine priests, and now there was much excited talk that it was about to be returned. Added to this, an epidemic was now raging, and many had died of it within a few days. 'The deaths of people close to me has made me think that I may soon be numbered among the dead as well,' he told me. 'I've been feeling so low that I decided to come and see you.'

Unusually downcast, he talked despairingly of the future. 'Whatever form my future rebirths may take, as long as I can continue to see you . . . Though I were reborn in the loftiest realms of paradise, I would be miserable if I couldn't live there with you . . . Even if my home is some mean little hut, if only you were by my side there . . .' All night he talked without a moment's sleep and before we knew it the day had grown bright.

His only way out was close to the main house, which was full of prying eyes, and his huddled disguise would only draw more attention as he left so he stayed with me that day. I felt very apprehensive. The only person who knew of his presence was a young attendant who understood the situation, and I was terribly nervous about what might be said in the main house. None of this seemed to bother him, however, which left me lost for words.

We talked quietly all day. 'After our dawn parting that day,' he said, 'when I heard that you had suddenly disappeared and I had no one to turn to in my anxiety, I set about copying the Five Great Sutras,[191] inserting one by one the words of your message into each volume, as a fervent prayer that I would bond with you once more in the human world. I was feeling quite frantic, you see. I completed the task, but I didn't dedicate them on the altar because I planned to do so with you when we were reborn here again together. I would store them in the great sutra storehouse of the Dragon Palace,[192] I decided, and in our next rebirth I would dedicate the entire two hundred or so volumes. To this end, I plan to take them with me by having them burnt on my funeral pyre when I die.'

I found these impossible delusions of his quite frightening.

'Why not pray to be reborn on a single lotus in the same paradise,' I urged.

'No no,' he replied. 'Love creates such attachment, I have chosen to be reborn again into the human realm, and when fate decrees that I should die and become an empty wisp of drifting smoke, even then I will never leave your side.' He spoke with pitiful earnestness.

Later he slept, then suddenly started awake, sweat pouring. 'What is it?' I asked.

'I dreamt that I had become a mandarin duck,'[193] he told me, 'and had entered your body. This terrible sweat must be because the intensity of my feelings has snared my soul inside you.'

Worried that he had stayed so long, he rose and left as the moon was sinking behind the mountain rim and the trailing clouds paled with the faint glimmer of first light above the eastern hills.

Tears of parting mingled with the dawn bell's mournful tolling, and I was left with longing thoughts haunting my heart, when his young attendant arrived with a message from him:

My yearning soul	*akugaruru*
has lodged	*waga tamashii wa*
within you there	*todome-okinu*
so what remains here	*nani no nokori*
yearning for you still?	*mono omouran*

My heart overflowing with sorrow and love, I replied:

Would that we could	*mono omou*
compare the tears	*namida no iro wo*
each sheds in yearning.	*kurabeba ya*
Truly, whose sleeve would prove	*ge ni ta ga sode ka*
more soaked with sorrow?	*shiore-masaru to*

I jotted this poem down just as it came to me.

I soon heard that he had gone to the Palace that day; then, I think on the eighteenth, word came that he had symptoms of the epidemic that was everywhere, and had summoned a doctor.

News followed that he was growing sicker, and I was in despair. Then came this from him, I think on the twenty-first:

'I never thought that our recent meeting would be our last in this world. Now in the grip of this illness, what haunts me more than the frailty of my life is the deep sin of the attachment that will continue to bind me to this world. What will be the outcome of the dream I dreamt that night?' He wrote much else besides, and ended with this poem:

For love of you	mi wa kakute
this body fades	omoi-kienan
yet all I ask	kemuri dani
is that its smoke still linger	sonata no sora ni
in the sky you see	nabiki dani seba

How could this not affect me deeply? Indeed, how heart-breaking that that dawn together should have been our last.

I would only see	omoi-kien
the lingering smoke	kemuri no sue wo
that marks your end	sore to dani
if I too could remain	nagaraeba koso
alive without you	ato wo dani mime

With all the comings and goings around him, I felt that it would only prove a hindrance to pour my heart out to him in detail, so this is all I sent. I couldn't bring myself to believe that this truly was the last farewell, but on I think the twenty-fifth of the eleventh month, I learned that he had passed away. It all seemed more unreal than a dream within a dream; words cannot express all I felt, haunted also by my own sense of guilt.[194]

I thought of how, back in the beginning, he had beseeched me with the poem, 'I yearn / for revelation of that moment / when this dream's fulfilled',[195] and recalled him in his poem, 'a lingering sorrow haunts / this moonlit night of autumn'. If that painful parting had indeed been permanent, I thought, I would not now be sunk in such sorrow.

That night the heavens themselves seemed to join in my grief, for rain drifted down and the clouds hung unusually heavy and low. The last poem he had sent me still lay forlornly in the nearby document box; the scent of his incense still lingered full of memories on the sleeve where I laid my head to sleep. Now is the moment to take Buddhist vows as I so yearn to do, I said to myself, but knowing the talk that would spread made me fearful. Guessing how his reputation would be sullied even beyond the grave if I did as I longed to do, I felt a wave of bitterness that this too was denied me.

As dawn was breaking I learned that the young messenger had come again. What dream is this? I wondered, and hurried out myself to meet him. His gown, in the withered-field combination with an embroidered design of pheasants, hung limply, and his sleeves clearly revealed a night spent weeping. Still in tears, he told me the full story of Ariake's death, and no brush can convey or words describe all that I felt as I listened.

Apparently he had kept the robe I had exchanged for his that day,[196] folded tightly and placed permanently beside where he sat to chant. Then on the evening of the twenty-fourth he had asked to wear it next to his skin, and instructed that he should be dressed in it when his body was committed to the flames. 'It was unbearably sad,' the lad said.

'He told me to give you this,' he continued, and handed me a large lacquer document box with a gold-inlay design of a sacred *sakaki* tree. In it was what appeared to be a letter. The writing was a mere scrawl, the characters quite unformed. It began with the words 'On that night', and further on I thought I could make out 'while I am still of this world' and other scraps, but nothing was clear. Ah, if the river of tears I shed then could bear me down to join him in the sea of death!

Half afloat half sinking	*uki-shizumi*
down that stream into death	*mitsuse-gawa ni mo*
I would gladly go in search	*ōse naraba*
abandoning this body	*mi wo sutete mo ya*
could I but meet him there	*tazune-yukamashi*

In the midst of grief it seems I still had presence of mind enough to compose a poem.

He had filled the box with bundles of gold. Tears soaking his sleeves as he spoke, the lad proceeded to tell me the details of how he had been cremated wrapped in my robe as requested, with the five sutras that he had copied added to the flames. When he left, still sobbing, I watched his retreating figure with eyes half blinded with anguished grief.

His Highness too was surely grief-stricken, given how close the two had been. A message from him saying that he was thinking of me in my sorrow only served to deepen my unhappiness:

The image of that face	*omokage mo*
the memories of him	*nagori mo sakoso*
must still remain for you	*nokorurame*
though clouds have shrouded	*kumo-gakurenuru*
that dawn moon itself	*ariake no tsuki*

he wrote, adding 'Painful partings are a given in this world of ours, but his love for you was no ordinary love, and it saddened me to see how deeply he bewailed his parting from you.'

At a loss how to reply, I seem to remember that I simply sent this:

Worthless though I am	*kazu naranu*
my misery is profound	*mi no uki koto mo*
as the memories	*omokage mo*
of that dawn moon	*hitokata ni ya wa*
are deep	*ariake no tsuki*

Neither words nor feeling seemed adequate. I spent my days and nights in tears, and this year, 'the spring passed before I was aware'.[197]

There was a constant flow of messages from His Highness, but they simply asked why I was staying away, and there were no summons to come at once as there used to be. Although he said nothing to indicate it in so many words, I began to suspect that somehow his feelings for me were cooling, which was not so surprising given how many times I had wronged him, though through no fault of my own. Under the circumstances, I felt disinclined to return to the Palace.

As the year drew to a close I felt as if my life was likewise approaching its end. I took out the letters I had received from Ariake and set out to copy the Lotus Sutra on their reverse side as a prayer for his soul, thinking unhappily as I did so of his sin in not dedicating his own copy of the sutras to his future salvation. And so the year ended.

Still deep in grief as I was, I felt no celebratory sense of the new year beginning. On I think the fifteenth of the first month, the forty-ninth day of mourning,[198] I visited a holy man I trusted in such matters. The usual full moon Repentance Ceremony[199] was being held, and I took along some of the gold that Ariake had passed to me and presented it by way of an offering for prayers for his soul. On the paper I wrapped it in I wrote:

May you be   *kono tabi wa*
a guide that leads   *matsu akatsuki no*
to the dawn beyond death   *shirube seyo*
though in this life   *sate mo taenuru*
our bond is ended   *chigiri nari to mo*

This monk was renowned for his fine delivery and he said many splendid things in the course of the sermon, but the words of the old poem 'the dawn to come' particularly struck me as I listened tearfully.

I remained in deep seclusion there until the fifteenth of the second month, the day that marks the Buddha's death with special ceremonies. This was hardly the first time I had cast my thoughts back to that event, but now the sorrow of that death chimed with my own grief-laden state of mind. It so happened that a series of Lotus lectures[200] was being held here for twenty-seven days, and I gladly took the opportunity to offer up recitations of the holy text each day. Unable to follow custom by naming the one on whose behalf the offering was

made, I just wrote sadly: 'For one with whom I have an unforgettable bond'. On the final day, I added the following poem:

The waiting heaven	*tsuki wo matsu*
of that dawn	*akatsuki made no*
is still so distant	*harukasa ni*
and sorrow fills me	*ima irishi hi no*
faced with the now set sun	*kage zo kanashiki*

His Highness had never once come calling while I was living
there in the eastern hills. So that's the way it is, I thought miserably as I made my forlorn preparations to return the next
morning to the capital.

That night four consecutive lectures were held, for which the
monks stayed up till dawn. I was dozing off in the audience hall
around dawn when I was startled by a vision of Ariake, just as
he had been in life. 'The dream of this life is a long dark path
of delusion,' he intoned, and he took me in his arms. I was
immediately stricken with a terrible fever, and lay there barely
conscious.

The holy man was so concerned that he begged me to stay on
that day to make sure I recovered, but it would have been difficult to send back the waiting carriage so I chose to go. But just
as I reached the western bridge along the Kiyomizu road I felt
that he who had just appeared in my dream had now entered
my carriage and sat there in the flesh, and I promptly fainted.

My companions attended to me as best they could and took
me to my nurse's place. I couldn't even drink, and seemed very
close to death. Finally, halfway through the spring, it became
clear that I was pregnant.

I had remained pure and not so much as exchanged glances
with any man since that last dawn parting from Ariake, so there
was no doubting that the child was his. For all the misfortune
of our bond, I was warmed by feelings of this deep connection
to him as yet unknown to others, and perversely felt an urgent
longing for the day when I would see this child.

Around the middle of the fourth month I was summoned to
the Palace 'on particular business', but my condition made me

reluctant to go so I replied that I was confined by illness and needed to stay at home. In response His Highness wrote:

So you still pine so much	*omokage wo*
for him you loved	*sa nomi mo ikaga*
though the dawn moon	*koi-wataru*
has gone	*ukiyo wo ideshi*
from this sad world?	*ariake no tsuki*

'I imagine there is more than one reason why tears continue to soak those sleeves of yours. Apparently I am now in your past . . . ,' he added.

I assumed that he must be unhappy about my continued feelings for Ariake, but in fact it was not that. It seems he had heard rumours that my nurse's son Nakayori – a trusted retainer of Kameyama's who had been promoted to fifth rank on his abdication and now served him as Lieutenant Major – had helped enable Kameyama to visit me in secret, that Kameyama had become quite infatuated with me, and that I was withdrawing my affections from His Highness. How could I have known any of this?

I was soon feeling better, and around the beginning of the fifth month I decided to present myself at the Palace, before my condition became too obvious. His Highness said nothing unusual and things at the Palace all seemed much as normal, but I remained sunk in depression. I stayed until the sixth month, when the death of a relative gave me an excuse to take leave again.

This time it was particularly important to keep the birth secret, so I withdrew to stay with someone I knew in the eastern hills. No one came visiting me there, and I felt a changed person. Around the twentieth of the eighth month I felt the birth pangs beginning. For the previous births, someone had always been with me even if in secret, but now I had only the crying deer on the nearby mountain to echo my own cries. But all went smoothly; the child was a boy, and my heart overflowed with love and pity for him.

Ariake's dream had seemed to foretell this child,[201] and now here he was. I was overwhelmed to think of it. My thoughts went to my own sorrow at having lost my mother so young and having no memory of her – now this child in turn would look back to think of a father who had died before he was born.

Pitying him, I kept him close. There was not even a wet-nurse at hand to feed him and none was to be found, so I fed him myself. Simply having him there with me made me ache with tenderness for him. It became quite wet where he lay, so I hastily picked him up and laid him gently beside me, and at this moment I felt a strong surge of motherly love and suddenly understood what my mother would have felt for me.

For a while I kept him with me, reluctant to part,[202] and looked after him myself, but after forty days or so a wetnurse arrived from Yamazaki to take over. Even then I continued to sleep with my little son beside me, and I felt less and less inclined to return to the Palace and His Highness.

Eventually winter arrived, and His Highness sent a message complaining that I couldn't continue to stay away like this, so early in the tenth month I reluctantly went back, and I saw in the new year at the Palace.

Poignant thoughts haunted me that New Year as I presented myself for service on the third day. His Highness did not exactly chastise me, but I could sense how distant he was, and life at the Palace felt increasingly forlorn and depressing. Only that man who now belonged to the past[203] constantly called on me, proclaiming the old adage 'bitterness turns again to love'.

In the second month I accompanied Their Highnesses to attend the Equinoctial Buddhist Service at Kameyama's Saga Palace, all the while haunted by the vivid memory of Ariake as I had seen him in last year's dream. Mournfully, I sent all my thoughts in prayer to the Manifest Buddha on the altar: 'Oh most holy one who vows to save all sentient beings, please save now that wandering soul and lead him to paradise':

Ah these tears	*koi-shinobu*
of yearning love	*sode no namida ya*
that pour like a great river	*ōikawa*
yet if it held a way to meet	*ōse ariseba*
I would gladly drown there	*mi wo ya sutemashi*

Prey to such thoughts, despondent and bitter against the world, I was sorting through and discarding old pieces of used writing paper when I found myself thinking of the fate of my little child. If I were to die and abandon him, who would be left to think of him with pitying love? So this is what is meant by the attachments that hold one back from the Buddhist path, I thought, as a yearning for him overwhelmed me:

Born on wild shores	*tazunu beki*
abandoned	*hito mo nagisa ni*
unvisited	*oi-someshi*
what fate awaits	*matsu wa ika naru*
that little pine?	*chigiri naruran*

On our return from the Saga Palace, I found some time to set out and visit the child, and it smote my heart to find him wonderfully grown, babbling away, smiling and laughing. Deeply reluctant, I returned to the Palace, and so the autumn began.

Then came a sudden message from my grandfather Count Takachika. 'You are to pack up your room and leave the court,' it said. 'I'll be sending a carriage for you this evening.' Mystified, I showed it to His Highness and asked what he made of it, but he gave no reply. Very puzzled, I then said to Lady Genkimon'in (who still went by the name Sanmidono at that time I think), 'What can this be about? I asked His Highness about this letter but he didn't reply.'

'I don't know either,' she said.

Well, there was nothing for it but to go, so I set about preparing myself. Now that I felt I was seeing for the last time the Palace that I had been a part of ever since the ninth month of the year I turned four, this place that I had so pined for whenever I was back at home, my eyes lingered over every last tree and flower that I knew so well.

Overwhelmed with tears, I suddenly heard that man who had forsworn bitterness[204] arrive and ask if I was in my room, and I went out for a moment to see him, feeling both touched and sad. Noticing that I had been crying, he asked what had happened. 'Asking only brings fresh pain', as they say. I was lost for words, and simply took out my grandfather's letter and showed him.

'This is why I'm miserable,' was all I said, as I tearfully drew him into my room.

'What on earth can this be about?' he said, but of course no one had any idea. The older ladies called in to see me too, but they also couldn't understand it. All I could do was weep while the day drew to an end.

I could only imagine that this must be His Highness's idea. Reluctant as I was to go to him again, I felt this would be my last chance to see him so I timidly presented myself once more, and found him chatting idly with a couple of nobles.

I was dressed in a thin glossed gossamer silk robe embroidered with a design of twining vines and plume grass in green thread, and a red Chinese jacket. His Highness threw a quick glance in my direction.

'So you're off tonight?' he said casually.

I could find no words to reply.

'Hoping to twine your way back into my affections, is that it?' he went on, referring to my robe. 'I don't like that twisted design of yours.' With that he rose and left, no doubt on his way to Her Highness's apartments.

How could I not bitterly resent him at this moment? No matter what he may be thinking, hadn't he sworn all these years that nothing would ever come between us? How had it come to this? I was filled with a hopeless longing to simply die then and there. But the carriage was already waiting for me. If only I could simply go off somewhere now and hide myself away. Yet I did want to understand what this was all about, and so I let the carriage take me to my grandfather's house at Nijō.

My grandfather came out in person to meet me. 'I'm old and ill,' he said, 'and who knows when I might die. Lately my health has gone from bad to worse, and nothing seems to help. Your welfare has weighed on my mind ever since your father passed away, and your uncle has since died as well, leaving you with even less support. This is worrying enough, but now Her Highness has sent this demand and I'm afraid there's no help for it, you must withdraw from court service.' With that he produced a letter and showed it to me.

'I do not care for the way she waits on His Highness while snubbing me. Remove her forthwith', it read. 'As her mother, your daughter, is no more, the responsibility for her lies with you.' The letter was written in Her Highness's own hand.

Well, I could at least comfort myself now with the thought that, given this, it would have been impossible to remain at the Palace, so I now felt somewhat more resigned to my departure. Nevertheless, through the long sleepless nights that followed it seemed that 'the thousand mournful voices of the fulling blocks' were speaking to my own sorrow as I lay there, while the dew that bowed low the bush clover around the house might have been the tears of autumn's wild geese overhead, weeping as they went.

And so time passed, and the year drew toward its end. I could take no pleasure in the preparations that were afoot to greet the new year, and planned to embark on a thousand-day retreat at Gion Shrine, something I had long sworn to do although all manner of things had prevented it until now.

On the second day of the eleventh month I paid a visit to Hachiman Shrine for the sacred Kagura performance. Recalling the poet who wrote, 'my heart's prayers are offered to the gods',[205] I composed this:

Endlessly I offer	*itsumo tada*
prayers to the gods	*kami ni tanomi wo*
yet all in vain	*yūdasuki*
and I am bitter	*kakuru kai naki*
at my wretched fate	*mi wo zo uramuru*

I stayed in retreat there seven days, and from there I went to Gion Shrine. I could have no further desire to remain in the world now, and in my prayers I begged that I be released from this world of delusion and enter the gates of salvation.

The eleventh month of this year marked the second anniversary of Ariake's death. The seven days of the Five Lotus Rites[206] were performed at the temple of the holy man in the eastern hills, and I spent my days there in the audience while my nights were spent at Gion Shrine. The last day of the Rites was the anniversary of his death. The insistent beating of the sutra bell prompted tears as I composed:

> The sutra's timely bell
> finds echoes
> in my sighs.
> What holds me longer
> in this dreary world?

> *oriori no*
> *kane no hibiki ni*
> *ne wo soete*
> *nani to ukiyo ni*
> *nao nokoruran*

Hesitant though I was to visit the child who was being raised in secret, I called there from time to time just to comfort myself, and in the new year it wrenched my heart to see how he was now running about and talking, innocent of the world's sorrows.

Even my grandfather Takachika had now died, gone with the autumn dews of that bitter year just passed, and this should only have deepened my sorrow, but my heart was already so heavy with the shock of all that had befallen me that somehow I hardly seemed to feel it. Yet as I sat intently chanting and praying at the altar through the long spring days, perhaps because my heart had found a little peace, it finally came home to me that he had been the last person left to connect me to my dead mother, and now at last I did feel sad.

When the cherry blossoms around the shrine began to reach full bloom, I recalled the oracular poem bestowed by the shrine's god some ten years earlier:

> If the shrine's garden
> fills with the bloom
> of a thousand cherry trees
> those who planted them
> find their lives blessed

> *kamigaki ni*
> *chimoto no sakura*
> *hana sakaba*
> *ue-oku hito no*
> *mi mo sakaenan*

A huge number of cherry trees were consequently planted in the grounds, and as this was the god's sacred promise, I hoped that I too might be a beneficiary. It seemed it would make little difference whether the offering was a rooted sapling or simply a branch, as long as it was in flower, so I asked the high prelate Shingen, a close relative of my father, to beg for me a branch of flowering cherry from Abbot Kōyo of Danna Temple, then head of Amida Temple. On the first Day of the Horse in the second month I presented this to the high prelate Enyō, executive temple head at Gion, along with a set of plum-red patterned unlined gowns and a fine silk robe as offerings for prayers to be said at the eastern sutra hall.

On this occasion I wrote on a pale blue-green poem card of thin paper the following poem:

Rootless though it is	*ne naku to mo*
may this branch	*iro ni wa ideyo*
blossom with my prayers	*sakurabana*
for the gods know	*chigiru kokoro wa*
what I have vowed	*kami zo shiruran*

Watching the branch take root and flower, I felt that my own vow to leave the world must surely also be fulfilled. Taking fresh heart from this, I committed myself for the first time to perform the Thousand Chants.[207] This was difficult in my present quarters however, so I moved into the more easterly of the two retreat huts in the grounds behind Hōdō Temple. And in this way another year ended.

At the end of the first month of the following year, a letter from Her Cloistered Highness the empress dowager arrived. 'Preparations are underway this spring to celebrate the ninetieth birthday of my mother Lady Kitayama,' she wrote. 'You have been back at home for a long time now, but there is no need to feel unwelcome here. I would like you to join us and place yourself at my mother's service.'

'Delighted as I am by your kind invitation,' I replied, 'I am at home owing to His Highness's displeasure, so it could give me no happiness to be present at this glorious event.'

'You surely need feel no compunction,' came the reply. 'After all, my mother has had a particularly deep connection both to your deceased mother and to yourself since you were an infant, so there is absolutely no reason why you should worry about being present at this momentous ceremony.' Insistent messages in her own hand kept arriving, and it seemed churlish to go on refusing so I ended by agreeing to be present.

I had now completed some four hundred days of my thousand-day retreat, but I installed a substitute to perform the rites on my behalf until my return. Sanekane arranged for an ox cart to fetch me and I went, dressed in a set of three plum-red robes under a silk robe in spring-shoot green on blossom pink. I was very ill at ease at the prospect of this magnificent event, since by now I felt thoroughly uncouth and countrified, and when I arrived I saw that it was indeed all very splendid.

I found Their Highnesses, together with Her Highness Higashi Nijō'in and Princess Yūgimon'in (who was not yet elevated to the rank of empress) already ensconced. Her Highness Shinyōmeimon'in[208] also quietly joined the gathering. The official celebration was set for the last day of the second month, so on the twenty-ninth Emperor Go-Uda and the Crown Prince appeared for the event.

First came the imperial procession, at around two in the morning. The imperial palanquin was lowered before the gate, where the priest blessed it and musicians from the Music Department performed. Superintendent Saemon then entered and announced the imperial arrival, and the palanquin was duly carried to the Middle Gate. At the point when the Nijō Captain was to carry the imperial sword in from the Middle Gate, the Crown Prince's procession arrived. Matting was quickly laid out to the foot of the gate. The temporary building used for the occasion had been set up by Fujiwara Akiie, who was in charge of the event, together with the Regent, the General of the Left, the Nijō Captain and others. The Custodian Chief Minister duly arrived with the Crown Prince.

On the day itself, the building was set up as follows: in the south-facing central area of the three-pillars-wide inner chamber a stand bearing a scroll depicting the Buddha was placed by the northern blinds. Before this was a table for the incense and flower offerings. Standing lamps stood to left and right. The priest's seat was in front of this; to its south was the worship platform, while a table for the two sutra boxes, containing the Zumyō and Lotus Sutras, was set up by the southern lattice shutters. The manuscript of the prayer petition was apparently drafted by Mochinori and formally transcribed by the Regent.

Every pillar of the Inner Chamber was festooned with religious banners and delicately carved decorative plates.[209] In the eastern section His Majesty's seat, in the form of a Chinese brocade cushion placed on two mats with decorative silk edging, was installed behind reed blinds. To its north were placed two mats with edgings in the imperial design where His Highness sat, while a similar arrangement was placed in the second section of the room for His Highness Kameyama. In the eastern section a standing screen was set up for Her Cloistered Highness, and standing curtains were placed to the south where His Highness's ladies were installed. It stirred considerable emotion in me to find myself observing this as a bystander. Another standing screen was set up in the western section of the room with two mats of silk edging topped by a Chinese damask brocade cushion, where Lady Kitayama was ensconced.

Lady Kitayama, the consort of the former Chief Minister Saionji Saneuji, was the mother of both the empress dowager Ōmiya'in and Her Highness Higashi Nijō'in, as well as grandmother to both His Highness and Kameyama, and the great-grandmother of the present emperor Go-Uda and the Crown Prince, so it was only natural that everyone should gather for this gala event. In secular life,[210] she had been the grandchild of the former Chancellor Takafusa and daughter of my maternal great-grandfather Count Takahira.

Not only was there a strong family connection, but my mother had grown up in the care of Lady Kitayama, and she had always treated me with equal fondness. It had therefore been suggested that I did not need formal wear for this occasion, and the empress dowager had decided that I should be part of Lady Kitayama's own retinue and dress in graded purple. She apparently changed her mind, however, and I was required instead to be in her own retinue, where the ladies all wore robes in graded shades of plum red with an unlined gown in a deeper shade, glossed scarlet over-robe and red Chinese jacket. However, thanks to the special offices of Sanekane I was provided instead with eight layered robes in plum red, an unlined robe of deep scarlet, an outer coat of kerria yellow over spring-shoot green, a blue Chinese jacket, glossed scarlet over-robe, another with decorative design and so forth. I had not expected any of this, and I found it all rather tiresome.

The ceremonials began. First came Their Highnesses, followed in succession by Emperor Go-Uda, the Crown Prince, the empress dowager and Higashi Nijō'in, Lady Imadegawa, Princess Yūgimon'in, and the Custodian Chief Minister. There followed the stirring sound of the gong announcing the sutra recitation. To the east of the stairs sat, in order, the Prime Minister, the Minister of the Left, the Minister of the Right, the Kazan'in Middle Counsellor, the Tsuchimikado Chancellor, the Minamoto Chancellor, the Ōi no Mikado Chancellor, the General of the Right, the Custodian Chief Minister (who very soon left), the General of the Left, the Sanjō Middle Counsellor, the Kazan'in Middle Counsellor, and the Household Prefect. To the west of the stairs sat the previous Shijō Chancellor Takayuki, together with many other high dignitaries.

The present emperor was dressed in a formal trailing cloak and gossamer silk *hakama* trousers; His Highness in cloak and graded blue gathered trousers, His Highness Kameyama in cloak and brocade gathered trousers; and the Crown Prince in cloak and raised design scarlet-purple gathered trousers. All were seated behind elegant reed blinds. The Left and Right Generals and the Right Guards Brigadier were also present, replete with bows and quivers on their backs.

The musicians struck up and the dances began. First was the stately 'Chōkōraku', in which the dancer beat a little drum slung around his neck. This was followed by a musical ensemble piece, with the dancers of left and right swinging lances. Next the flute played in the Ichikotsu mode and musicians and dancers turned towards where the waiting priests were gathered and performed a piece to welcome them in. They duly filed in in two lines, entering from the middle gate and passing to left and right of the stage, climbed the stairs and took their seats.

Once the Kenjichi Grand Abbot, the Shujo Abbot in charge of sutras, and the Abbot in charge of spells and prayers were all seated, the priest in charge struck the sutra gong. At this point the young flower boys Shigetsune, Akinori, Nakakane and so forth stood by on two sides, and while the prayer priest intoned a hymn they distributed flower boxes. The musicians played Shingachō, and lotus-petal papers from the boxes were ceremonially scattered to the accompaniment of a hymn. The drummer now knelt before His Majesty, and Mansion Superintendent Tamekata conveyed a gift of robes to Hisasuke, one of the dancers.

The ceremonial dove-headed rod, a ninetieth-birthday gift from His Majesty to Lady Kitayama, was next set aside and a dance was performed. Watching them as they moved hither and yon, apparently heedless of the fine threads of spring rain that had begun to drift down upon them, I felt quite dispirited by the endless nature of it all.

The pieces performed were: on the left, 'Manzairaku', 'Gakuhyōshi', 'Gaten' and 'Ryōō'; on the right, 'Chikyū', 'Engiraku' and 'Nasori'. Ōno Hisatada then danced the Imperial Gift dance, and now the Minister of the Right rose, summoned the left dancer Chikayasu and presented him with a gift. At this point he was to perform another dance of thanks, but now a dancer (Chikyū) and a musician (Masaaki) from the right both likewise received gifts. His Majesty particularly praised the admirable way that Masaaki, *shō* in hand, prostrated himself and rose to his feet again.

The head priest descended from his altar dais and the musicians played, after which alms were distributed to the monks by Middle Captain Kin'atsu and others, wearing formal cloaks and bearing ceremonial quivers. Their swords, mostly narrow swords, hung from special leather straps. As the gathered monks retired, 'Kaikotsu' and 'Chōgeishi' were performed, after which the musicians and dancers also withdrew.

At this point, the meal was served to the empress dowager, Higashi Nijō'in and Lady Kitayama, the latter served by the Shijō Premier assisted by Superintendent Saemon.

The following day, the first of the third month, began with a ceremonial meal served to His Majesty, the Crown Prince, His Highness and Kameyama. The stage from yesterday's performances was removed, and the four sides of the Inner Chamber were enclosed with drapery; a standing screen was placed in the west corner, and in the central area two decorative-edged tatami mats were placed, topped with a Chinese brocade cushion, to form His Majesty's seat.

Their two Highnesses were seated in the Inner Chamber. A decorative-edged mat and a Chinese damask brocade cushion were placed in the eastern section, apparently for the Crown Prince's seat. The Prime Minister performed the raising of the blinds for His Majesty and Their Highnesses on their arrival. The Custodian Chief Minister, who was to perform this function for the Crown Prince, arrived late and the Lieutenant Major acted in his stead.

His Majesty wore the usual cloak, with the edge of an under-robe of scarlet glossed silk brocade revealed at the hem. His Highness was dressed in pale mauve gathered trousers of tight-weave brocade, while His Highness Kameyama was in a raised-weave brocade cloak and the same gathered trousers, also with an under-robe of scarlet glossed silk brocade revealed at the hem. The Crown Prince arrived wearing gathered trousers of raised-weave brocade, with a plain under-robe at the hem.

The meal was duly served. His Majesty was served by the Kazan'in Chancellor, aided by the Shijō Premier and the Sanjō Captain Premier. His Highness was served by the Ōinomikado Chancellor, while the Lieutenant Major served His Highness Kameyama. The Crown Prince was served by the Sanjō Captain Premier with the aid of Shijō Takayoshi. He too looked impressively ceremonial for the occasion, clad in a cloak in the blossom combination of white over saffron red, pale mauve gown, the same gathered trousers and scarlet unlined robe, with a cylindrical quiver and formal decorative sprays at his ears.

The meal over, it was time for the imperial musical performance. Tadayo carried in His Majesty's flute, by the name of 'Katei', in a box, and the Prime Minister took it and laid it before him. The Crown Prince played a *biwa* named 'Genjō', brought in by Chikasada and presented by Sanekane. Separate boxes contained the retainers' flutes. The Tsuchimikado Chancellor and the Superintendent were on the *shō*, while Kaneyuki played the *hichiriki* flute. The Japanese *koto* was played by the Ōinomikado Chancellor, the *koto* by the Commander of the Left. On the *biwa* were Sanekane and the Provisional Chancellor. The rhythm was played by the Tokudaiji Chancellor. The Tōin Captain played *koto*. Masafuyu sang the accompanying songs. The songs in the Ryo scale were 'Ana Tōto' and 'Mushiroda'. The music was the middle and final movements of 'Tori', the Ritsu songs were 'Aoyanagi', 'Manzairaku', and the final section of 'Sandai'. I believe this was the programme.

The performances were followed by a poetry session. The chamberlains and courtiers set up the recording desk and woven straw cushions, and the pages were presented in order beginning with those of the lowest rank. Tanemichi, robed in a formal cloak and wearing a narrow sword hung from a leather strap and cylindrical quiver, placed his own page on his bow when he ascended the podium, and transferred it to the recording desk, then the rest of the courtier's pages were collected and placed on the desk by Nobusuke. Provisional Lieutenant Major Akiie had ascended before Tanemichi and set the Crown Prince's straw cushion to the east of the desk, where the Crown Prince remained seated as the poems were read out, a resurrection of an earlier tradition that everyone praised as very striking.

The many assembled nobles took their allotted turn to compose. All were clothed in formal nobleman's cloaks, but the General of the Right revealed at the hem a wave-pattern damask brocade in kerria yellow over spring-shoot green, and bore a sword at his side. He also held his page against his formal mace when presenting it. The other nobles of military rank carried bow and arrows on their backs.

The Kazan'in Chancellor now summoned the Reader,[211] and Kin'atsu presented himself. The Minister of the Left had been assigned the role of Reader's Aide, but circumstances prevented him so the Minister of the Right took his place. Count Takachika and the Fujiwara Middle Counsellor were also summoned.

When Lady Gonchūnagon, who was in the empress dowager's

service, presented a poem written on thin scarlet paper from behind her blind, His Highness Kameyama enquired why I was not presenting a poem as well in that case. 'I imagine she is feeling indisposed,' replied Her Cloistered Highness.

'Come now, why not at least submit a poem?' Sankekane urged me.

'I was told by Lady Kitayama that Her Highness Higashi Nijō'in expressly requested that I not do so,' I replied – but silently I recited to myself:

> Long since   *kanete yori*
> I learned that I   *kazu ni morenu to*
> was not among that number.   *kikishikaba*
> A poem was never   *omoi mo yoranu*
> further from my mind.   *waka no uranami*

The poems composed by Their Highnesses were received by the Prime Minister. The Crown Prince's was not treated in this exalted fashion, however, and was simply read out by the Reader. His Majesty's and His Highness's poems were read by Superintendent Saemon, with the Prime Minister sometimes doing the reading.

Once the readings were over, the Crown Prince retired, at which point gifts were presented to the nobles, and the Konoe Minister Kanehira wrote out a fair copy of the poem composed by His Majesty, as follows:

A poem composed in celebration of Her Ladyship Fujiwara Kitayama on the occasion of her ninetieth birthday:

> Surely it promises   *yuku sue wo*
> yet longer life   *nao nagaki yo to*
> to come,   *chigiru kana*
> this long spring day   *yayoi ni utsuru*
> that welcomes a new month   *kyō no haruhi ni*

Iemoto was the scribe for His Highness Kaneyama's poem. The introduction was as above, with the omission of her name:

Their hundred voices	*momoiro to*
sing you a hundred years	*ima ya nakuran*
those *uguisu*	*uguisu no*
that celebrate	*kokonokaeri no*
your ninety springs today	*kimi ga haru hete*

The Minister of the Right wrote out the Crown Prince's poem, which was introduced with 'Composed at the behest of the emperor for the ninetieth-birthday celebration of Lady Fujiwara, on a spring day at the Kitayama Mansion', followed by the words 'hereby offered', no doubt in line with ancient precedent:

Limitless	*kagiri naki*
the years that reach	*yowai wa ima wa*
beyond this spring day's ninety	*kokonosoji*
so may your years stretch on	*nao chiyo tōki*
through countless years to come	*haru ni mo aru kana*

I have recorded the other poems elsewhere.[212] Sanekane composed:

Your years have risen	*yoyo no ato ni*
wave upon wave	*nao tachinoboru*
past generations	*oi no nami*
and all perhaps	*yoriken toshi wa*
for the sake of this great day	*kyō no tame kamo*

All present seemed full of appreciation for this sentiment.

Some said that it was on a par with the poem composed by the former Chief Minister Saneuji for the Great Sutras service, when Go-Saga composed 'As with the flourishing blossoms so flourishes my line', and Saneuji responded with 'Flower, blossoms, for a garland to adorn that flourishing line', to such acclaim.

Next came the court football, where a fine variety of clothing was on display. His Highness, the Crown Prince, Kameyama, the Prime Minister, Iemoto and others were a wonderful sight in their various robes. The preliminary kick was performed by His Highness Kameyama, according to a precedent established early in the century. After the games were over His Majesty reluctantly departed, as he needed to hurry back to preside at the spring promotions ceremony.

His departure meant that the following day there weren't many guards to be seen, and those who were there looked quite relaxed. Around noon, matting was laid between the northern pavilion and the worship hall, and there followed a procession of Their Highnesses in formal lacquered hat and robes, together with the Crown Prince, who wore tucked trousers in the hunting style. After pausing to pay their respects at the various worship halls, they made their way to the hall dedicated to Myōon, divine protector of music.

Seemingly in expectation of this visit, a single cherry tree still held its blossoms, almost as if it had somehow learned that fine old poem that bids the mountain cherry bloom after others scatter. A throng of ladies had gathered to hear the musical performance, faces shielded from view, and I mingled with this crowd of silk-robed ladies and watched as the three made their way into the hall.

The performance took place on the veranda. The Kazan'in Chancellor was on the flute, Superintendent Saemon on the *shō*, Kaneyuki played the *hichiriki* flute, the Crown Prince was on the *biwa*, Sanekane on the *koto*, Tomoaki played the big drum and Norifuji the side drum. A number of pieces were played[213] in the Banshiki mode and Kaneyuki sang 'Bright Flowers Bloom in the Upper Garden'. The various tones blended so beautifully that he performed it twice, after which His Highness sang 'How Cruel the Girl who Wove this Heavy Robe'. Kameyama and the Crown Prince joined in, and how marvellous it was to hear them all singing together. Once the concert was over the performers retired, leaving everyone longing for more and agreeing that it was truly a spectacle to remember with emotion.

Witnessing all this general splendour and jollity made me feel rather wretched, and I wished I hadn't agreed to be part of it. Sorrow had flooded me at the sound of His Highness's dear voice singing at the Myōon Hall, and though another game of court football followed I chose to stay away.

Then Takayoshi came to deliver a letter to me. I demurred,

telling him it must surely be for someone else, but at his insistence I finally took it. This is what I read there:

Might it be possible	*kaki-taete*
to sever ties and live	*arare ya suru to*
without you? I wondered.	*kokoromi ni*
So the days and months go by	*tsumoru tsukihi wo*
yet you do not complain	*nado ka uraminu*

'I cannot forget you,' His Highness had added. 'Surely this means that our ties remain unsevered still. Relieve me of my long unhappiness tonight.'

In reply I only wrote:

Still spoken of	*kakute yo ni*
as living in the world	*ari to kikaruru*
as the years have passed	*mi no usa wo*
all my complaint	*uramite nomi zo*
is of that misery	*toshi wa henikeru*

The football game was over, and at around seven that evening I had lain down to sleep when suddenly he arrived. 'The boating is on now,' he said. 'Come.'

Seeing absolutely no point in joining the event, I made no move to rise. 'Just come as you are,' he insisted, and he set about tying the loosened strings of my *hakama* trousers and setting my clothes to rights. Since when can he have turned tender again like this? I wondered in bewilderment. It was hardly consolation for these past two years of bitterness, but since it was impossible to refuse him I brushed away my tears and presented myself at the gathering.

Darkness was drawing in as everyone boarded boats at the Pond Pavilion. In the Crown Prince's party were Lady Dainagon, Lady Uemon no Kami and Lady Kō no Naishi, all in formal attire. Their Highnesses were to ride together in a small boat with myself in attendance wearing triple robes plus a fine silk robe and Chinese jacket, but instead I was called across to the Crown Prince's boat. Musical instruments were taken on board, and the nobles boarded another small boat which was attached to ours as an outlier. Music-making followed, with the Kazan'in Chancellor on flute, Superintendent Saemon on *shō*, Kaneyuki on *hichiriki* flute, the Crown Prince on *biwa*, Lady Emon no Kami on *koto*, Tomoaki on the big drum and Sanekane on the smaller drum.

The mode was unchanged from that of the earlier concert at the Myōon Hall, which His Highness had found so tirelessly delightful. The pieces included 'Waves on the Green Sea', 'Song of the Bamboo Grove', 'Crossing Heaven' and others, repeated over and over. Kaneyuki launched into a performance of 'Mountain After Mountain', which Their Highnesses followed with 'The Dancing Girls with Varied Gestures Dance', till one could imagine the very mud beneath our boats astonished at the beauty of the sound. As we rowed farther out and away from the Pond Pavilion, the interlacing branches of the ancient, mossy pines on the central island and indeed the water itself somehow suggested the poetic illusion that we were rowing upon some vast ocean, and His Highness Kameyama made reference to the line that speaks of 'travelling two thousand leagues from home', then intoned 'making our way through waves of cloud and mist'.[214]

He turned to me. 'You have firmly sworn never to play the strings again, I know, but do add a line to this,' he said, and so I reluctantly intoned, 'into such distance may your time continue'.[215]

Sanekane took up the song with the line, 'with gifts of tribute far surpassing all that came before'.

Tomoaki sang, 'your light will shine protected by the gods'.

The Crown Prince added, 'year upon year still climbing past old age'.

Kameyama: 'though life is difficult when lived so long'.

'Yet bearing steadfastly the pain within one's heart,' I sang.

'I know just what lies in your heart behind those words,' His Highness said to me, and he sang, 'that dawn moon shines still in those endless tears'.[216]

'What's this about the dawn moon?' said Kameyama. 'I don't follow it.'

When it grew dark, the Crown Prince's attendants lit pine torches here and there and presented themselves to urge him to return, which created a fine and unusual spectacle. The boats made their way back to the Pond Pavilion and their Highnesses disembarked, with evident reluctance to end the evening's pleasures.

Others must surely have been able to guess my feelings, perilously afloat as I now was on the waters of uncertain fate, but alas this was not that river where heavenly lovers meet,[217] and I was left bereft of any friend to show concern for me.

Oh yes, the Crown Prince's military aide Tachihaki Kiyokage was dressed that day in a glossed lavender ceremonial robe and trousers embroidered with a pattern of pine and wisteria, and it was remarked that both his conduct and the formal decorative sprays at his ears were most impressive. When he was sent as messenger to the imperial court he apparently crossed paths with Count Tō no Ōkura Tadayo, who was on his way there from the court.

The empress dowager's gifts on this occasion were, I believe, as follows: to His Highness a *biwa*, and to the Crown Prince a Japanese *koto*. The rewards given for the occasion were: from His Majesty to Toshisata, the lower fourth rank, while the Crown Prince gave Koresuke a lower fifth. Sanekane's gift of a *biwa* was given to Tamemichi, and much else was also given but I won't record it all.

A general gloom descended after the departure of the Crown Prince. There was to be another visit to the worship hall, and messages kept arriving urging me to take part, but it seemed to me that nothing would alleviate my sadness, and my poor heart could find no room for any urge to go.

BOOK 4

(1289–1293)

I set out from the capital as the second month's waning moon was rising.[218] Although I had severed myself from my old home with barely a backward glance, now thoughts of the uncertainties of this world where there can be no promise of return crowded in to draw belated tears to my sleeves, till 'even the moon reflected in those drops seemed to me a tearful face'.[219] And so, unnerved by my own faintheartedness, I made my way to the Barrier Gate of Ōsaka.[220]

I could not find even the lingering traces here of Semimaru's[221] famous hut of old, where he once lived and wrote the poem 'whether in palace or in lowly hut / life will pass', and the form I saw reflected when I bent to the Barrier's pure spring waters moved me with the unfamiliar traveller's guise of my departure's first steps on the long journey, halting my feet. A single cherry tree stood there at the height of its blossoming, and even this my eyes were loath to farewell.

There in the blossoms' shade four or five others on horseback were also resting, apparently country folk though neatly turned out. Perhaps they saw those flowers with the same feelings as myself:

These cherry blossoms	yuku hito no
halt the heart	kokoro wo tomuru
of the passerby –	sakura kana
barrier guards of sorts	hana ya sekimori
on Ōsaka Mountain	ōsaka no yama

With such thoughts I set off again, and arrived at a waystation called Kagami, or Mirror. It was just coming on dusk, and the sight of courtesans wandering about in search of a night of love filled me with a deep melancholy at the sad ways of this world. I was touched to sadness too by the dawn's temple bell that sent me on my way again next day:

Though I come to gaze	*tachi-yorite*
at mirroring Kagami	*miru to mo shiraji*
it cannot know	*kagami yama*
the image of that lingering face	*kokoro no naka ni*
that still haunts my heart	*nokoru omokage*

Days went by, and I came to the waystation of Akasaka in the land of Mino. Unused to travel as I was, the passing days had been hard on me, so in my weariness I paused to stay here. The innkeeper had two courtesans, sisters who played elegantly on the *koto* and *biwa*. This brought back earlier and happier days for me, so I ordered up sake for them and asked them to perform. The one who seemed the older of the two was evidently deeply troubled by something, for though she was distracting herself by plucking the *biwa*, tears filled her eyes, and I watched her full of sympathy, imagining that she was surely suffering much as I was.

These tears of mine at memories of lost love, so unbecoming to a nun's black sleeves, must have troubled her, for she wrote this poem on the tray that held the sake cups and handed it to me:

Whatever in your heart	*omoi-tatsu*
prompted you to rise	*kokoro wa nani no*
and leave the world behind you	*iro zo to mo*
haunting as Fuji's smoke that drifts	*fuji no kemuri no*
on to some unknown end?	*sue zo yukashiki*

Taken completely by surprise at this unexpectedly elegant gesture, I responded with:

Mount Fuji's peak	*fuji no ne wa*
lies in the land of Suruga	*koi wo suruga no*

linking it with love[222]   *yama nareba*
so that smoke surely rises   *omoi ari to zo*
from love's fierce fires   *kemuri tatsuran*

Prone as my heart was to linger over all I loved, even this passing encounter was hard to leave behind me, yet there was nothing for it and I went on my way again.

Arriving at Yatsuhashi of the eight bridges, I found no flowing streams there as of old. Not even the famous bridges were to be seen, and I felt as if bereft of a friend:

My heart still enmeshed   *ware wa nao*
with thoughts as tangled   *kumode ni mono wo*
as those spidery streams   *omoedomo*
but at Yatsuhashi now   *sono yatsuhashi wa*
all sign of any bridge is gone   *ato dani mo nashi*

I paused on my way to worship at Atsuta Shrine in the land of Owari. Praying at the sacred fence, memories flooded me. This shrine had been part of my late father's domain, and by way of a personal prayer offering in the fifth month he would always send a messenger with a sacred horse[223] for the shrine festival; the year of his final illness he added a gossamer silk robe, but then the horse died suddenly en route at the way-station of Kayatsu. Dismayed, they found a substitute to offer from among the resident officials, we learned, but I remember that it troubled my mind, for it seemed to me that the gods had refused to accept his offering. All this came back to me now, and I spent the night there deep in sorrow and pining over the past.

It was past the twentieth day of the second month when I left the capital, but being so unaccustomed to the road, though my heart urged me forward I was travelling slowly, and it was by now the beginning of the third month. Seeing the evening moon rise resplendent in the sky recalled to me that same sight above the capital, and I seemed to see before my eyes again the dear face of His Highness.

In the shrine precinct the cherries were at the very height of their blossoming, puffed with pride at their own splendour, yet I found myself wondering sadly for whose sake they had decked themselves in such beauty:

Now the lovely flowers	*haru no iro mo*
come to spring's sky	*yayoi no sora ni*
as I to Narumigata	*narumigata*
yet how soon now will they pass	*ima ikuhodo ka*
leaving a dark grove of green	*hana mo sugimura*

This I wrote on an offering card which I attached to a cedar tree that stood before the shrine.

Having prayers I wished to make, I stayed in retreat here seven days, then set off once more. As I made my way ever onward over the tidal sands of Narumi, I paused to look back at Atsuta Shrine and glimpsed the vermilion of its sacred fence, now hazed with mist, majestic in the distance, prompting unstoppable tears at my father's memory:

Look on me, oh gods,	*kami wa nao*
with pity still	*aware wo kakeyo*
though the rope of my life	*mi-shimenawa*
is twined a different way now	*hiki-tagaetaru*
and I wander here forlorn	*ukimi nari to mo*

I crossed the Barrier of Kiyomi by the moon, my heart full of sad ponderings on all that was past and to come. With thoughts more numerous than the white-spread sands of the beach that stretched before me, on I went around the skirts of Mount Fuji across Floating Island Plain. Snow still lay deep on Fuji's peak, and as I gazed it seemed quite plausible that the poet Narihira should have found the dappled snow still lying even in the fifth month.[224] How pointless, I thought, to pile thought upon thought like these layered snows, when I must come to nothing in the end. Fuji's smoke too was now no more, it seemed[225] – what was any longer left to 'trail lingering in the wind', as the old poem has it?

Then I crossed Mount Utsu, but seeing no sign of Narihira's famous vines and maples thronging the path, I was quite unaware of where I was and failed to take it in, only learning later when I asked that I had already passed it:

Where was that ivy	*koto no ha mo*
that has so thronged	*shigeshi to kikishi*
this road with words?[226]	*tsuta wa izura*
Not even in my dreams did I	*yume ni dani mizu*
see it as I crossed Mount Utsu	*utsu no yama-goe*

Pausing to pray at Mishima Shrine in the land of Izu, I found that the offertory ceremony was just like that of the Kumano pilgrimage,[227] with a most awe-inspiring dragon image. A distinguished lady in traveller's garb was performing the Ten Thousand Venerations on the shore, a practice begun by the late Shogun Yoritomo,[228] and seeing her wretched figure pacing endlessly to and fro brought home to me that I was not alone in my sorrows.

Well into the night, the long-awaited moon rose. Brief nights are cause for sorrow,[229] as the old poem tells us, but here it was beguiling to watch the shrine maidens making their strange gestures as they danced the sacred *kagura*. The over-gown that they wear for shrine duties is somewhat like a child's *akome* gown. They danced something called the Eight Maidens Dance, and the sight of three or four at a time weaving around each other was so engrossing that I stayed up all night to watch, only leaving the shrine when the cocks' crowing signalled the dawn.

It was after the twentieth day when I arrived at the island of Enoshima, a place so lovely that words in fact fail me. I spent the night in one of the many rock retreats on the island, which lies far out over the boundless sea, a place called Senju Cave where an aged mountain ascetic was performing austerities as he must have done for many long years. Crude though his dwelling was, hedged only with the mist and with bamboos for screen, yet the place had true elegance. He was most hospitable, serving up shellfish and other local delicacies. When I presented him with a fan and various gifts from the capital produced from my companion's satchel, he declared that, living where he did, he heard no news from the capital. 'The visiting winds certainly never bring me such gifts as these,' he went on. 'I've met with old friends this evening!' I could well appreciate what he meant. Nothing more was said, and we all settled down for the night.

The night grew late, but lying there on the renunciate's mossy mat in the 'long-worn robe'[230] of my far journey, thoughts piling one upon another, I did not doze enough even to dream. Sleeves soaked with the muffled tears I hid from others, I rose and went to stand outside the cave, where billowing cloud mingled as one with billowing smoke. Then the night's roiling clouds evaporated to reveal the moon seemingly suspended there motionless, high and bright in the sky, and I felt that I had indeed wandered the poet's 'two thousand miles from home'.[231] From a mountain somewhere behind came the sudden shriek of a monkey – it rent my heart, and I felt all the sadness in me rise up as fresh as ever. I had left the capital, I thought miserably, hoping perhaps to find a way to dry the tears of my lonely thoughts and griefs, but the sorrows of this world had covertly come along with me:

A simple cedar hut	*sugi no io*
rough pine for pillars	*matsu no hashira ni*
hung with coarse blinds –	*shino-sudare*
could I but leave	*ukiyo no naka wo*
the sad world far behind me	*kakehanareba ya*

The following morning as I approached Kamakura I paused to visit Gokuraku Temple, and watched nostalgically as the priests went about their business in precisely the same style as back in the capital.

From Kehai Hill I looked out over the city of Kamakura, a scene very different from the view of the old capital seen from its eastern hills. Here the rows of houses rose one upon another up the hillside, all crammed together like objects stuffed into a bag, and the longer I gazed the drearier and the more unattractive I found the sight.

I went out to look at a place called Yui Beach where there is a large shrine gate, with Wakamiya Shrine visible in the distance.

Its deity is the sworn protector of the Genji clan[232] above all others. It was surely not for nothing that I was born into this illustrious clan. So why, I wondered, should this sad fate have been mine? Then I remembered that I had prayed to this god that my father should be reborn in paradise, and in return received the message that his happiness in the next life would be secured in exchange for my own happiness in this one. Not that I say this in bitterness. No, it means that I have no cause to bewail my fate, even though I find myself reduced to a begging life.

As I paid my respects at the shrine, my head was full of thoughts of the poet Ono no Komachi[233] – who was forced to spend her old age in poverty, a rough basket over her arm and a straw coat wrapped about her, though she was descended from the lovely Princess Sotoori – and of her words, 'I alone am sunk in sorrow'.

It could be said that this shrine, with its view over the sea, presents a finer scene than the parent Hachiman shrine of Iwashimizu. It is also very strange to see domain lords who visit the shrine dressed not in the customary white robes but wearing the warrior's formal *hitatare* gown in various colours.

I went on to visit other temples, including Egara, Nikaidō and Ōmidō, after which I sent a message to Lady Komachi, a relative of my second cousin Tsuchimikado Sadazane, who was living in the Ōkuradani area in service to the Shogun. A reply came saying how astonished she was to hear that I was there and inviting me to stay, but this would actually have been rather awkward so instead I took lodgings nearby. Concerned that I might not have all I need, she kindly sent over all sorts of things for me, and so I rested there and recovered for a while from the rigours of the journey.

Unfortunately, the person I had asked to guide me on the forthcoming Zenkōji pilgrimage[234] had fallen gravely ill around the end of the fourth month, and there were fears for her life. This was bad enough, but no sooner had she begun to recover a little than it was my turn to fall ill.

Everyone was worried now that two of us were sick, but the doctor pronounced it was nothing serious, just the return of a chronic illness brought on by the strains of unaccustomed travel. I felt at death's door, however, and words cannot express my misery. Back when I was a girl, if even so much as a cold or a sniffle continued for more than a few days, all the doctors and Yin-Yang Masters[235] would be prevailed on to do all in their power for me, and even household heirlooms and the finest horses would be offered at shrines and temples to pray for my swift recovery. Exotic delicacies, extravagant fruits – my father went to endless trouble and all for me. Now day after day I lay on my sickbed feeling utterly different from that child, with no one to pray for me and no means of securing food or medicines, my days and nights spent simply lying there.

But fate determines how long we live, after all. From around the sixth month I began to improve a little, although I still had no inclination to set off and resume my pilgrimage. More time passed while I drifted about, aimless and unsettled, until the eighth month at last arrived.

On the morning of the fifteenth day, a message from Lady Komachi arrived. 'Today is the day for the Ceremony of Release[236] back home at Iwashimizu's Hachiman Shrine. What memories does this evoke for you?' she asked.

My reply:

> There is no point   omoi-izuru
> in my remembering   kai koso nakere
> for in me now   iwashimizu
> the waters of that lineage[237] onaji nagare no
> flow only to a murky end   sue mo naki mi wa

Lady Komachi's response:

> Hold fast your faith   tada tanome
> for where the heart offers   kokoro no shime no
> prayers and invocations   hiku kata ni
> the gods must surely   kami mo aware wa
> respond with pity   sakoso kakarame

A Ceremony of Release was also held at Kamakura's New Hachiman Shrine, and curiosity drew me to go and see it. The

Shogun was present, dressed in impressive finery given the place.[238] The domain lords all wore hunting costume, and their armed retainers and so forth, clad in formal *hitatare* robes each after his own style, made an unusual spectacle. When the Shogun descended from his carriage at a place called the Red Bridge, he was accompanied by just a handful of nobles and courtiers. The impression was really quite vulgar and unprepossessing. Taira no Munetsuna, oldest son of the Government Superintendent lay monk Taira no Yoritsuna, attended in the role of Undersecretary of Operations but behaved rather as a prime minister would, very grand. There seemed little point in watching the horseback archery and other festive events, so at this point I went home.

Not many days after this, a rumour went round that something was afoot in Kamakura. Who is involved? we all wondered. It appeared that the Shogun was preparing to return to the capital,[239] and when I learned that he was about to set out I went along to see.

A very undistinguished matting-sided palanquin[240] was drawn up to the edge of the adjacent building. Someone, I think Superintendent Tango no Jirō, signalled that His Excellency was to board, at which point Taira no Munetsuna arrived as the emissary of Hōjō Sadatoki,[241] with orders that the palanquin follow precedent and be turned to face backwards.[242] What's more, before the Shogun had even boarded, a group of lowly underlings entered the main building without so much as removing their straw sandals and set about pulling down the reed blinds and generally dismantling it. I couldn't bear to watch.

When the Shogun's palanquin set off some of his ladies emerged from the building, without even covering their heads and though no palanquins awaited them, weeping and begging to know where His Excellency had gone. Certain domain lords who were no doubt particularly attached to His Excellency had ordered some of their young retainers to accompany him, but it seemed that they were waiting until the cover of darkness to quietly dispatch them. Words cannot describe the various scenes of parting.

His Excellency first travelled to a place called Sasuke no Yatsu, where he stayed five days before proceeding on to the capital, and since I was eager to see this departure I went to a nearby temple where the deity Oshite no Shōten was enshrined. On enquiry I learned that he was to depart at around two in the morning. Rain had been falling since evening, and by now it had turned to a downpour, accompanied by wind. In such weather strange spirits might well be afoot, but the procession was not to be delayed so they duly prepared to set off, the Shogun's palanquin wrapped in straw matting against the elements. It looked so dreadful that I had to avert my eyes.

The palanquin was drawn up to the landing and it seemed His Excellency had boarded, but then for some reason it was lowered again in the garden, and a little later he was heard to blow his nose. It was done very quietly but the sound was repeated several times, and one could all too well imagine the tears he must be weeping.

Now this man was not just some upstart barbarian who had seized power by brute force.[243] His father was, I believe, Prince Munetaka, referred to as the second son of Emperor Go-Saga, who was actually born some months earlier than his brother the Mikado, Go-Fukakusa.[244] If his father had become emperor he in turn would have inherited the throne, but this failed to happen owing to the inferior lineage of his father's mother, and instead his father became Shogun. Nevertheless, he retained the status of his royal birth and was referred to as a prince, and his son too was of course similarly exalted. His mother was rumoured to be only a lesser imperial concubine, but she came from the imperial regents' branch of the great Fujiwaras. Tears spring to my eyes when I consider how impeccable his lineage was on both sides:

> Remembering that this man   *isuzugawa*
> issues from that sacred stream   *onaji nagare wo*
> from which emperors spring   *wasurezu wa*
> how moved with pity   *ika ni aware to*
> the gods would be to see him   *kami mo miruran*

I could only too well imagine how tearful he felt as he made his way to the capital, and it was just a pity that no poem of his from this journey has come down to us, considering that he was the child of the man who composed the fine 'daybreak on the snows of Kitano'.[245]

In due course it was announced that His Highness's young son Prince Hisaakira was to come to Kamakura as the new Shogun. The shogunal headquarters were renovated for the occasion, and in the midst of all the celebratory bustle the news arrived that seven domain lords would go to greet him, among them Taira no Yoritsuna's second son Iinuma (who had not yet received his later title of Shinzaemon). It was said that he took the alternative route over Mount Ashigara rather than 'follow in the footsteps of an exile',[246] as he put it, which everyone said was going to ridiculous extremes.

There was great excitement when word spread that the new Shogun would soon arrive. Early one morning a few days before the grand event, a letter for me arrived from Lady Komachi. Intrigued, I read it and discovered it was about something quite unexpected. Apparently Her Highness Higashi Nijō'in had sent a set of five robes to Yoritsuna's wife, a lady by the name of Lady Onkata, but the pieces were unsewn and she wished to consult me about how to assemble them.

At first I declined, but she was persistent. 'Having taken religious orders, you are surely free to come and go as you please,' she urged, 'and besides, no one will recognize you. All she has been told is that you are "someone from the capital".' It was all very difficult, and though I repeatedly refused, in the end a letter from the Regent himself arrived to back up the request. Since Lady Komachi gave assurances that she would take care of any problems and besides, it was really a trivial matter and not worth the bother of all this fuss, I finally agreed and went to call on Lady Onkata.

She lived in what I believe was called the Corner Building, part of Regent Yoritsuna's estate. While the Shogun's own residence was furnished in the standard manner, this place was studded with gold and silver and glittered in a way that called to mind the polished radiance of the fabled Phoenix Mirror. Although not quite the splendours of paradise, the ladies were swathed in finest silks, and everything from standing curtains to trailing drapes seemed aglow with light.

Lady Onkata appeared, a tall, large-framed woman, impressive of feature and stately in bearing, clothed in a Chinese weave double robe with a raised design of a large tree in autumn leaf done in varying shades of scarlet-purple thread on a light blue weave ground, and a white train. I gazed in awe, but this magnificent impression was rather spoiled by the arrival of the lay priest her husband, who came trotting in clad in a simple white short-sleeved gown and settled down cosily next to his splendid wife.

The clothes sent by Her Highness were produced, a set of five robes dyed in rusty plum reds graded from paler to richer shades, together with a blue unlined gown. The outermost layer had a ground of very pale reddish purple with a checkered pattern done in rich scarlet-purple and blue on one sleeve, which had been wrongly put together in sewing. The inner layers, which should have been in progressively darker shades, were instead progressively paler, so that the topmost reddish-purple layer was followed by a rich scarlet-purple one and so forth. It was all most peculiar.

'Why did they do such a thing?' I asked, and it was explained to me that everyone in the government's official clothing bureau had been too busy to do it, so the pieces had been assembled like this in ignorance by the household ladies. I was most amused.

As I was instructing them on how to re-sew the layers correctly, a messenger arrived from the Regent to the effect that the external furnishings of the Shogun's residence were being set up by the men according to written instructions, but he wanted the interior furnishings of the private quarters shown to 'the lady from the capital' for consultation.

I was considerably annoyed by this, but since it was on my way, and besides it wouldn't do to express my irritation, I went as asked.

The place wasn't too dreadful really; it was acceptably set up in the proper way, and there wasn't anything that needed immediate instructions, so I simply questioned the placement of the cabinet shelves and the robe hanger before returning to my quarters.

It was the day of the new Shogun's arrival, and the crowds were packed tight along Wakamiya Street. The first group of men who had gone to accompany him here from the border had apparently already passed by at the head of the procession, and now twenty, then thirty, forty, fifty horsemen rode imposingly past. The main procession began to arrive, and about twenty men in *hitatare* robes who appeared to be attendants (termed 'minor escorts' I believe) came running by, followed by successive little clusters of provincial lords dressed in varied *hitatare*. After five or six city blocks of procession had finally gone past, the Shogun, wearing I think a valerian inner robe in a raised design, finally arrived, carried in a palanquin with the blinds raised. Behind him rode Yoritsuna's son Iinuma in a hunting costume of spring-shoot green over white. The whole thing was quite splendid.

Various men of importance, among them the Regent and his right-hand man Ashikaga Sadauji, were gathered at the Shogun's headquarters, robed in unpatterned hunting costumes. The Viewing of the Horses[247] was an impressive affair. I heard marvellous reports of the Shogun's visit on the third day to the Regent's mountain retreat, which filled me with moving memories of the old days at His Highness's court.

The end of the year drew near. I was disappointed that I hadn't managed to make the planned pilgrimage to Zenkōji Temple that year, but Lady Komachi . . .

The page has been cut with a blade at this point. If only we knew what had been written below.[248]

. . . It was a great shame. So the time passed.

One Wakabayashi Jirōzaemon brought frequent messages from Iinuma, who was known as a poet and a man of fine taste, with polite requests that I join him in a session of continuous composition,[249] so eventually I went along. I was pleasantly surprised by his refinement, and we met on a number of occasions to enjoy ourselves with linked verse and poetry sessions.

When the twelfth month arrived, the tonsured widow of the

Kawagoe lay priest told me that she was planning to go to a place called Kawaguchi in the province of Musashi, and to travel on from there in the new year to make a pilgrimage to Zenkōji Temple. Overjoyed at this opportunity, I duly set off with her for Kawaguchi.

Snow was falling, and lay so deep along the way that we could scarcely make out the road, but after two days' travelling we arrived. It was a remote and wretched place on the bank of I think the Iruma River, with on the opposite bank a post town called Iwabuchi where there was a courtesan house. There is not a mountain to be seen in this land. Far and wide over the Musashi Plain the tangled undergrowth of sedge stretched withered and frost-seared. My thoughts went out to the lonely dwellings of those who had made their way in to these distant parts, and to my own dear home back in the capital, receding ever further as I went on, and pity and sorrow mingled in my heart as the year drew to its close.

I turned over the past in my mind – how I had lost my mother at two, too young to remember her face, and how later, at the age of four, around I think the twentieth of the ninth month I had been summoned to join the entourage of His Highness Go-Fukakusa. Since the day I first began to serve at his Palace I had been blessed with his favour, learned the accomplishments of a lady, and spent many years bathed in the favour of his warm love, of course nursing the secret hope that I might bring honour to my family through the child I bore him. But it is decreed that one must leave behind the bonds of love and enter the Buddhist Way. 'Family, riches, kingly might – none will go with you at your hour of death,' as the sutra[250] says. The worldly realm that I had turned from is truly a place of sorrows, as I well knew, yet I found myself yearning for that familiar world of the Palace that had been mine for so long, nor could I forget His Highness's love, and the rich tears that soaked my sleeves were my only comfort.

As I sat gazing forlornly out into the gloom of the falling snow and darkening sky, which seemed to be severing me from any last traces of the way home, my companion the Kawagoe nun sent across to me a message inquiring how I felt in all this snow. In reply I sent:

Think of me with pity	*omoiyare*
sorrows piled high	*uki koto tsumoru*
as this white garden snow	*shirayuki no*
who like the snow	*ato naki niwa ni*
will vanish without trace	*kie-kaeru mi wo*

Her solicitous question served to provoke more painful thoughts and I struggled to contain my tears, held back only by the thought of those around me, and in this way the new year arrived.

The song of a warbler flitting through the plum blossom by the eave awoke me to the new spring, yet I found myself bewailing time's inexorable passing. Thoughts of the past turned my sorrowing heart back even as the turning year drew me forward, and as the old year fell away so too my tears fell on.

Towards the middle of the second month I resolved to make my pilgrimage to Zenkōji Temple. I climbed over Usui Pass and trod in person the suspension bridge of Kiso, and perilous it was indeed as the old poem says of it. I longed to pause and take in the famous places along the way, but I was with a great crowd of other pilgrims who hurried me along, so regretfully I passed by with barely a glance. At Zenkōji I announced that I would stay in retreat there for a while in fulfilment of a vow, and when the others all left I remained behind.

It worried them to be leaving me on my own like this, my companions told me, but in reply I said: 'Who will be with me on my journey beyond death? It was alone that I came into the world, and alone I must leave it at the end. All who meet must part. All who are born must die. The peach tree is lovely in its blossoming, but to the root it must return at last. The deep-dyed leaves of autumn in their glory wait only for the wind to soon bear them away. This sorrow at parting is no more than a passing emotion.' So saying, I stayed on there alone.

Zenkōji does not boast a grand view, but its deity, the bodhisattva Amida, is believed to have appeared there in human form

to save humankind. Filled with reverence, I devoted my stay
to performing the Ten Thousand Recitations.[251] While there,
I was invited by some of the other practitioners and nuns to
join them in visiting the home of a nearby lay monk known as
Iwami of Takaoka, a man of fine sensibility who enjoyed composing poetry and holding musical events. It was a most refined
place, far above the normal standard for that remote area. One
way and another there was much here to ease my heart, and I
stayed on until the autumn.

The eighth month had begun. A desire to wait until I could
see the famous autumn scenery of Musashino had kept me here
all this time, and I now decided to return that way. The temple
of Asakusa was said to have a miraculous Eleven-Headed
Bodhisattva Kannon which I longed to see, and I made my way
towards it across a wide plain swathed in a dense growth of
Musashino's famous bush clover, together with valerian, silver-
grass and mugwort, all of a height that could be judged by the
fact that even a man on horseback was invisible in its midst. For
three days I pressed on through it all and still there was no
end. Little side roads led off to the occasional inn, but the plain
stretched on far and wide behind and before me as I went.[252]
The Kannon temple was on a low rise in the midst of the
treeless plain, and I thought of that poem about Musashino
that goes, 'as from the grassy moor / the moon emerges',[253] for
indeed this was the night of the full harvest moon. My thoughts
went back to the wonderful musical performance that is always
held at the court under this full moon, and I recalled the scene
in *The Tale of Genji* where on this same night the exiled Genji
too weeps to think of that courtly music, gazing at the special
robe he carries as keepsake in exile as he quotes Sugawara's
famous words, 'the robe is with me now'[254] – though in my case
I had proffered my special keepsake robe from His Highness as
alms to the bodhisattva Hachiman for the sutra copying ceremony, so it was not in fact with me now. Like these exiled men,
I too could not forget the court, and my sorrow and longing
was as deep, I thought, as Sugawara's long ago as he bowed in
exile to the emperor's scented robe.

The full moon that rose from the grassy plain grew in brilliance as the night deepened, and the dewdrops that clung to the tip of every blade of grass seemed to me like flashing jewels:

This moon beyond the clouds	*kumo no ue ni*
I saw then in exalted realms	*mishi mo nakanaka*
but now this night	*tsuki yue no*
the memories it carries	*mi no omoide wa*
are of a sadder fate	*koyoi narikeri*

I felt afloat on waves of tears:

The full moon rises	*kuma mo naki*
bright and brighter yet	*tsuki ni nari-yuku*
and as I gaze	*nagame ni mo*
my memory fills	*nao omokage wa*
with thoughts of that dear face	*wasure ya wa suru*

Daybreak had come and I could no longer stay out there on the plain, so I returned to my lodgings.

On I went, wondering whether I was now somewhere close to the area around the famous Sumida River.[255] Then, crossing a large bridge in the style of the Gion and Kiyomizu bridges back in the capital, I met with two respectable-looking men, so I asked them where the Sumida might be.

'This is the very river,' one said. 'This bridge is called Suda Bridge. There was no bridge here back in the old days and people had to be carried over by ferry, but to avoid all that trouble they built a bridge instead. Sumida was probably a more elegant name for the river, but the commoners around here just refer to this as the bridge over the Suda.

'Over there on the far bank, that was once called Miyoshino Village,' he went on, 'but the rice that the folk cut and dried there bore next to no grain. The local governor asked the name of the place, and when he heard it he declared that this name was the problem,[256] so he changed the name to Yoshida Village and ever since the rice there has fruited up beautifully.'

I recalled the famous episode in *The Ise Tales* where

Narihira on his northern journey asks the 'capital birds' on this river to give him news of his distant beloved. I saw no such birds there now:

Pointless to have come	*tazune-koshi*
all this long way	*kai koso nakere*
to Sumida River	*sumidagawa*
when no trace remains	*sumiken tori no*
of those birds that once lived here	*ato dani mo nashi*

The river mists hung thick before me and behind, blinding me as, in blinding tears, I made my way along this far road, and the cries of the wild geese high in the heavens seemed to echo this moment's feelings.

Beneath a traveller's sky	*tabi no sora*
and lost in tears	*namida ni kurete*
how sorrowful the cry	*yuku sode wo*
of the wild geese	*koto tou kari no*
who speak of my sorrows	*koe zo kanashiki*

Nothing remained of Horikane Well of poetic fame; only a single dead tree stood there now. I longed to travel further in along this way, but 'the path of love leads on / to guards that bar the way',[257] as they say, so I thought better of the idea and instead went back to Kamakura with the plan of returning from there to the capital.

I stayed a while in Kamakura. Towards the middle of the ninth month, the evening before I was to depart at daybreak, various friends whom I had come to know there called to bid me a sad goodbye. Among them was Superintendent Iinuma, who arrived with several parting gifts and suggested that we compose some farewell linked verse together. Moved by this wonderfully warm gesture, I stayed up composing long into the night with him.

The last time we had met, I had asked if he knew the actual location of the river known as the River of Tears,[258] and he had replied that he had no idea. Now, as we enjoyed ourselves with poetry through the night, he inquired if I really intended to leave next morning. 'There is no halting life's journey,' I replied. Then, as he was leaving, he wrote a departing poem for me on the bentwood tray that held the sake cups.

Now I know	*waga sode ni*
the River of Tears flows	*arikeru mono wo*
in my own sleeves	*namida-gawa*
since I have no right to beg	*shibashi tomare to*
that you stay on a while	*iwanu chigiri ni*

Very soon after, while I was still considering a poem in reply, a gift of travelling robes arrived from him. With it came this poem:

Only wear this for me	*kite dani mo*
and keep it wrapped about you	*mi wo ba hanatsu na*
as you travel on	*tabi-goromo*
though you and I	*sakoso yoso naru*
must forever be remote	*chigiri naru to mo*

We had often met up like this while I was staying in Kamakura, and I heard that some had wondered aloud whether our relationship had in fact been somewhat less than properly 'remote', so with this in mind I drew on the old expression for a false rumour, 'to cast wet clothes on someone', in my response:

That wet robe that was cast	*kawakasazarishi*
I left undried	*sono nureginu mo*
and now it must	*ima wa itodo*
decay with loving tears	*koin namida ni*
as I remember you	*kuchinu-beki ka na*

Although there was no reason to hurry back to the capital, I couldn't simply linger on in Kamakura, so when the morning sun was well risen I set out.

Various friends arranged for a series of palanquins to take me from one inn to the next as I travelled, and very soon I arrived at the pass of Saya no Nakayama. Recalling the famous poem composed here by Saigyō, 'life has brought me back',[259] I composed:

Hard it is to cross	*koe-yuku mo*
Saya's dark pass	*kurushikarikeri*
and if I live on	*inochi ari to*
will I return	*mata towamashi ya*
to cross this way again?	*saya no nakayama*

Along the way I paused to worship again at Atsuta Shrine,[260] and spent a night there in prayer. While I was there I spoke to a band of religious practitioners who told me they had come from the Grand Shrine of Ise.[261] Is it far off? I asked, and when they told me I could get there by boat over the Tsushima Crossing[262] I was delighted and made up my mind to go myself.

Before I went there I should stay on here at the shrine, I decided, until I had completed a copy of the remaining thirty books of the Kegon Sutra[263] in fulfilment of an earlier vow. I gathered up all the travelling robes and so forth that I had received in Kamakura, as payment for my stay, and was prepared to set in on the task, but the head priest or whoever he was created all manner of difficulties that upset my plans. Then, while I was hesitating over what to do, another bad bout of my old illness struck. All plans to complete my vow in tatters, I ended by going straight back to the capital.

I arrived there around the end of the tenth month and stayed on for a while, but life in the capital was far from easy for me, so I made the decision to go on to Nara. Not being a descendant of the Fujiwara family, I had seldom had reason to go there,[264] but it was not far from the capital and it seemed like a good place to stay while I recovered from the rigours of the journey.

Knowing no one, I went alone.

First I prayed at the great Kasuga Shrine. The two-storied gate and the splendid roofs of the four shrine buildings were deeply overawing, while the fierce winds that blew from the nearby peak sang loud enough to waken one from the ignorant sleep of earthly passions, and the stream that flowed below might wash away the stains of this sinful world, it seemed to me. I then went on to pay my respects at nearby Wakamiya Shrine, where the sight of the shrine maidens was redolent of times past. The evening sun slanted over the shrine roof and lit the treetops on the ridge beyond as the two shrine maidens danced the sacred dances together over and over before the altar.

I spent that night in the shrine corridor in prayer, listening to people endlessly singing the sacred songs, and felt again the well-known truth of the deity's awe-inspiring manifestation in this sullied world, and the power of foolish words and specious phrases to nevertheless lead the ignorant to the truth.[265]

I was further deeply moved when I heard the tale of how Abbot Rinkai, when he was still an acolyte of Abbot Shinki who lived in Kōfukuji Temple's Kita monastery, was so annoyed by the beating of drums and jangling of bells at the shrine while he was performing his own practice that he swore that if he ever found himself in charge he would put a permanent end to this cacophony. He did indeed attain this powerful position in due course, and put his long-cherished plan into action by banning sacred performances at Kasuga Shrine. The shrine precincts in their beautiful vermilion enclosures were left forlorn and silent and the dancers and musicians bewailed their fate, but the sacred order from on high prevailed.

The Abbot declared that he had attained his final desire in this world, and he now hoped only that the deity would grant him rebirth in paradise. He secluded himself in the shrine and fervently offered to the deity the wealth of Buddhist learning he had gained, but the Kasuga deity appeared to him in a revelatory dream and this is what it said: 'I have pierced the realm of the absolute and given myself into this sullied world out of the compassionate urge to save the ignorant such as yourself, only to have you hinder the chance for salvation by extinguishing the sounds of drum and bell. I bitterly resent this, and I hereby refuse these offerings of your fine Buddhist learning.' And so to this day, the sacred performances are maintained no matter what complaints and demands are made.

The following morning I made my way to the nunnery of Hokkeji Temple, where I visited the nun Jakuen, Minister

Fuyutada's daughter,[266] who lived there in the Ichinomuro quarters, and we talked together of the dreariness of this ephemeral life. I was tempted to settle down for a while and make a home for myself in a place such as this, but I realized that I didn't have it in me to quietly devote myself to religious study. Drawn to wander on by the heart's endless delusion, I set off once more for Nara's Kōfukuji Temple, going first to the home of the head of Kasuga Shrine, one Sukeie.

I didn't realize whose house it was at first, but as I passed I noticed the imposing gabled roof of the gatehouse and went in, assuming it must be some temple hall. But no, I saw that it was the home of someone of consequence. The garden's white chrysanthemum hedge spoke of the owner's taste, its elegantly faded hues just the sort of thing one might find at the Palace. A couple of young men emerged as I was admiring it and asked where I had come from. 'From the capital,' I replied, whereupon one said, 'Oh dear, our chrysanthemum hedge is nothing to look at I'm afraid.' This refined youth turned out to be Sukeie's son, Sukenaga, brother of Suketoshi who was vice-governor of Mino:

My colours too	kokonoe no
have turned like these flowers	hoka ni utsurou
with distance from the court	mi ni shi areba
and tales of that far world	miyako wa yoso ni
sound to me ephemeral as dew	kiku no shiratsuyu

I jotted this on a poem card which I attached to a chrysanthemum before going on my way, but it must have been discovered for someone was sent running after me to convince me to return. I was treated most hospitably and urged to stay there for a while, which I did.

Chūgūji Temple, a nunnery built long ago by Prince Shōtoku, houses a mandala woven for his salvation by his widow, so I went to see it. The head nun, one Shinnyobō, was someone I had met back at the court long ago. Yet after all these years she seemed not to recognize me, so I didn't bother giving my name but simply spoke to her in passing. For some reason, however, she was wonderfully kind to me, and at her insistence I ended by staying on there for a while.

From Hōryūji Temple I went on to Taima Temple, about which the following wonderful legend is recorded. Long ago, a maiden by the name of Princess Chūjō, daughter of the Yoko-haki Minister, lived here as a nun, and she made a solemn vow to offer prayers to the embodiment of the bodhisattva Amida. Thereupon a strange nun appeared before her and offered to weave a mandala depicting the glories of paradise if she could supply ten loads of lotus stems. She ordered the lotus stems and from them spun thread which she rinsed in the well water of the Clothing Bureau at the Palace, and when the thread emerged it was dyed in the five colours of salvation.[267] When all was prepared, a lady appeared, asked for a supply of lamp oil and set to work, and between ten in the evening and six the next morning she wove a marvellous mandala before departing.

'How can I meet you again?' Princess Chūjō asked when she left.

'In this place long ago, Buddha's disciple Kashō preached the Buddhist Law. On yonder mountain now, the bodhisattva Hōki pursues his holy practice. You have desired rebirth in Buddha's western paradise, and so I came. Worship this and you will be forever spared all suffering,'[268] came the reply, and with that the lady rose and flew off to the western paradise.

I was very moved by the grave of Prince Shōtoku,[269] which with its impressive rocks is all that the grave of such a great person should be. I was copying the Lotus Sutra at the time, and in my delight at this contact with such holiness I made an offering of a robe before going on my way again.

And so another year ended.

Around the second month I think it was, as I was on my way back to the capital I paused to pay my respects at Hachiman Shrine. It was quite some distance from Nara and I arrived as the sun was setting. Climbing Inohana Slope, I went to call at the Tamamae Garden before the shrine, where I fell in with a dwarf who said she was from Iwami province. We went on together, discussing what karma from a previous life might have caused her to be reborn in this form, till we arrived at the building overlooking the riding grounds.[270]

We found it open, which generally happened when the shrine administrator was in residence. No one along the way had mentioned that on this occasion it was because His Highness had arrived on pilgrimage. Quite ignorant of this, I went on past, then as we were climbing towards the main gate some fellow who looked like a palace official approached with the request that I return to the riding-grounds building.

'Who is there?' I asked. 'I can't imagine who might have discovered who I am. Or perhaps you are addressing this dwarf?'

'No, there's been no mistake. The message is for you. His Highness Go-Fukakusa has been here on pilgrimage since yesterday,' he replied.

I was speechless. All this time my heart had never forgotten him, but years ago when I left my aunt Lady Kyōgoku's apartments where I was staying to beg formal leave from him,[271] I believed it would be the last time we would ever meet. Now in dark nun's robes, haggard from frost, snow and hail after all my time on the road, a faded shadow of my former self, surely no one would recognize me. Yet someone must have, I thought, not realizing that the summons came from His Highness himself. One of the ladies must have noticed me and been puzzled, and sent this official just to check whether I was indeed who she thought I was, I decided. But as I was turning all this over in my mind, a palace guard came running up with orders for me to hurry.

There was no avoiding it. I went and stood timidly by the side door.

'You're only making yourself more obvious there. Come on in.' It was his voice, exactly as he had always sounded. In complete confusion I remained rooted to the spot, my heart bursting.

'Quick! Come on!' he urged, and rather than disobey him, in I went.

'I still recognized you instantly,' he said. 'That should convince you of how deeply I still feel about you all these years later.' So he began, and he went on to speak of all that had happened, and how sad were the ways of this impermanent world of ours. In this way we talked on without sleeping through the all too brief night.

The sky was beginning to brighten. 'You must stay here at the shrine as long as I am here,' he said, 'and we will meet and talk quietly together like this again.' Before he left he took off the three inner robes he wore next to the skin and gave them to me. 'My secret keepsake for you,' he said. 'Wear them always.' As I took them, unspeakable sorrow and emotion overwhelmed me, and my heart forgot all past and future and the darkness of the world to come.[272]

Dawn had arrived, and it was awkward to stay longer. 'Goodbye then,' he said and left, drawing the door closed behind him. The lingering scent of his dear familiar incense seemed to have imbued the very sleeves of my poor nun's robe, so close had he been. Unseemly sorrow overwhelmed me as I put on his three keepsake robes beneath my own to avoid attention, and I composed this:

Gone are those nights	*kasaneshi mo*
our two sleeves lay together	*mukashi ni narinu*
now your robes lie	*koi-goromo*
beneath these ink-black sleeves	*ima wa namida ni*
soaked deep with tears	*sumizome no sode*

The futile memory of his face still lingered in my tears as I was leaving. It seemed a dream within a dream. Could I somehow stay there at least for the day and manage to spend a little more time with him? I wondered as I went on my way. No, confronted with the shocking sight of me in my present state, he had surely felt that this transformation had come about because of my own weakness and error. If I stayed on brazenly seeming to be waiting for another meeting I would look even more foolish. Imagine my feelings, then, as I forced myself to overcome my longing to stay and decided instead to go straight back to the capital that day.

I still wished to catch another glimpse of him from a distance, even as he went about his pilgrimages to the various sub-shrines, and since I was worried that he would recognize me if I was in my usual nun's habit, I slipped on over it the robes he had given me and mingled with the crowd of other women pilgrims. It touched me deeply to see how different he looked now in his monkish robes.[273] As he climbed the stairs to the shrine, Middle Counsellor Suketaka, who would then have been a Councillor I believe, held his arm. I still heard the words he had spoken the previous night: 'Now that we are both in religious robes it brings us closer', and my head was full of the other things he had spoken of too, even recalling the days when I was still a little girl. I left the shrine with his image still held in the tears I shed. Although my feet carried me north to the capital, my soul seemed to linger still on that holy mountain.

I could not stay in the capital, however, and so I took myself off to Atsuta Shrine once more, hoping to fulfil my vow and complete the sutra copying to offer there.

I was sitting there writing through the night when suddenly a fire broke out[274] above the shrine building. You can just imagine the uproar among the attendants! Being of divine origin, this fire was not a thing that ordinary mortals could extinguish, and in no time the building had all gone up in smoke.

Next morning carpenters arrived to begin the task of rebuilding this heap of ashes, and the head priest and the Master of Prayers went around inspecting the situation. The building known as The Sealed Hall had been established there long ago in the age of the gods by the shrine deity as his dwelling, and on its foundation stone, with great beams still alight just beside it, they found a red lacquer box about a foot wide and four feet long. Everyone gathered to look in amazement. The Master of Prayers, whose dealings with the deity were particularly close, approached it, picked it up and slid open the side just a little to see what was in there. He announced that it held what must be the sacred sword[275] inside a red brocade bag, so the Yatsurugi Shrine[276] was opened and it was placed in the altar there.

Now there is a quite extraordinary story about this sword: when the deity of this shrine, an incarnation of Prince Yamato Takeru who was born in the tenth year of the reign of Emperor

Keikō,[277] was ordered to defeat the eastern barbarians, he first went to the Grand Shrine of Ise to beg leave of the deity there, who gave him a sacred sword and a brocade bag.

'This sword I received from you in your previous life when you were the god Susanoo no Mikoto. You took it from the tail of Yamata no Orochi, the Eight Crossroads Snake, in Izumo,' she told him. 'And here is a brocade bag. If the enemy attacks you and you fear for your life, you must open it.'

When Yamato Takeru was later threatened by fire on the plains of Mikarino in Suruga, the sword at his side drew itself out and proceeded to slash back the grass all around him to keep the fire away. Then with the flint that was in the brocade bag he in his turn lit a fire that enveloped and blinded the enemy, thereby defeating them. This is why the place was also known as Yakitsuno or Burned Fields, while the name of the sacred sword is Kusanagi or Grass Mower. This story is recorded in the legendary history of the shrine, which survived the fire. When I heard this I thought of the words of my dream[278] and was awed and astonished.

What with all the fuss over the fire, it felt less and less like a good moment to continue my sutra copying there, so instead I set off over the Tsushima Crossing to visit the Grand Shrine of Ise.

It was early in the fourth month, and the rich green treetops were unusually beautiful. I first went to the New Shrine. At the cedar grove on the Plain of Yamada[279] I found on my lips those words of the poet Saigyō, 'here I will take my stand'.[280] The Religious Affairs Building was full of shrine priests, from the First and Second Priests down. I had heard that members of Buddhist orders such as myself should refrain from worshipping at the shrine, so I was at a loss to know where I should go and how to proceed, but they told me that I was probably allowed to enter as far as the sacred garden at the second gate.

The place felt deeply holy. As I was lingering near the main building, a couple of men who appeared to be shrine priests emerged and asked where I had come from.

'I have come here from the capital to gain religious merit,' I replied.

'Those in Buddhist garb like yourself are usually not permitted here,' one of them said, 'but you look so exhausted that the
gods would surely excuse you.'

He asked me in and kindly looked after me, offering to show
me around, although I was instructed to worship only from a
discreet distance owing to the prohibition. I was taken to the
sacred Thousand-Boughed Cedar and the sacred pond.[281] Here
the shrine priest performed a solemn purification over me and
I made an offering, but as I left I felt miserably that even such a
purification as this might not be able to cleanse a heart as mired
in delusion as mine.

On my way back I took lodgings in a little nearby house, and
asked there who it was who had shown me around so gener-
ously. A man who introduced himself as Third Priest Yukitada,
the head of the establishment, told me that it had been the second
son of the current First Priest, a man called Tsuneyoshi,[282] and in
memory of his many kindnesses I composed this:

Surely it was	*oshinabete*
as one who represents the gods	*chiri ni majiwaru*
who manifest to save us	*sue tote ya*
that he showed such kindness	*koke no tamoto ni*
to this poor Buddhist nun	*nasake kakuran*

I wrote this on a scrap of sacramental mulberry paper which I tied
to a sprig of sacred *sakaki*[283] and sent to him. His response was:

Know then	*kage yadosu*
that even we later twigs	*yamada no sugi no*
of the great sheltering cedar	*sueba sae*
on Yamada's sacred plain	*hito wo mo wakanu*
are bound to save one and all	*chikai to wo shire*

I stayed in seclusion here seven days, hoping to invoke the
gods to aid me in my quest for enlightened release from the
cycle of life and death. While I was there, various shrine priests
sent poems, and there were constant linked verse gatherings. It
was all very refined.

Unlike at most shrines, sutras were chanted not in the shrine itself but in a place called the Hōrakusha or Law-delighting Hall, some half a mile from the shrine. Here I devoted myself all day to chanting, and when evening drew on I went to a nearby nunnery called Kannondō and sought lodgings there. They firmly refused me, however, and I was coldly turned away:

Though we wear the same	*yo wo itou*
ink-black robes to show	*onaji tamoto no*
we have renounced the world	*sumizome wo*
what worldly colour do you see	*ika naru iro to*
to spurn me in this way?	*omoi-sutsuran*

Breaking off a sprig of sacred bamboo that grew near the building, I sent it in with this poem, written on a piece of sacramental paper.

They sent no reply, but instead they did lend me a room, and we proceeded to become friends.

Seven days passed and I was preparing to go on to the Inner Shrine when the priest who had first shown me around sent this:

It seems to me now	*ima zo omou*
that poetry	*michi yuku hito wa*
which drew me first to know	*narenuru mo*
this traveller on the Way	*kuyashikarikeru*
makes our parting only keener	*waka no uranami*

My response:

Why this regret?	*nani ka omou*
Even were I not	*michi yuku hito ni*
a traveller on the Way	*arazu to mo*
surely none in this world	*tomarihatsu-beki*
can stay forever	*yo no narai ka wa*

At the Inner Shrine there were people particularly committed to the refined arts. Rumour of my presence at the Outer Shrine

had reached them, and I learned that they were waiting in hopes
that I would be coming on there eventually. I felt rather uneasy
about this, but I couldn't really stay any further where I was so
I finally moved on to the Inner Shrine.

Next door to where I stayed at a place called Okada was a
house belonging to a lady who seemed of high birth. Soon after
I arrived, a young girl from there appeared with a letter:

Hearing that you came	*nani to naku*
from the capital	*miyako to kikeba*
sad memory floods me	*natsukashimi*
so that I find	*sozoro ni sode wo*
tears soak my sleeves afresh	*mata nurasu ka na*

She turned out to be the widow of Second Priest Nobunari.[284]
Her letter went on to suggest that she come for a visit.

In reply I wrote:

I too cannot forget	*wasurarenu*
the past –	*mukashi wo toeba*
were you to ask, my sorrow	*kanashisa mo*
would rob me of the words	*kotaeyaru-beki*
with which to answer	*koto no ha zo naki*

In the brief summer night before the moon rose, I paid a visit
to the shrine. Here too my Buddhist robes meant I could not
enter, so I stood upstream to worship the distant shrine itself
by the Mimosuso River that flows through the shrine precincts.
Double-flowered *sakaki* trees stood thickly crowded, so that
the sacred fences surrounding the shrine felt very far away.
Learning that the shrine's projecting cross-beams are cut level
along their upper surface, signifying divine protection of the
nation's ruler, I was deeply moved to find myself uttering the
words, 'May no harm befall his sacred person.'[285]

The colour of my heart	*omoi-someshi*
is still unchanged	*kokoro no iro no*
since first I loved you	*kawaraneba*

| so now still I pray | *chiyo to zo kimi wo* |
| that you may live forever | *nao inoritsuru* |

The night wind singing in the sacred forest filled my heart with awe, the waters of Mimosuso River ran softly on, and the rising moon that now made its way through the treetops of nearby Mount Kamiji seemed to swell in brightness here, sending my thoughts like its moonbeams out to distant lands beyond our own.

Having successfully made my prayers I retreated, passing the Religious Affairs Building on my way. The moonlight was particularly impressive at the quarters of First Priest Hisayoshi, but all the doors and shutters were tightly closed and no one was admiring it. The Outer Shrine is known as the Moon Shrine, so I composed this:

Why should you feel	*tsuki wo nado*
this moonlight is inferior	*hoka no hikari to*
to that other light?	*hedatsuran*
Though of course I know	*sakoso asahi no*
you live in the sun's brilliance[286]	*kage ni sumu to mo*

I wrote this on sacramental paper, tied it to a sprig of *sakaki*, laid it on the veranda of the Religious Affairs Building, and went back to my lodgings. It seems Hisayoshi opened and read it, for this soon arrived for me tied to a sprig of *sakaki*:

How could I despise	*sumu tsuki wo*
the clear bright moon?	*ikaga hedaten*
It was an old man's sleep	*maki no to wo*
that kept my humble door	*akenu wa oi no*
shut up against it	*neburi narikeri*

I stayed here a further seven days, then when it was time to leave, my thoughts turned to nearby Futami Bay and I asked the way there, explaining that I longed to see this place that had meant so much to the deity.[287] I was promised a guide, who turned out to be the shrine priest Munenobu.

Off I went with him, taking in Purification Beach, the Gold Lacquer Pines,[288] the rock that a thunderbolt split apart and other places of note, and arriving at Sabino Myōjin Shrine which stands on the shore of the bay. From here I took a boat out to see various islands such as Tateishi, Gozen and Tōru. Gozen or Sacred Offering Island is so called because the local shrine priests gather the abundant seaweed that grows around it and offer it there to the Sun Goddess. Tōru or Passing Island gets its name because boats can pass through a gap beneath its roof-like overhang of rock. This splendid expanse of sea is full of wonderful views.

I was told a moving story here about the deity of a shrine called Koasakuma. Apparently the sacred mirror made by this deity, which reflected the image of the Sun Goddess, was once stolen from the shrine. It was rescued from where it had been sunk deep in the water and placed back on the shrine's altar, whereupon the deity announced, 'I have sworn a solemn vow to bring salvation to the fish of the sea', and with that it rose and left the shrine and reappeared on a rock. Beside this rock grows a cherry tree. When the tide is high the mirror resides at the top of the tree, and at other times it returns to live on the rock next to it.

This wonderful story of the god's vow of salvation filled me with awe, and I felt the urge to stay there a few days to make my devotions to it, so I found lodgings with the shrine head at a place called Shioai.

He treated me with such sensitive kindness and the place was so comfortable that I stayed on here too, and about three days later I went with some other ladies down to the beach, as the moonlit nights of Futami Bay were reputed to be particularly lovely. It was indeed quite delightful, and more moving than words can describe, and we stayed all night enjoying ourselves on the shore. Returning as the dawn sky lightened, I composed this:

Never will I forget	*wasureji na*
the lovely face	*kiyoki nagisa ni*
of the clear moon lingering	*sumu tsuki no*
in the dawning sky	*ake-yuku sora ni*
above this pure white beach	*nokoru omokage*

Teruzuki, a lady in service in the palace kitchens who was a relative of the head of the Ise Shrine, had somehow heard that I was here at Futami, and now a letter arrived 'from a lady at His Highness's court'. I was astonished and puzzled. Opening it, I read these words written on His Highness's behalf: 'Have you grown so accustomed to the moon of Futami that you forget the face of us "cloud-dwellers"[289] at court? I would love to have another such talk with you as we recently so unexpectedly had.'

I was shaken beyond belief. In reply I wrote:

Think only	*omoe tada*
that the midnight moon	*nareshi kumoi no*
I knew among those clouds	*yowa no tsuki*
can never be forgotten	*hoka ni sumu ni mo*
though it shines elsewhere now	*wasure ya wa suru*

I could not linger here forever, so I made my way back to the Outer Shrine, and since things had now settled down again at Atsuta Shrine I prepared to go back there to complete my sutra copying. Reluctant to leave this place, I paid one more final visit to the shrine, and composed this:

Lead me	*ari-haten*
as I wander to my end	*mi no yuku sue no*
in this sad world	*shirube seyo*
you gods	*ukiyo no naka wo*
of Watarai's shrine[290]	*watarai no miya*

I was preparing to leave at first light when this arrived from First Priest Hisayoshi: 'You leave fond memories of your stay with us. Be sure to come again in the ninth month for the shrine's ritual festivities.' Touched by his thoughtfulness, I replied:

In this world	*iku sue no*
ruled by our long-lived emperor	*hisashikaru-beki*
may you too live long	*kimi no yo ni*

| and I will come again | mata kaeri-kon |
| in the long ninth month[291] | nagatsuki no koro |

No one could know the real prayer that was in my heart.[292] 'How could I not respond to such kind wishes for myself and the emperor?' came his response late that night, together with the gift of a wrapped bundle of two rolls of silk, which he explained was a local gift from Ise. With it was this poem:

Like the long-lived pine	kamigaki ni
I will wait long	matsu mo hisashiki
by the sacred fence	chigiri ka na
for that far-off autumn month	chitose no aki no
of the return you vow	nagatsuki no koro

I set off that night for the port of Ōminato to catch the boat that left at dawn on the rising tide, resting along the way by a lowly fisherfolks' salting hut.[293] Lying there, I thought of that old saying, 'Among far rocks where cormorants perch, along whale-haunted shores, I would bravely wait if I could meet my love.' What had I come to? I wondered. Wait though I may, there could be no comfort for my pain; no mountain that I crossed would lead me to that pass where lovers meet.[294]

In the dark of the night just before the dawn when I was to set out, a message arrived from the Outer Shrine priest Tsune-yoshi[295] with the apology that this should have been sent to me while I was at the Inner Shrine. With it was this poem:

Hearing that you go	tachi-kaeru
like the travelling waves	namiji to kikeba
my sleeves are soaked	sode nurete
and that far bay of Narumi[296]	yoso ni narumi no
sounds cruel to my ears	ura no na zo uki

In reply I wrote:

| I have long sworn | kanete yori |
| to part from here | yoso ni narumi no |

and travel on to Narumi   *chigiri naredo*
but my sleeves too are soaked   *kaeru nami ni wa*
by these travelling waves   *nururu sode ka na*

The rebuilding of Atsuta Shrine was proceeding apace and there was all manner of disruption, but I was reluctant to let any more time pass before the fulfilment of my vow, so I set up a retreat for myself there and settled in to copy out the remaining thirty volumes of the Kegon Sutra, which I presented at the altar. The officiating priest for the occasion was an unimpressive country fellow who had no real understanding of such things, but my aim was really to please the Ten Guardians of the sutra,[297] and after the various dedication ceremonies were completed I returned to the capital.

That extraordinary meeting with His Highness while he was at Hachiman Shrine would stay in my memory beyond the grave, and he had since sent a number of messages through a mutual acquaintance to my old home, but I had no inclination to respond, so although I was moved and grateful for his continued goodwill, time passed and still we did not meet.

A year later,[298] around the ninth month when His Highness was staying at the Fushimi Palace, he sent a string of messages to say that things were quiet so this would be a good time to meet unnoticed. My old feelings of love once more overpowered my frail heart and convinced me to comply, and I secretly made my way as bidden to a place near the southern building of the Fushimi Palace.

Our go-between came out to show me the way in, which struck me as ludicrously unnecessary, but as I waited for His Highness to come I stepped out to the railing of the worship hall and looked about me, and felt a sudden flood of tears rise in me like the mournful waters of the nearby Uji River.[299] I stood there recalling the old poem about the waves of Akashi that seem to turn the bright moon dark.[300]

Finally, when the night was well advanced, His Highness arrived. In the bright moonlight the sight of that face so changed from of old was clouded by my tears. He spoke of many things long since passed, from those early days when I was still a child who lived beside him day in day out until the day I left the Palace knowing this to be the end, and distant though those days were now, how could I not be deeply moved as I listened?

'Life in this sorry world cannot but be full of griefs and troubles for you,' he said, 'yet why have you not told me of them all this time?' I could only think of how unhappy I felt at this futile existence of mine. There was no other comforting friend with whom I could share my feelings and my woes, but they were not things I could speak of to him. As I sat intently listening to his words, a deer on Mount Otowa cried out as if to summon my tears, and the dawn bell of nearby Sokujōin Temple rang as if announcing the lightening sky.

With the deer's sad cry	*shika no ne ni*
now comes the tolling	*mata uchi-soete*
of the temple bell	*kane no oto no*
speaking afresh of tears	*namida koto-tou*
as day dawns in the sky	*akatsuki no sora*

I kept this poem secret in my heart, and so our meeting ended. The dawning day made it difficult to stay longer and I prepared to leave, sleeves wet with tears and the image of His Highness still vivid in my heart.

'For my own part, I long to find another chance such as we have had this moonlit night to see you again in this world,' he said before we parted, 'yet you speak only of that distant dawn of salvation when we will meet beyond the grave. Who else is it you love? It's quite acceptable for a man to travel hither and yon, to the eastern provinces or even to China, but it's said that all kinds of things stand in a woman's way to hinder her in this kind of wandering practice. Just who have you taken up with along the way to help you through your difficulties? You surely can't have travelled about like this all on your own. That man who discovered his River of Tears at parting from you, that chrysanthemum hedge you visited at Mount Mikasa, that promise to return to Mimosuso River in the ninth month[301] – such poems were surely not just casual words. Surely these have been long and deep relationships, and there must have been other men too who travelled with you on all those wanderings of yours.'

To all this close questioning I replied, 'Ever since I left the misty heights of the Palace and set off to seek my way along those cloudy roads, I have settled nowhere in this illusory world of suffering. My present unhappy fate brings home to me the wretched karma of my past. I have forsworn relations with men and that is that. Though I am born of Genji stock and trace my line back to Hachiman, I can hope for no good fortune in this present incarnation. My first point of worship on my eastern pilgrimage was the shrine of that bodhisattva. My prayers are both for what lies in my own heart and more widely for the extinction of sin and enhancement of karma.

'Hachiman has vowed to bathe the honest in his light, and this sacred vow is strong. My travels took me east as far as Musashino and the Sumida River, but if I had ever spent so much as a night with any man, I would fall from the grace of salvation promised by Hachiman's avatar Amida, and sink into the limitless pits of hell. When I visited Ise's pure stream, if I had given my heart to any man, Dainichi Nyorai himself, that embodiment of the two ways,[302] would have known of it and inflicted divine punishment upon me. My visit to the house with that autumnal chrysanthemum hedge at Kasuga was solely for the sake of the poems that spoke my heart there. If there were any man south of Nara Hill with whom I formed such a bond or in whom I placed my trust, when I worshipped at Kasuga Shrine those four great deities would refuse protection to me and I would be inflicted with the Eight Impediments of the Three Hells.[303]

'The sadness of never knowing the face of the mother I lost when I was only two, sorrow at the father who died when I was fifteen and whose love I so missed, still soak my sleeves with loving tears at their memory. But you deigned to take me in and bestow your deep pity on me when I was only a little child. Sheltered by the protection of your care, all the pain at losing my parents was salved. Then when I grew to adulthood you gave me your special love, and for this of course my gratitude is deep. Fools with dull, unfeeling hearts are no more than beasts, yet even they value the fundamental obligations of this life.[304] How then could I, human as I am, forget all I owe Your Highness? In childhood your gift of love was more marvellous to me than the light of sun and moon; as an adult you were dearer to me than my very parents.

'Then I found myself forced to part from you, but in those empty years that followed, whenever I happened to see you on one of your imperial expeditions tears flooded me to recall the past; if I learned of the success of other families in the court appointments lists or of promotions among the other ladies of the court I always winced with pain. Eventually these deluded thoughts receded, and I set off to wander hither and yon, hoping to quell my feelings and their foolish tears.

'In those wanderings I sometimes stayed in monastic quarters and sometimes I mixed with the company of men. Many were the days and nights devoted to poetry spent among others who treasured the finer feelings, and there were quite a few in the capital and in the provinces who found this suspicious, but although I have heard of others who have struck up casual alliances with wandering monks or ruffian renunciates[305] and the like, somehow fate has spared me any such inclination, and my nights have been spent alone and unloved. If ever I had loved another here in the capital, if ever I had lain with another sleeve on sleeve, it would have kept at bay the wintry winds on clear frosty nights, but there was no such man, no one who waited for me, and instead I spent my spring days idle under the blossoms, and sighed in autumn, hearing the dwindling song of insects on the plain as if it was my own, and many nights I lay in wild unpeopled fields with grass as my traveller's pillow.'

'No doubt you offered up your prayers chastely at a great many shrines on your pilgrimages,' he replied, 'but I note that these chaste prayers don't include the capital, which surely indicates that an old relationship here has been revived.'

'I have no hopes for a long life,' I responded, 'though I am not yet forty and who knows what the future holds. But to this very day there has been no such relationship, either old or new. If this is a lie, then those two thousand days I spent chanting the essentials of the Lotus Sutra in which I have placed my faith, all those times I reached for the brush to copy its holy words, will only serve to consign me to hell, all my hopes of paradise will be in vain, and I will never see "the awaited dawn of that new day"[306] when we meet again in Amida's paradise, but be condemned to the eternal sufferings of unending hell.'

Whatever thoughts these words provoked, His Highness remained silent for some time when I had spoken. Finally he said, 'Well, one should never jump to conclusions about things. It's true, after first your mother then your father died I felt I was the only one who must protect and care for you, but then things went awry between us and I decided our bond had been only a shallow thing after all. I was heedless of how deeply you felt for me until the bodhisattva Hachiman revealed it to me, for that is surely how I came to recognize you that day at the shrine.' This and other things he said, until the moon tilted in the west and sank behind the mountain rim and the light of the rising sun in the east began to brighten.

Clad in nun's robes as I was, I would have made a strange sight to prying eyes, so I hurried away. 'We must meet again soon,' he said as I left, and these parting words seemed to me almost a beacon lighting my way to the world hereafter.

After His Highness had returned to the city, an unexpected messenger arrived from him. I was profoundly grateful for the kind and thoughtful gifts he sent. Unlooked for as it was, the merest casual word from him filled me with delight, so you can imagine how I felt at this sign that his feelings were sincere, and at the care he took to keep others from knowing. I was quite overwhelmed. He had never treated me in a way that might raise eyebrows, heaven knows, and I had received nothing from him that could be construed as a sign of his special affection, but in his heart it seemed he had truly felt for me, and now looking back over the past I was indelibly struck by this realization.

Years passed, and I decided to return to the Bay of Futami, since after all its name suggests that even the deity 'looked twice' here,[307] and pray at Ise for enlightenment release from the cycle of life and death. I set out along the Ise Highway from Nara, calling first at a place called Kasaoki Temple . . .[308]

BOOK 5

(1302–1306)

I now decided to go on to the shrine of Itsukushima in Aki province,[309] following the vanished wake of those white waves that marked where Emperor Takakura[310] had long ago made an imperial pilgrimage there. I went by the usual route, first taking a river boat from Toba,[311] then transferring at the mouth of the river to a sea-going vessel and a lonely time spent on the waves. Suma Bay was pointed out to me as we passed, and I thought of Yukihira there in days gone by, and longed to ask the passing breeze to show me where his sad dwelling had been, where he 'gathered the salt-hung seaweed / soaked with tears'.[312]

It was by this time early in the ninth month, and from the frost-withered grasses rose the soft intermittent cries of autumn insects that now sang their last. When the boat drew in to shore and we spent the night at anchor, the 'thousand, nay ten thousand beats'[313] of fulling blocks carried to me, bearing thoughts of wintry villages on dark nights, a sorrowful sound to hear from my listening pillow on the waves. It was moving, too, to see the boats on Akashi Bay, 'slipping away in morning mist / lost among islands',[314] bound who knew where. I felt I knew to the full how Prince Genji felt when he longed for the moonlit roan to carry him back to the capital,[315] as we rowed on down the coast until we reached Tomo in Bingo province.[316]

Offshore from the busy port town lay a little island by the name of Taika, where some former courtesans had turned away from the world to live together in a group of huts. Destined from birth to ply that deeply squalid trade that condemned them to endless rebirth in the lower realms, they had long lived a life of scented robes, their one thought to find a man to love more fully, wondering as they combed out their hair each morning upon whose pillow it would tangle again that night, waiting at evening for customers, at daybreak left to sigh over another parting, and I was impressed and moved that they had turned their back on all that to live here now in seclusion.

'How do you follow your religious practice?' I asked. 'How did you come to awaken to the Buddhist Way?'

One of the nuns replied, 'I am the leader of the women on this island. Once I collected lovely girls and sold their various charms to passers-by, happy when someone paused, lamenting if he went on his way. I swore eternal love to unknown men, beguiling them with drink and affection "transient as the dew beneath the flowers", until, past fifty, impelled perhaps by some karmic prompting, I awoke one day to the truth of this mutable world of ours, and once awakened there was no returning. So I came to this island, where my practice is each morning to climb the hill and gather flowers, which I offer to the buddhas of the three worlds.'

Envying them their life, I stayed here several days before the boat took me on my way again. 'When will you return to the capital?' they asked as I left, and I thought to myself, 'It may be that I go no more'.

For all the nights I pause	*isa ya sono*
to sleep and wake with dawn	*ikuyo akashi no*
port after port	*tomari to mo*
there could be no sure way	*kanete wa e koso*
to set my passage	*omoi-sadamene*

I arrived at the island of Itsukushima, where from afar the great shrine gate soars up from the flooding waves, and a vast expanse of roofed galleries stands over the water, with a huge crowd of boats drawn up to them.

There was to be a great religious ceremony, and all the priestesses were bustling hither and yon. On the twelfth day of the month a stage was set up over the water, surrounded by galleries, and the priestesses emerged from the shrine corridor for a rehearsal of the performance. There were eight of them, all wearing variously coloured short-sleeved robes beneath white cloaks. The music was the usual shrine music, but memories flooded me when I learned that the dance was the one that the famous Chinese beauty Yang gui-fei performed for her emperor.[317] The formal brocade clothing worn by the dancers, red on the left and green on the right, on the day of the performance was just like that of bodhisattvas,[318] and the glittering headdresses and ornamental hairpins of the dancers made them seem very much as one imagines Yang gui-fei would have looked. As the darkness drew in, the music soared still more beautifully, and I was particularly struck by the sound of the piece called 'Autumn Wind'.

The ceremony ended at nightfall, and the great crowd of people all returned to their various lodgings. The shrine was left forlorn and empty, with only a few besides myself who stayed on through the night to pray. The near-full moon that rose from the mountain behind might almost have emerged from the very shrine itself; reflected in the rising tide all about, it seemed almost to inhabit both the sky above and the water's depths below. Moved by the power of the deity who had forged a way through the vast ocean of Truth, borne on the winds of liberation from all suffering, to come and dwell here, a manifestation of the bodhisattva Amida, I prayed, 'May your divine light illuminate the ten worlds and save those who pray to your holy name, leading all to paradise.' If only I could be of purer heart, I thought fretfully.

I stayed at Itsukushima just a few days, then set off back up the coast. On the boat was a seemingly well-born lady who told me she was from Wachi in Bingo province. She had come to the shrine to fulfil a long-held vow, she said, and she invited me to come and see where she lived. Explaining that I planned first to go to Ashizuri peninsula in Tosa,[319] I promised to visit her on my way home from there.

On this peninsula there is a little hall dedicated to the bodhisattva Kannon. The hall is a single open room, and there is no incumbent priest. The only people who come here are religious practitioners and passers-by, and high and low mingle here freely. Its story is as follows:

There was once a monk who spent time here pursuing his practice. He had with him a young lad in training for the monkhood, who valued compassion above all things. Along came another young monk from who knows where, and when they ate the morning and afternoon meals the first young monk would always share his own food with him.

The older monk scolded him, saying, 'Once or twice would be one thing, but you mustn't keep giving him food so constantly.'

The next morning the second young monk came again at the usual time. 'I would like to give you food,' said the first young monk, 'but my master has scolded me. Please don't come again. This is the last time', and he shared his food with him once more.

'I won't forget the kindness you have shown me,' said the second young monk. 'I would like you to come and see where I live. Come along', and the young monk went with him.

Suspicious, his master secretly watched the two depart together, and saw them arrive at the edge of the peninsula, board a little boat and set off to row south.

'You're deserting me!' he cried. 'Where are you going?'

'We are going to Kannon's Fudaraku paradise,'[320] came the reply.

Before his eyes the two young monks were transformed into bodhisattvas, standing there in the boat astern and aft.

Weeping, the old monk ground his foot into the earth in rage and grief. And this is why this peninsula has the name Ashizuri, meaning Grinding Foot. Leaving the mark left by his foot in the rock, the old monk went back home bereft.

'I live here now with this moral in mind, that intolerance of heart leads to misfortune such as his,' finished the man who told me this story. When I heard it, I was filled with awe to think that here was surely an instance of the thirty-three manifestations of Kannon.[321]

Satō Shrine in Aki is dedicated to the Cow-headed Deity, which brought to mind the Gion Shrine[322] back in the capital. Moved by this connection, I stayed a night there in peaceful prayer.

Shiramine and Matsuyama in Sanuki drew me to visit them

for their association with the exiled emperor Sutoku,[323] and since I also wanted to call on a relative nearby, I took a boat there. Visiting Sutoku's mausoleum, I found a service for him in progress. Surely, I thought, his soul would find salvation with this, no matter what hell it had sunk to. My mind went to the poem Saigyō composed to his spirit here, 'what now is left you / in this afterlife?', and I thought too with feeling of Emperor Tsuchimikado in exile, and of his poem, 'fated to be thus':[324]

Remembering	*mono omou*
your sad self	*mi no uki koto wo*
lamenting in this world	*omoideba*
have pity on me	*koke no shita ni mo*
from your mossy grave	*aware to wa miyo*

I still had far to go with my vow to make a complete copy of the Five Great Sutras,[325] and I felt the urge to stay in this area while I copied out a little more, so I prepared myself for the task, sought out a little hermitage not far from Matsuyama which I made my retreat, and set about performing the preparatory repentance rites. It was by now the end of the ninth month, the voices of the autumn insects had long since weakened and disappeared, and I was bereft of anything to call company. Three times a day at the prescribed hour I chanted the repentance prayers.

His Highness's words lay unforgotten in my heart, and I well remembered how when I was still a child he had taught me tunes to play on the *biwa*, and had given me a plectrum. I had long since given up playing, of course, but the plectrum lay beside me now as I sat before the altar, in memory of those dear familiar hands that had once taught me:

Nothing remains now	*te ni nareshi*
of that instrument	*mukashi no kage wa*
my hands knew so well	*nokoranedo*
but seeing this keepsake	*katami to mireba*
my sleeves are wet with tears	*nururu sode ka na*

During this retreat I copied twenty of the Daijō Sutra's forty volumes, which I dedicated at Matsuyama. I had relied on a local person of my acquaintance to help set me up for the copying and recitations. For the dedication ceremony I brought along as an offering the second of the three robes that His Highness had given me, one having already been given with the dedication ceremony at Atsuta Shrine, and I composed this:

This robe must be	tsuki idemu
a keepsake till that day	akatsuki made no
we meet at last in heaven	katami zo to
yet why did he not	nado onajiku wa
swear as much when he gave it?	chigirazariken

It was surely deeply sinful of me to choose, come what may in the next world, to cling to this robe that had once known his body.

What with this and that the end of the eleventh month came round, and I happily seized the chance to board a boat that was going back to the capital. On the way we were beset by wild and stormy seas and fierce snow and hail, and progress was slow. I was a pathetic bundle of nerves. Learning that Wachi, the name that the lady I had met on the boat had written when inviting me, was not far inland from where the boat had paused in Bingo, I left it and set off to find where she lived.

I easily located her home, and was pleased to spend several days there. As for her husband, I observed that he brought along four or five men and women each day, and treated them so badly that I couldn't bear to witness it. What could be going on? I wondered. Then I discovered that he was hawking. A great many birds were being killed and collected, and they brought in wild animals as well. He was most certainly mired deep in sin.[326]

A close connection of his, a tonsured lay monk from Kamakura by the name of Hirosawa no Yosō, announced that he would be calling in on his way through on pilgrimage to Kumano,[327] and the household and indeed the whole district was swept up in preparations for his visit. The sliding doors were papered with sheets of silk, and hearing that the master wanted pictures painted on them I happened to remark that if only I had painting utensils I would do it myself. There turned out to be some in nearby Tomo, and someone was promptly sent running there to fetch them. I deeply regretted having spoken, but there was no help for it now, so I duly painted some pictures with what had been brought. The master was so delighted that he urged me to settle down and stay there, which I found quite amusing.

Hirosawa himself now arrived and was treated to a fine welcome with banqueting and so forth. Noticing the paintings on the doors, he declared that it was extraordinary to come across such brushwork in a remote place like this. 'Who can have painted these?' he asked.

'A nun who is staying here,' came the reply.

'She's bound to compose poetry too,' he said. 'That's generally the way with such religious practitioners. I'd like to meet her.'

This was all very annoying, but, knowing that he was on his way to Kumano, I managed to escape the situation by suggesting we have a poetry session on his way back.

Two or three ladies had come for the occasion, and they told me that the master's older brother lived in a place called Eda where a daughter of one of them also lived. 'You're so good at painting,' they said, 'you should come and see this lovely place.' This was certainly a very difficult household to stay in, and I was warned that the snow would prevent me from returning to the capital, so since it seemed likely I would be in the area until the year's end I made my way to Eda.

The husband back in Wachi was astonishingly angry at this. I was a long-standing servant who had run away and been found at Itsukushima, he claimed, only to be now abducted to Eda. 'I'll murder her!' he cried. I could make no sense of this at all, but someone who didn't know the full story said to me, 'This is dreadful. I advise you to stay put', and so I did. There were a number of young girls at Eda and it seemed a kindly place. It was not really somewhere to attract me, but I could certainly

feel more relaxed than I had back at Wachi. Still, the whole
episode puzzled me.

At this point, the lay monk Hirosawa came through again
on his way back from the Kumano pilgrimage. The husband
now complained to him that an outrage had occurred – his
brother had made off with his servant, and he was bringing
a suit against him, he declared. Well, the lay monk Hirosawa
was not only uncle to these brothers, but also the local stew-
ard. 'What's all this about?' he demanded. 'What a ridiculous
accusation to make. What manner of person is she? After all,
it's perfectly normal to go off on pilgrimage, and besides, who
knows what high-ranking lady she might have been back in the
capital. How shameful to carry on like this!'

Word of this reached me, followed by the news that Hirosawa
was coming on to visit Eda, and a great bustle of preparation
ensued.

The elder brother explained the situation to him. 'We two
have fallen out, and all because of some insignificant pilgrim,'
he complained.

'It's astonishing,' Hirosawa agreed, and he ordered that
someone be provided to accompany me into the neighbouring
province of Bitchū when I left, for which I was very grateful.

I called on him and explained how things stood. 'Too much
talent can sometimes get one into trouble,' he said. 'It was
because of your skills that he wanted to keep you, which led to
him claiming all this.'

We proceeded to compose linked verse and continuous poetry
together, and on closer observation it came home to me that I had
seen him at a linked verse session with Superintendent Iinuma[328]
back in Kamakura. He was astonished when I told him.

He afterwards went back to where he was staying at a place
called Ida.

There was a great fall of snow, and I was struck by the
unusual sight of it on an open-weave bamboo fence:

> Renunciate that I am   *yo wo itou*
> my life can only be   *narai nagara mo*

piled high with sorrows	*takasugaki*
yet winter here piles higher yet	*uki fushibushi wa*
sad snows on this bamboo fence	*fuyu zo kanashiki*

The year had ended, and I began to hope I could return to the capital, but the bitter cold continued. Everyone was dubious at the idea of the boat trip, so I stayed on fretfully until the end of the second month.

Learning that I was preparing to go at last, Hirosawa came visiting from where he was staying in Ida for one more session of continuous composition, and as he was leaving he gave me a number of thoughtful parting gifts for the journey. He was the guardian of Prince Munetaka's young daughter, who was under the care of Lady Komachi[329] in Kamakura, which I thought may be how he came to be so particularly attentive to me.

On the return journey, I first went to a place called Ebara in Bitchū province.[330] Here I came upon cherry trees in full flower, and I broke off a twig which I gave to my guide to deliver to Hirosawa with this poem:

Though misty distances	*kasumi koso*
may stand between us	*tachi-hedatsu to mo*
remember me	*sakura-bana*
oh flowering cherry	*kaze no tsute ni wa*
when the spring breeze blows	*omoi-okoseyo*

Hirosawa sent someone on the two-day journey back to me just to deliver his reply:

Not the flowers alone	*hana nomi ka*
but I too cannot forget you	*wasururu ma naki*
though words	*koto no ha wo*
could not convey these thoughts	*kokoro wa yukite*
my heart yearns to tell	*katarazarikeri*

Kibitsu Shrine[331] lay on my way to the capital, so I paused to worship there. It was quite unlike the usual shrine in its furnishings, with standing curtains and so forth – very odd. The days were longer now and the wind had dropped, so from there I made my way on to the capital in no time.

Well, it had been a very strange adventure, and if the lay monk Hirosawa had not happened to arrive from Kamakura heaven knows what might have become of me. Protest though I might that that man was not my master, no one would have taken my part. When I imagined what might have ensued in that case, I lost all taste for further pilgrimages, and settled down to stay in Nara with occasional forays . . .[332]

News of events in the capital sometimes reached me, and I think around the first month I learned that Her Highness Higashi Nijō'in was ill. I knew no details and was privately very concerned, but there was no one I could ask. Then someone told me that the situation was hopeless and she was being moved to the Fushimi Palace. Transience is the way of this world, of course, but I did wonder just why she had to leave the home she had known so long. As one who had sat in state beside the emperor supporting his rule by day and at night slept by his side, surely she should be afforded the same dignities in her final days. I couldn't understand it. Then in no time there was a great commotion with the news that she had passed away.

I happened to be staying close by in the capital at the time, and I felt an urge to go and see what was happening at the Fushimi Palace. The first thing I saw when I arrived was a couple of lesser palace guards drawing up the carriage in which Her Highness's daughter Yūgimon'in would be leaving. The Imadegawa Minister of the Right[333] was also there preparing to leave, but after some discussion it was agreed that Her Highness[334] Yūgimon'in's departure should be hastened. Her carriage was duly drawn up, but then a delay was announced while she apparently went back inside again. This happened several more times. It was terribly sad to imagine how reluctant she must be feeling to say her final farewell to her mother. There was a great crowd of onlookers, so I made my way over to the carriage. 'No sooner is she on her way out than back she goes yet again,' they were saying to each other. When she did finally emerge, it was heartbreaking to see how utterly distraught she seemed. Even mere bystanders wept at the sight, as did all who saw her, whether tender-hearted or not.

Her Highness had had a number of children but all had pre-deceased her. Yūgimon'in was the only one left, and I could only too well imagine how they had loved each other. The depth of her feelings were plain to see, and I felt that in my own small way I understood from my own experience of my father's death.

Watching Her Highness's funeral procession, I thought of just how deeply this would have affected me had I still been in my former life at the Palace:

Worthless though I am	*sate mo kaku*
yet still alive	*kazu naranu mi wa*
with what sorrow	*nagaraete*
I witness now	*ima wa to mitsuru*
that passing dream of life	*yume zo kanashiki*

The funeral was held at the Fushimi Palace. I learned that both His Highness and Yūgimon'in were present, and I could too easily imagine how wretched they would be feeling, but these days I had lost all means of communication and there was no way to convey my sympathy to them. And so the days passed in fruitless sorrow, and at length the sixth month of that year arrived.

Now word reached me that His Highness himself was ill. It was said to be an intermittent fever, and I privately hoped that very soon I would hear that he was recovering, but instead he grew sicker. Then I heard that prayers for his recovery were being offered to Enma.[335] Desperate to know more, I went to the Palace, but I found no one I could ask and ended by turning for home again with nothing gained:

If not in dream	*yume narade*
how might he ever	*ika de ka shiran*
know of these tears	*kaku bakari*
I weep alone	*ware nomi sode ni*
for him	*kakuru namida wo*

Rumours flew thick and fast that his fevers were coming and going daily, and it was now said that he may be nearing his end. Utterly miserable, I began to imagine my sorrow if I were never to see him again in life. From sheer wretchedness, on the first of the seventh month I went into retreat at Iwashimizu's Hachiman Shrine and performed a thousand purifications to the deity Takeuchi to implore that nothing untoward should befall him. At dawn on the fifth night I dreamt of a solar eclipse, with the message that the sun would not reveal itself . . . *Transcribed as found. The page has been cut at this point and the following content is unknown. Transcribed from the cut page.*[336]

Desperate to know how His Highness was, I now went to the Kitayama retreat of Saionji Sanekane.[337] I presented myself at the door, where I explained that I was someone who had formerly been at the Palace and requested a brief audience with him, but no one seemed inclined to convey my message, no doubt despising this figure in nun's garb. I then wrote a note and gave it to them, hoping that they would at least transmit a letter for me, but though I begged them to show it to him they were still reluctant.

Finally, late that night, a servant by the name of Shun'ō appeared and took the letter in. 'I have grown old, and I'm afraid I can't really recall you,' came his reply. 'But by all means call again in two days' time.' This at least made me happy, and I came again on the night of the tenth as instructed, only to hear that he had gone to the capital as His Highness's condition was now serious.

The news threw me into despair. On my way back to the capital past the Right Palace Guards Horse Grounds, I stopped at Kitano and Hirano Shrines, threw myself on the ground and prayed that my life might be taken instead of his. If my prayers were granted and I were to perish, I thought miserably, he would have no way of knowing that it was for him that I had died:

If I should die before him	*kimi yue ni*
for his sake	*ware saki-databa*

may the white dew	*onozukara*
that lies upon my grave	*yume ni mo mieyo*
appear in dream to tell him	*ato no shiratsuyu*

I spent my days sunk in sad thought and all night long lamenting until dawn, until on the night of the fourteenth I went back to Kitayama, and this evening Sanekane himself came out to meet me. He spoke to me at length of the past, and told me that there was no hope of His Highness's recovery. Hearing this, my heart was overwhelmed with grief.

I had gone there with the thought that I would ask him to help me see His Highness one last time, but I was at a loss how to put this to him. However, he himself told me that I must go to the Palace and explain that he had instructed me to do so. Managing to repress my tears before others, I returned.

It was the time of the Festival of the Dead, and as I went I passed crowds of people coming and going to the burial grounds to tend the graves of their dead, and thought sorrowfully that I too must soon be among that number:

They come and go	*adashino no*
to tend the grassy graves	*kusaba no tsuyu no*
where life's dew has faded	*ato tou to*
but ah they too	*yuki-kau hito mo*
will soon have vanished	*aware itsu made*

On the night of the fifteenth I went to the Palace through the Nijō Kyōgoku gate, sought out Sanekane, and then like a dream I was taken before His Highness.

Around noon it would have been, on the sixteenth, word came that His Highness had passed away. Prepared though my heart had been, when the news actually came I was overcome with inconsolable sorrow and emotion, with none to tell my woes to.

I went to the Palace, where the priests were emerging after dismantling the altar where the special prayers for recovery had been offered. People were coming and going, but no sounds broke the hush, and the lamps in the southern hall were unlit.

The Crown Prince had already left, probably while it was still light, and moved to the Nijō Palace,[338] and fewer and fewer people were about.

In the evening, the Rokuhara Constables[339] called to present their condolences, presenting a grand sight as their accompanying military retinue lined up, that of the North Constable in front of Tominokōji Street where they had pine torches lit before the houses. The South Constable sat on a raised seat before basket torches in front of Kyōgoku Street, his retinue forming two lines. It was a most imposing scene.

The night grew late, but I had no inclination to go home. I lingered alone in the empty garden, haunted by memories of the past. Each memory evoked the face that I still seemed to see before me now. Inexpressibly sad, I watched the clear bright moon rise.

Even the moon	*kuma mo naki*
clear and unshadowed	*tsuki sae tsuraki*
brings me pain tonight.	*koyoi ka na*
How happy I would be	*kumoraba ika ni*
to see it dark and shrouded	*ureshikaramashi*

Long ago, it is said, when the Buddha died, the light of the sun and moon was eclipsed and even the insentient birds and beasts were sunk in sorrow. Truly, I realized, the pain I felt as I gazed now at the moon with such a heavy heart was deep indeed.

I left when daylight came, but I was still restless with grief. Learning that a relative of Heichūnagon[340] was in charge of the funeral procession, I called on a lady of my acquaintance who was related to him and begged that I might be allowed to see the coffin, even if only from a distance. I was refused, however, so I helplessly cast about for some other way to approach it.

Next I tried draping a court lady's robe over my head and loitering about the Palace all day, but to no avail. Finally, around the time when the shutters were lowered with the approach of evening, I tiptoed over to peep through the reed blinds into the room where I thought perhaps his coffin now lay. All I could make out in the low lamplight was a shape that might have been the coffin, but at this thought the world grew dark before me and my heart was crazed with grief.

Then the preparations were complete, the hearse drawn up, and the coffin was on its way. His Highness Retired Emperor Fushimi[341] accompanied the hearse to the gate of the Palace before returning, and I could all too well sense how he must be feeling as I sadly watched him wiping his eyes with the sleeves of his cloak.

I set off hurriedly for Kyōgoku Street to go after the hearse as it travelled along, but having been at the Palace all that day, when it came to the point and the funeral procession set out I was in such a state that I couldn't find my shoes, so I set off barefoot down the road to follow him.

As the hearse turned west into Gojō Street it caught on some bamboo that was propped there and one of the reed blinds was in danger of being torn off. The procession paused while a retainer climbed up to fix it back in place, giving me the chance for a closer look. There standing beside the hearse I saw the Yamashina Captain, now a lay monk, and it touched me deeply to observe him wringing the tear-soaked sleeves of his black monk's robes.

I now began to feel I should really go no further, but I had no desire to turn back so on I went, stepping gingerly as my bare feet grew more and more painful, and falling further and further behind. At length, somewhere around Fujinomori I came across a man and asked him whether the funeral procession had gone by ahead of me.

'It wouldn't have been able to pass in front of Inari Shrine,'[342] he replied, 'so they'll have chosen some other route. I don't think you'll come across anyone around here. It's terribly late,' he added. 'How can you go on at this hour? Where are you off to? Don't run into trouble, will you. Here, let me see you home.'

It would have broken my heart to give up and turn back at this point, however, so I went on alone, weeping as I went. When first light came I finally arrived, to find that all was over.

I stood watching the last trail of smoke rising from the funeral pyre, that sight I had hoped never to live to witness.

From there I went on to look at the nearby Fushimi Palace. This spring when Her Highness Higashi Nijō'in had died, His Highness and Lady Genkimon'in had both been present to share the mourning, but now it was Lady Genkimon'in alone who was there, and imagining the depth of her sorrow, I composed:

Gone like the dew	*tsuyu kieshi*
his last journey done	*nochi no miyuki no*
this sorrow sends me back	*kanashisa ni*
to our past days together	*mukashi ni kaeru*
soaking these sleeves with tears	*waga tamoto ka na*

All the doors were closed and there was no way to confide my heart to another, nor anyone to commiserate with. I couldn't go on lingering any longer, so finally towards evening I went home.

Hearing that Her Highness Yūgimon'in was now wearing mourning robes, I imagined how deeply dyed[343] would have been the robes that I too wore had I still been at the Palace. I remembered that when His Cloistered Excellency Go-Saga passed away,[344] back when I was at court, my father proposed that for various reasons I should be included among the official mourners and dress in full mourning robes, but His Highness declared that since I was still very young, normal sombre clothing would be most suitable. All too soon the eighth month came round, and I found myself dressed in mourning for my own father. All this and much else I now recalled, and I composed:

Nun that I am	*sumizome no*
no dye can deepen	*sode wa somu beki*
the deep black of these robes	*iro zo naki*
yet my heart still mourns	*omoi wa hitotsu*
as hers does	*omoi naredomo*

Hoping to find some comfort for these thoughts that I could tell to no one, I took myself off to Tennōji Temple, renowned as the place where the Buddha preached the Law.[345] Drawn by its reputation, I stayed there quietly reciting sutras, trying to quell my grief for a while. From the sad thoughts that filled my own mind, I could imagine how Her Highness Yūgimon'in must be feeling:

When spring came your sleeves   *haru kiteshi*
were sorrow-misted   *kasumi no sode ni*
now the fogs of autumn   *aki kiri no*
dampen those sad sleeves   *tachi kasanuran*
to a still darker hue   *iro zo kanashiki*

In due course the time of the forty-ninth-day ceremonies[346] came round, and I made my way back to the capital. When I arrived at the Fushimi Palace the service had already begun, and standing there among the many gathered mourners, I thought sorrowfully that their grief was surely less than mine. The service ended, and as I watched each in turn present their offerings at the altar, sadness filled me at the thought that this marked the end of the official mourning. It was early in the ninth month, and I thought with sympathy of the ladies behind their blinds and how their tears would be mingling with the damp fogs of autumn.

I learned that His Highness Fushimi was now in the same palace as His Highness had lived in, and sighed to remember how I used to see him as a little boy before he became Crown Prince[347] and moved to the corner palace building. One way and another, I was beset by moving and unhappy memories. First my father and now His Highness – 'Why should autumn hold such special sorrow?' as the old poem has it.[348] Unworthy as I am, I had longed to offer my own life in place of His Highness's, yet it was not to be and here I was, still lingering in our sad world. Now the mourning period for his death was at an end. How pointless life seemed.

There is a story about the Fudō deity of Jōjūin sub-temple in

the Miidera temple complex.[349] It is said that when the court
priest Chikō was nearing his end, his disciple the high priest
Shōkū prayed saying, 'I owe a deep debt for having received
the Buddhist teaching from him. Unworthy though I am, may
my life be taken in his stead.' He prevailed upon the Yin-Yang
Master Seimei to perform a transformation ceremony for him,
whereupon Fudō appeared and said to him, 'You have vowed
to take your teacher's place, so I will in turn take yours', and in
this way not only did Chikō recover but Shōkū also lived longer.
The debt I owed to His Highness was surely greater than Shōkū's
to his teacher. Why then should my fervent prayers have gone
unanswered? It is said that the deity Hachiman is named Bodhisattva because of his vow to take on himself the sufferings of the
masses. Why should my own unworthiness have mattered? The
failure of my prayer must be because, despite his deep piety, His
Highness's karma would not allow it, I decided.

Turning all this over in my mind, I made my way back, but
once home I could not sleep:

Hearing the soft cries	*kanashisa no*
of autumn insects	*tagui to zo kiku*
as my friends in sorrow	*mushi no ne mo*
through the lengthening nights	*oi no nagame no*
I lie, wakeful with age	*nagatsuki no koro*

Thoughts of the past flooded my spread sleeve with tears
as I lay alone pondering the past – my father's death, his life
gone with the dews of autumn, and now His Highness's life
gone too with autumn's lifting mists, so that the sky itself was
hazed with the sorrow of his passing. Might he have turned
to rain, I thought, or cloud, in that insubstantial journey into
death?

Why is there	*izukata no*
no wizard who can know	*kumoji zo to dani*
even in what distant cloud	*tazune-yuku*
he dwells now	*nado maboroshi no*
to go in search of him?	*naki yo naruran*

I had yet to finish copying the last twenty volumes of the Five Great Sutras and my plan was to complete them before the hundredth-day commemoration of His Highness's death, but I had no spare robe that would serve as an offering for their presentation, and I couldn't very well take off the one I wore. I could barely sustain myself with what little I had, and I could think of nothing that I could part with.

I was at my wit's end and feeling very low when I recalled that I had some keepsakes left me by my parents. When my mother died, she had asked that I be given a flat lacquer box she owned whose lid had a round design in gold dust of a loving pair of mandarin ducks,[350] containing combs, mirror and so forth also lacquered with the same design. From my father I had received a lacquer inkstone box with a raised gold-dust lozenge-shaped design of cranes on the lid. On its side was written in my father's own hand the auspicious Chinese quotation 'in this glorious time', incised in gold.

I had long believed I would never part with these precious things until death, that they would rise with my own cremation smoke; later, when I set off on my journeying, I left them in someone's care with the same pangs one would feel to leave a little child, and whenever I returned I made sure to retrieve them with all the joy of meeting my parents again. My mother's box had been with me these forty-six years, my father's inkstone box for thirty-three. You can well imagine how much they meant to me.

I thought and thought, but no fine jewel is more precious than a human life, and I decided that for the sake of His Highness I should relinquish them. Such treasures have meaning only in this world below, and I essentially had no child to pass anything on to.[351] If my vow to offer myself in his stead had been realized, these things would only have ended up in the possession of some other family. Rather, I would offer them to the Three Jewels of Buddhism as a means to ensure the salvation of His Highness's soul and for the sake of my parents, I decided. I retrieved the boxes, and though these dear long-familiar objects could not speak or smile, how could I not grieve over them like children?

Then, as chance would have it, a lady who was going to the East to marry said that she was in need of just such things, and by the grace of the Buddha, when someone came to fetch them I was paid far more than I had expected. I was delighted that I could now fulfill my vow to offer the remaining sutras, but when I sent off my mother's box I composed:

This precious box	*futaoya no*
that was to me a keepsake	*katami to mitsuru*
of my departed parents	*tamakushige*
I part from now	*kyō wakare-yuku*
with double sorrow	*koto zo kanashiki*

On the fifteenth of the ninth month I began the repentance rites in preparation for sutra copying, at the temple known as Sōrinji in the eastern hills of the capital. The first twenty volumes of sutras . . .[352]

Many a time I had sighed to think of His Highness, recalling my time at the Palace and unable still to forget my love for him, but now I dedicated myself waking and sleeping to repetition of the prayer that his soul should attain enlightenment. It was indeed a sorry fate that had brought me to this pass, I thought.

The melancholy cries of the deer on nearby Kiyomizu Mountain were companionable to my ears, while the murmuring insects in the bamboo fence might have been gently asking why I wept. Rising late at night for the pre-dawn repentance rites, I watched the moon that rose over the eastern mountain now sinking in the west. The early sutra chanting in the surrounding temples had ceased, and now all that could be heard was the uncanny voice of a solitary hermit high on the mountain above, chanting the *nenbutsu* invocation:[353]

How might I	*ika ni shite*
find my way	*shide no yamaji wo*
along the path of death	*tazune-mimu*
where his soul perhaps	*moshi naki tama no*
still lingers?	*kage ya tomaru to*

I employed a monk to go up to Yokawa on Mount Hiei to fetch a supply of the paper and water I needed for copying,[354] and went with him as far as Sakamoto at the mountain's eastern foot. From there I went to pray at Hiyoshi Shrine, with which my grandmother the nun had had a devout connection and where she had often taken me on her frequent visits to the shrine . . . *The page has been cut with a blade at this point. If only we knew what had been written below.*[355]

I learned that they had asked at Yokawa on whose behalf the sutras were being copied, which of course provoked a fresh wave of sorrow in me. I would have liked to present them at His Highness's grave, but this would arouse suspicions, so I then recalled his particular devotion to the deity of Kasuga Shrine in Nara and took the sutras there to dedicate them on the sacred mountain behind.

The deer on the peak seemed knowingly to lend their cries to the occasion:

Even the sad cries	*mine no shika*
of deer on the peak	*nohara no mushi no*
and insects in the grass	*koe made mo*
seem to befriend me	*onaji namida no*
chiming with my tears	*tomo to koso kike*

This was the thirty-third year since my father's death, so I held a small memorial ceremony for his soul. By way of an accompanying poem to these prayers, I sent the officiating monk the following:

My pitiable life	*tsurenaku zo*
lived to this day –	*meguri-ainuru*
now three and thirty years	*wakaretsutsu*
since that far moment	*tō zutsu mitsu ni*
when death parted us	*mitsu amaru made*

Going to the burning grounds of Mount Kagura to visit the site of his cremation, I found the ancient moss thick with dew, and I made my way beneath the trees along the leaf-buried

path until I found his mournful grave tablet, still standing there
in mute remembrance. How sad, I thought, that none of his
poems had been included in the recent imperial anthology.[356] If
I had still been at court I would certainly have put in a word for
his selection. After all, his poetry had been chosen for inclusion
in every imperial anthology since the *Zoku Gosenshū*.[357] For
myself, too, it grieved me to think that our family's poetic lineage of eight generations, from our princely ancestor[358] down,
was now perhaps on the verge of extinction. Pondering all this,
and my father's dying words, I composed:

I grieve	*furinikeru*
over our ancient fame	*na koso oshikere*
a nun now cast adrift	*waka no ura ni*
like some abandoned boat	*mi wa itazura ni*
idle on poetry's stream	*ama no sutebune*

All this I lamented by his grave before returning, and that
night my father appeared to me as he had been in life. I sat
before him, seemingly the person I once was, and when I told
him these bitter thoughts he said, 'Generations of our family
have been imperial poets,[359] from your Koga grandfather the
Grand Minister who wrote the poem "dew on the fallen leaves
/ takes up their colour", to my own "is it not also spring / over
the Koshi Road?" Then there was your maternal grandfather
Count Takachika, who on the occasion of an imperial visit to
his Washino'o Villa composed the poem "today above all other
days / the flowers are tinted bright". Given this heritage, you
cannot be overlooked as part of our poetic line. Our inheritance stretches all the way back to Prince Tomohira, and in all
that time the pulse of poetry has never ceased.' As he was leaving, he recited:

Dedicate yourself	*nao mo tada*
to gathering your poems	*kakitomete miyo*
for in this world	*moshiogusa*
fine poems move the heart	*hito wo mo wakazu*
regardless of who writes them	*nasake aru yo ni*

As he left I woke, that ghostly form still lingering in the tears that soaked my sleeve, his words still resonant in the pillow where I lay.

Now more than ever my urge to follow the Way of Poetry deepened, and not long after this I took myself off and stayed seven days praying at the grave of the great poet Hitomaro.[360] On the seventh day I spent the night there and dreamed the following:

Fated to be born	*chigiri arite*
a late leaf	*take no sueba ni*
on that long-famous plant	*kakeshi na no*
must I wither	*munashiki fushi ni*
unseen upon its stem?	*sate nokore to ya*

At this, an old man appeared to me and spoke. I later drew a picture of him, and wrote down his words in a document that I titled 'Hymn to Hitomaro'. If it pleased him, he would surely grant what I prayed for, and if my wish was indeed granted, I planned to perform a ceremony before this image of him that I had made. With this hope, I put it carefully in the bottom of my box and there it stayed until the eighth of the third month of the following year, when I did indeed set it up and made offerings to it.

The fifth month came round, and the anniversary of His Highness's death approached. I had succeeded in copying three of the five sutras, but two still remained. There was no time to waste, for who knows what tomorrow may bring? I had already offered my mother's precious box on the previous occasion, and now there was no reason not to do the same with my father's parting gift. However long it remained with me, it could never accompany me in my journey beyond the grave, I told myself firmly, so I prepared myself to part with it.

I should really offer it to some relative to buy rather than see it become the property of a stranger, I thought, but as I pondered the question further I decided that it would never do to be seen by those with no knowledge of my secret vow as someone who had cast away her father's precious keepsake to the treacherous shallows of worldly cash simply to make ends meet. While I was turning this over in my mind, it happened that the provincial undersecretary of Tsukushi,[361] just then in the capital on his way back from Kamakura to Tsukushi, heard that I hoped to sell the inkstone box and purchased it from me. So now my mother's precious keepsake had gone to the east, and my father's was on its way to the sea in the west. It was terribly sad:

Bereft, my tears flow	*suru sumi wa*
as that precious ink	*namida no umi ni*
down to the sea	*irinu to mo*
but may its current lead me	*nagaren sue ni*
to meet again on that far shore	*ōse araseyo*

Towards the middle of the fifth month I undertook the copying of the two remaining sutras. Having some business in the vicinity of Prince Shōtoku's grave in Kawachi,[362] I stayed there and copied out the twenty volumes of the Daibon Hannya Sutra, presented them at the grave, and returned to the capital at the beginning of the seventh month.

The anniversary of His Highness's death arrived. I first visited his grave in Fukakusa, then went on to the Fushimi Palace where his memorial service had already begun. The officiating priest was the Shakusen'in Abbot, and the service was offered by His Highness's son, the Retired Emperor Fushimi. I learned that the sutra being presented was a copy made by His Highness Fushimi himself on the reverse of something written by His Highness's own hand, and felt both honoured and sad to think that he and I were of one mind. Then it was the turn of his daughter Yūgimon'in to host the service, with the brother of the high prelate Kenki as officiating priest, and among the many sutras being offered I noticed that she too was presenting one written by her on the back of some of His Highness's writing.

Today marked the close of the mourning period, and there was a feeling that grieving was finally over. Hot though it was in the sun I didn't really feel it as I lingered there alone in the garden outside the worship hall. The services were at an end, and the imperial participants came flooding out, while I stood there feeling unable to unburden myself to anyone:

Never do these sleeves	*itsu to naku*
dry from the tears	*kawaku ma mo naki*
I weep still	*tamoto ka na*
yet they say today	*namida to kyō wa*
marks the end of grief	*hate to koso kike*

Through the blinds I glimpsed the forms of His Highness Fushimi and his son Go-Fushimi on their way to the audience room, and noted that Fushimi's mourning robe was particularly dark. This was the last day he would wear it, I thought sadly. Then I watched Retired Emperor Go-Uda[363] come along and join them in the audience room, and I was struck by how marvellous it was to witness these generations continuing the glory of the imperial line after His Highness's demise.

It must have been around this time that I first heard of His Cloistered Excellency Kameyama's illness. At first it was rumoured to be quite minor and unlikely to last long, and there was no reason to think he was approaching his end, but very soon people were reporting that there was no hope of recovery and he had been moved to his Saga Palace.[364] Distant though my life was from the imperial misfortunes that had struck in this and the previous year, they filled my heart with sorrow.

I had vowed to finish copying the remaining twenty volumes of the Hannya Sutra this year, and had long wanted to do this in the holy mountains of Kumano,[365] so towards the middle of the ninth month I set out, planning to travel before the water froze too hard. Kameyama's condition was still unchanged when I left, and I wondered what news of him would finally reach me. Yet I did not feel the same grief this time as I had last year at His Highness's illness and death. What a sorry thing is this fate of ours, doomed to the pain of parting from those one loves.

I stayed at Nachi and completed the copying, following the ritual of dawn and evening purifications in the sacred waterfall.

Towards the end of the ninth month, as a stormy wind buffeted
the mountain peak and the sound of the waterfall vied with my
tears, overcome with sorrow I composed:

> How often   *mono omou*
> have these tear-soaked sleeves   *sode no namida wo*
> been dyed in sorrows?   *ikushio to*
> If only someone somewhere   *semete wa yoso ni*
> cared enough to ask   *hito no toe kashi.*

The days of my reclusion sped by. Sad to think that I was
due to leave this sacred mountain so soon, I spent the night
in prayer. The Kumano deity must have deigned to accept my
resolution to relinquish everything down to the last of my precious keepsakes to complete my vow, for when I dozed off
around dawn, I was vouchsafed a dream.

I was sitting beside my father, who announced that His Highness was visiting. Then I saw His Highness himself, dressed
in a persimmon-dyed robe with a raised embroidery design of
two large birds. He was leaning a little to the right. I entered
through the blinds to his left and sat facing him. He now went
into the Shōkō shrine building,[366] lifting the blind slightly and
smiling a little, looking very cheerful.

He announced that Yūgimon'in had also arrived, and I saw
that she was wearing white *hakama* trousers with a simple
robe. She partly raised the blind inside the Nishi no Gozen
shrine and from opposite sides drew out two white gowns. 'I
am deeply moved by your resolution to part with your parents'
precious keepsakes to opposite sides of the land,' she said. 'Here,
take these two robes in return.' I received them and returned to
my seat.

Then I turned to my father and asked, 'What karma has
caused this man who has attained the exalted position of
emperor to be deformed[367] like this?'

'He is protecting a painful swelling below,' he replied, 'a hurt
caused by the dependence beneath him of all the foolish masses
such as ourselves, and the pity and care he feels for us. It is
through absolutely no fault of his own.'

I looked again. His Highness was still smiling cheerfully, and he told me to approach. I rose and knelt before him. He now produced two sticks rather like white chopsticks, the bases shaved back to bright whiteness and on each tip a pair of *nagi*[368] leaves, and as he gave them to me I awoke to discover that the Repentance Service had begun in the Nyoirin Hall.

Vaguely groping around beside me, I discovered a white fan with cypress wood ribs. It was not the season for fans so it was very strange that such a thing should be there, and it seemed quite wonderful. I took it and placed it in the meditation hall, and when I later told this story a priest at the temple, one Kakudō from the province of Bingo, said, 'The fan is a manifestation of the thousand-armed bodhisattva Kannon.[369] You have clearly been blessed.'

My tear-damp sleeves on waking still held the image of His Highness I had seen in dream. When I had finished the sutra copying, I decided that I could not go on clinging forever to the last of the robes he had given me, so I brought it out and presented it as an offering, though I wept to part with it. Here is what I composed:

This robe that for long years	*amata toshi*
I have wrapped close about me	*nareshi katami no*
through the night	*sayogoromo*
I will see no more	*kyō wo kagiri to*
from today's sad final glimpse	*miru zo kanashiki*

Having offered up everything at Nachi, I returned to the capital:

Waking from dream	*yume samuru*
with on my pillow still	*makura ni nokoru*
the dawn moon	*ariake ni*
I hear the waterfall	*namida tomonau*
that echoes my falling tears	*taki no oto ka na*

It was comforting to feel that the fan I had found by my pillow was a new keepsake from His Highness.

I learned on my return that Kameyama had passed away.

Although knowing that it is the cruel way of this mutable world for such misfortunes to follow thick and fast, it was melancholy to find myself the sole survivor where others had vanished into smoke. And so the year ended.

At the beginning of the third month I followed my long-established custom of a new-year visit to Hachiman Shrine.

I had been in Nara since the beginning of the year and out of touch with news, so I had no way of knowing that there would be an imperial visit there. Climbing the usual approach up Inohana Slope, I noticed as I passed that the building overlooking the riding grounds was open, and memories of the past[370] came flooding back. Then in the shrine forecourt I saw preparations to welcome an imperial visitor. Who was coming? I asked, and was told it was Her Highness Yūgimon'in. I was deeply moved at the fate that had brought me to coincide with her here, and went so far as to connect it back to my memory of the dream I had had in Nachi.

The next morning before first light, I observed an older lady who had the look of a palace attendant going through the gestures of worship, and on inquiry I learned that she was Otoranu, a lady in service in the palace kitchens. Filled with emotion, I casually asked her how things were at the Palace.

'All the people from long ago are dead and gone,' she said, 'and there are only young folk there now.'

Longing to find a way to let Her Highness Yūgimon'in know who I was, or to at least observe from a distance as she visited the various shrines, I didn't even bother returning to my lodgings to eat but lingered there until I heard an announcement that preparations were completed. Then I lurked inconspicuously to watch as her truly magnificent palanquin arrived and she went in to pray.

The Saionji Provisional Lieutenant Major was in charge of presenting her sacred offering, and as I watched I felt I could see his resemblance to his father, the now lay monk Sanekane, back in his youth when he had been Governor of the Left Guard, and this too moved me deeply.

Today was the eighth, and there was a ritual pilgrimage to the Togano'o sub-shrine. This time her procession was carefully inconspicuous, consisting of just two simple basketweave palanquins.[371] If she is making such a discreet pilgrimage, I thought, perhaps I might be able to draw her attention to my presence, or at least catch a glimpse of her if I approached. At this point I fell in with a couple of younger ladies who arrived on foot. At the shrine I stood behind, watching the figure that I felt must be her, and now I could not hold back my tears. I had no impulse to withdraw, however, and when she had completed her worship, she rose and saw me.

'Where are you from?' she asked.

I longed to speak to her of everything that had happened since those days long past, but I only replied, 'I have come from Nara, Your Highness.'

'From the Hokkeji nunnery?' she asked, but whatever she said to me all I could do was weep. She must find this behaviour quite mystifying, I thought, but though I decided it would be best to say little and leave as soon as possible, sorrow continued to hold me there. Then it was time for her departure.

I could not bear the thought that she would go, and noticing her difficulty stepping down into the courtyard, I went to her and offered my shoulder for her to lean on as she descended. She looked at me strangely then, and I blurted out, 'I knew you well long ago when you were very young. Perhaps you don't recognize me.' I was crying hard now.

After gentle questioning, she ended by telling me I must call on her anytime I wished. I recalled my dream, and reminded myself that it was here at this same shrine that I had also had the unexpected meeting with His Highness. So my private faith in this deity has not been in vain, I thought with joy. Only my tears knew what lay in my heart.

One of the ladies on foot whom I had arrived with had been particularly communicative. On enquiry I learned her name was Hyōe-no-suke. Her Highness was to leave the following morning and that night there was sacred *kagura* dancing and various amateur performances. Early that evening I sent a sprig of cherry blossom to Hyōe-no-suke to pass on, with the message that before these petals scattered I wished to call at the Palace back in the capital.

I was inclined to set out before Her Highness's departure next morning, but since I felt that it was thanks to the great bodhisattva Hachiman that I had chanced to coincide with her visit here, I chose to stay on three more days to offer my prayers of thanks.

Having left the shrine, I went up to the capital and sent Her Highness a letter. 'How are those blossoms I sent, I wonder?' I wrote, adding:

Perhaps the blossoms	*hana wa sate mo*
have been lured away	*ada ni ya kaze no*
and lost on a heartless wind	*sasoiken*
since more days than promised	*chigirishi hodo no*
were lost before I came	*hikazu naraneba*

In reply she wrote:

How could you think	*sono hana wa*
the wind would scatter	*kaze ni mo ikaga*
blossoms so precious	*sasowasen*
though days passed	*chigirishi hodo wa*
while still we waited for you	*hedate-yuku to mo*

We went on to exchange a certain number of messages after this, and it felt like old times for me.

Around the beginning of the seventh month, Her Highness Yūgimon'in moved to the Fushimi Palace to attend the third-year memorial ceremonies for His Highness's passing. I yearned to take part in the melancholy event, but the final section of the sutras I had undertaken to copy was still unfinished and I had now relinquished the last of the precious robes His Highness had given me so I had no offering I could present. Miserable that another year had passed with my task still uncompleted, I went to the vicinity of the Palace to watch the ceremonies from a distance.

Early on the morning of the fifteenth I visited His Highness's mausoleum to pray. How could it but be deeply moving to pay my respects to the newly made image of him that had been installed there? There was no hiding my tears, and the others gathered there, attendant priests and so forth, were so puzzled by the sight that they encouraged me to come forward. Overjoyed, I approached the tomb to pray. It seemed I had still more tears to weep, and I composed the following:

That passing dew	*tsuyu kieshi*
that was his life is now	*nochi no katami no*
embodied in his portrait	*omokage ni*
and once more the dew	*mata aratamuru*
of tears soaks my sleeve	*sode no tsuyu ka na*

The full moon shone clear and unclouded. I called on Hyōe-no-suke, and we talked on and on together of things past and present. My heart was still full when I left and went to linger for a while at the Myōjōin Pavilion.

Suddenly, I was bewildered to hear a voice announcing an imperial entrance. Then I saw the image of His Highness that I had seen that morning at the mausoleum being borne into the building. It was resting on some kind of dais carried by four serving men of some sort. Two men in priestly robes, evidently sculptors of sacred images, were directing. There were also a palace official and one or two palace guards.

It felt very dreamlike to see his image carried in like this, wrapped in a patchwork of paper. Once he had been the sacred emperor with a hundred officials at his beck and call; that time had passed before my memory of him, but I recalled those long-ago days when I had been in his service after he had received the exalted title of Retired Emperor, how even in his most modest excursions from the Palace his carriage was attended by nobles and senior courtiers, and pondering what paths beyond death he must now be wandering alone, fresh sorrow overcame me as if for the first time.

The next morning, the Madenokōji Chancellor Moroshige sent a message saying, 'You were just close by, I hear. How must you have felt at yesterday evening's sad service?' In reply I wrote:

With sorrow full	*mushi no ne mo*
as the sad moon and mournful	*tsuki mo hitotsu ni*
as autumn insect song	*kanashisa no*
I saw that dear face	*nokoru sumi naki*
flooded in bright moonlight	*yowa no omokage*

On the sixteenth there was a further memorial service in the form of a Lotus Tribute[372] or some such, in which the Buddha and the bodhisattva Tahō share the lotus pedestal upon the altar, and a series of services were held in the hall. The present Retired Emperor had arrived some time earlier, and there were strict protocols in place against outsiders both in the garden and in the hall, with anyone in religious robes particularly forbidden, to my sorrow. I looked about for a suitable position nearby, finally placing myself near the dripstone at the corner of the eaves to hear the service. If only I had my status of old, I thought, finding myself longing for that past that I had long since relinquished in despair.

Right through from the end of the presentation of the prayer of petition until the Repentance Service was over, my tears flowed unceasingly, and the kindly monk beside me asked who I was to be grieving so. But I couldn't bring myself to speak of the departed, so I replied simply that I was feeling particularly sad because I had lost someone who had been a kind of parent to me and the mourning period had only just ended, and with this I left.

The Retired Emperor departed that evening, and it saddened me to see how few people were left to attend on Her Highness Yūgimon'in, who remained sorrowing behind. Reluctant to leave, I lingered in the Palace area.

My cousin the former Koga Minister, mindful of our family connection, maintained occasional contact with me, and in reply to a letter I had sent he now replied with this poem:

Autumn in the capital	*miyako dani*
holds pathos enough	*aki no keshiki wa*
but sorrowing in Fushimi	*shiraruru wo*
how many nights have you	*ikuyo fushimi no*
lain gazing at the moon of dawn?	*ariake no tsuki*

His kind question provoked fresh pain. Unable to repress my feelings, I sent in reply:

Three autumns now	*aki wo hete*
have gone since he lived	*suginishi miyo mo*
and three nights have I lain	*fushimiyama*
here in Fushimi sorrowing	*mata aware sou*
afresh to see the moon of dawn	*ariake no sora*

His response:

Indeed that past	*sazo nage ni*
must rise afresh before you	*mukashi wo ima to*
in sorrowful memory	*shinoburan*
prompted by autumn's pathos	*fushimi no sato no*
in the lonely village of Fushimi	*aki no aware ni*

Meanwhile, on the fifteenth I had sent my precious fan to Her Highness Yūgimon'in with the idea that she might give it to the priest as an offering, and on the paper it was wrapped in I wrote:

I never thought	*omoiki ya*
that three long autumns	*kimi ga mitose no*
since his death	*aki no tsuyu*
that season's dewy tears	*mada hinu sode ni*
would soak these sleeves still	*kaken mono to wa*

Since His Highness's death I have ceased to feel the need to unburden myself to others. I think now of the astonishing coincidence of having worshipped at the grave of the poet Hitomaro back on the eighth of the third month of the previous year, and on the same day this year having coincided with the shrine visit of Her Highness Yūgimon'in; and I think too of how that precious dream meeting I had at Nachi later became real. What will be the final outcome of my vow? Surely these long years of faith and prayer will not prove to have been in vain.

Yet it is not enough simply to turn over in my own mind the

story of my life. My urge to go on wandering pilgrimage was
first aroused by the envy I felt at the tale of the poet Saigyō's
religious wanderings, and it is from a desire not to let this
impulse count for nothing that I have written this foolish tale
of mine. I have no hope that it will remain for future generations to remember me by.

*The copy I have used adds the following: The page has been
cut with a blade at this point. If only we knew what had been
written below.*[373]

Acknowledgements

I would like to thank Dr Lori Meeks for kindly taking the time to answer my questions, together with all the friends who have supported me during this translation, most particularly Rebecca Jennison, Stephanie L'Heureux and above all Patricia Clarke, with whom I shared Lady Nijō's unfolding story as I worked.

Notes

BOOK 1

1. *the special red*: Aka was a colour normally permitted only to those of the highest rank.

2. *the New Year's Day ritual herbs for His Highness*: The important New Year's Day formalities held on the first day of spring included drinking a medicinal tea to ensure long life and freedom from illness. The ceremonies depicted here are taking place at the Palace of Retired Emperor Go-Fukakusa, then twenty-eight.

3. *the Exchange of Cups*: A ritual series of exchanges of sake cups, consisting of three sets of three exchanges, to mark a celebratory occasion, accompanied by a banquet.

4. *'This spring I want the "little wild goose"'*: A coded poetic reference to Koga Masatada's daughter Nijō.

5. *a certain man*: Nijō is being secretly courted by a high-ranking man at court, later named by her 'Yuki no Akebono' (Snowy Dawn), whom she coyly doesn't identify.

6. *Today this letter seeks to make its mark . . . in hopes of perpetuity*: This is a poetically coded proposal that Nijō become the writer's lover. The new year marked Nijō's fourteenth year, when she officially became marriageable.

7. *Her Excellency Lady Kitayama*: Nijō's great-aunt. For her relationship with many of the key figures in this story, see the List of Principal Characters.

8. *because of a directional taboo*: In Yin-Yang divination, certain directions of travel were forbidden on certain days, and to avoid them a traveller had to spend the night in a different direction to the intended destination.

9. *the* setsubun *evening*: The official changes of the seasons (*setsubun*), particularly the evening before the first day of spring, were ritually significant times that involved directional taboos.

It was customary at the spring *setsubun* to offer a travelling guest a lavish meal.

10. *my father's wife*: Nijō's stepmother. Her own mother had died when she was two.

11. *a special robe hanger*: A pole on which clothes were hung.

12. *'Leaving the next morning looking smug'*: A quote from *The Tale of Genji* about a lover's dawn departure, here intended ironically.

13. *a letter*: It was customary for a lover to return home and send a next-morning letter containing a poem, to which the woman should reply by return messenger.

14. *something written in another hand*: If the woman could not compose a poem herself, it was sometimes acceptable for someone to write it on her behalf.

15. *an unexpected quarter*: The man who had earlier sent her the gift of clothing.

16. *a coloured design of the poem ... that hide Mount Yearning*: 'Let me die and disappear / until all trace / of this secret love / is gone like the clouds / that hide Mount Yearning' (Fujiwara no Masatsune). The poem formed the background patterning in the paper.

17. *if only words were never false*: 'If only / words were never false / with what delight / I would listen and believe / these words of yours' (anon.).

18. *My uncle the Zenshōji Counsellor*: Her maternal uncle Shijō Takaaki, a Senior Counsellor.

19. *'Left and right each sleeve' ... to borrow Prince Genji's words*: A quotation from *The Tale of Genji*. Genji's tears are a combination of resentment and affection for the emperor.

20. *the corner palace building*: A building in the north-east corner of the Palace compound, somewhat removed from the main residence.

21. *'His Highness should restore her to the usual position'*: She should be officially established as one of his ladies rather than kept in limbo like this without official status.

22. *'one day I would recall / with longing fondness'*: 'If I live long / will I one day recall / with longing fondness / this past time when life / was so unhappy?' (Fujiwara no Kiyosuke).

23. *somewhat older*: She was forty that year.

24. *come to the aid of Shōkū*: A reference to the legend that the Buddhist deity Fudō Myōō intervened to save the life of Shōkū, the founder of Jōjūin Temple. See page 206 for this story.

25. *to expel the evil spirits*: Illness and difficult childbirth were believed to be caused by evil spirits invading the body.

26. *The Yin-Yang Master*: A master of the art of Yin-Yang divination and magical healing. The ceremony he performs here is to purify the ritual defilement of childbirth.

27. *sacred white horses*: White horses were presented as a ritual offering to the gods. The great shrines were those, such as Ise and Kamo, that had strong imperial connections.

28. *It all struck me as very splendid*: Historical records show that in fact this event occurred the year before, when she was unlikely to have personally witnessed it.

29. *the ritual steamer was tipped to the north*: After an imperial birth the child's sex was announced by rolling a pot from the rooftop either to north or south. This infant girl became Yūgimon'in, Nijō's friend and ally in later life.

30. *the fifth and seventh night ceremonies*: Special celebrations held on the fifth and seventh nights after a birth.

31. *A divination . . . the god of longevity*: Unusual or inexplicable events were believed to be portents or the doing of wandering souls. This is taken to be a portent of Go-Saga's imminent death. Taizan Buku, a Chinese divinity, was invoked to restore the soul to the body and prevent death.

32. *bustling about applying moxibustion*: The application to acupuncture pressure points on the body of moxa (medicinal herbs), which are burned in place to promote recovery from an illness.

33. *he removed to his Saga Palace*: The move to his detached palace to the west of the city signifies acceptance of his approaching death, and is to avoid defiling the place where he normally resides.

34. *attended by Lady Mikushige*: One of Go-Fukakusa's consorts.

35. *Tsunetō*: A close retainer of Go-Saga's.

36. *the two Rokuhara constables*: The two men deputed by the Kamakura military government, which was now the seat of secular power, to oversee the governance of the old capital.

37. *the Saionji Counsellor Sanekane*: Sanekane was Nijō's secret lover 'Akebono'. She uses these two names to scrupulously distinguish between his public and private roles.

38. *had just been attacked and killed*: Tokisuke was killed on the orders of his fellow constable on the grounds of a suspected plot.

39. *the Three Attachments*: The three attachments that the dying soul still clings to – attachment to the family line and fortunes; attachment to the body; attachment to thoughts of one's place of rebirth.

40. *Yakusō Temple*: In the grounds of the Saga Palace.

41. *the princely abbots*: The sons of Go-Saga who became abbots of these imperial temples.

42. *Tsunetō ... no doubt take holy orders now*: For Tsunetō see note 35. Close retainers often took the tonsure and retired from active life when the person they served died.

43. *'even the flowers must bloom in mourning black'*: From a poem by Ueno Shinyū.

44. *the disinheritance problems with my mother*: The reference is unclear, but may refer to a quarrel between his stepmother and his older brother over his deceased father's estate.

45. *passed the age of fifty*: An expression signifying that he had entered old age. He was in fact forty-five.

46. *the forty-nine days of mourning*: The first forty-nine days after a death required daily ceremonies to assure the soul's safe passage.

47. *various difficulties ensued*: An oblique reference to the confrontation between Go-Saga's two sons, Go-Fukakusa and the reigning emperor Kameyama, over the imperial succession (see Introduction).

48. *Moxa*: See note 32.

49. *Taizan Buku ceremony ... Hachiman Shrine*: For Taizan Buku see note 31. Enryakuji Temple on Mount Hiei is the headquarters of the powerful Tendai sect. Hie is an associated shrine. *Dengaku* is a form of ritual music and dancing. Hachiman is an important shrine south of the capital.

50. biwa: A five-stringed instrument of the lute family, close relative of the Chinese *pipa*.

51. *at the time of his exile*: Go-Toba (1180–1239) was exiled to the island of Oki in 1221 as a result of a failed uprising against the Kamakura government.

52. *this bond lasts*: A servant's karmic bond with the master was said to continue through three lifetimes.

53. *childbirth band*: It was the custom to wrap the stomach of a pregnant woman, to ensure safe childbirth. This special band was ritually wrapped in a ceremony usually performed around the fifth month of pregnancy, but this was only Nijō's fourth month.

54. *my father was still here to witness it*: The childbirth band signified formal acknowledgement of Go-Fukakusa's paternity.

55. *the steamed plaintain to spread under the invalid*: Plaintain was used in Chinese medicine against a variety of afflictions. It seems to have been spread around or under an invalid each day.

56. *yam balls*: Grated yam and rice-flour balls wrapped in seaweed and seasoned with miso. This was one of the foods prohibited for pregnant women.

57. *Yasaka Temple*: At the time one of the important temples in the eastern foothills of the capital. Yasaka pagoda is all that now remains of it.

58. *Kawara Temple*: Kawara Temple was a temple in the south of the city.

59. *Nakamitsu, Nakatsuna's eldest son*: Fujwara Nakatsuna was a retainer of her father's. His wife had been Nijō's nurse, which placed Nakamitsu in a close relationship to Nijō and her father.

60. *the* nenbutsu *invocation*: A repeated chant invoking the bodhisattva Amida as a means to salvation.

61. *the ninth year of Bun'ei*: 1272.

62. *Nakatsuna arrived in monk's robes*: Following the custom of a loyal retainer, Nakatsuna had taken religious orders on the death of his master.

63. *The thirty-seventh day ceremonies*: Daily prayers are offered for the soul for the first forty-nine days after death, the thirty-seventh being one of the most important.

64. *mother of the Crown Prince*: Her six-year-old son was the future 91st emperor Go-Uda.

65. *spirit possession*: Malevolent spirits of the dead and sometimes of the living could possess someone and cause illness or madness.

66. *filled my yearning heart*: This descriptive passage weaves together allusions from a number of poetic sources. Cloth was fulled (softened and glossed) by being beaten with a wooden block.

67. *only Major Counsellor Mototomo failed to appear*: Horikawa Mototomo had been a rival of her father.

68. *a certain man*: A discreet reference to her secret admirer Sanekane ('Akebono') (see note 5).

69. *look suspiciously like a lovers' tryst if I'm seen*: It is implied that the visit was in fact chaste.

70. *The Sanjō Bōmon Counsellor ... the Zenshōji Counsellor*: High-ranking family members.

71. *a different source*: Her secret admirer Sanekane.

72. *made his way here in secret*: The soft rather than starched silk is to avoid detection from the swish of his clothing.

73. *Nakatsuna*: See note 59.

74. *her upbringing in the old palace ... in the old tale*: Her mother
    had been a lady-in-waiting to the daughter of Emperor Go-
    Shirakawa. She is likened to the crass and vulgar foster mother
    of Princess Imahime in *Sagoromo monogatari* (twelfth century).
75. *some games of flip-stones*: A game in which competitors flick *go*
    stones across the board to try to capture each other's stones.
76. *to avoid the ritual pollution*: Owing to her association with the
    deceased.
77. *Shōkutei-In in Daigo ... Abbess Shingan*: Shōkutei-In was a
    small nunnery in the grounds of Daigo Temple, east of Kyoto.
    Shingan is unidentified.
78. *to keep her tiny thread of smoke ... to higher ends*: This sen-
    tence weaves together quotations and allusions to various poems
    to give a poetic description of the simple ascetic life of Buddhist
    reclusion.
79. *the usual family shrine*: Hachiman Shrine, the clan shrine of the
    Genji, of which the Koga family were a branch.
80. *I have written elsewhere*: This description has been lost. It was
    a common practice at the time to record significant dreams, par-
    ticularly those associated with shrines.
81. *His Highness was not in a happy frame of mind*: He was engaged
    in an ongoing struggle with his brother Kameyama over the line
    of succession (see Introduction).
82. *Ninnaji Temple*: An important temple to the north of the capital
    whose abbot was chosen from among the imperial princes.
83. *the exorcist priest*: A priest who was present at a birth to per-
    form protective prayers and incantations. This and the following
    bow-twanging ceremony were to ward off possible spirit posses-
    sion at this vulnerable time.
84. *made all this feel a dream ...* : The rest of the sentence is inde-
    cipherable, and the following description abruptly begins a year
    later.
85. *that widowed crow that disturbs the night*: A poetic conceit that
    a recently widowed crow caws fitfully through the night, falsely
    suggesting the coming of dawn.
86. *Rokujō Palace ... on his behalf*: The Rokujō Palace included a
    Buddhist hall. The copies would have been made as an offering
    to mark the anniversary of his father Go-Saga's death.
87. *ritual childbirth band*: See notes 53 and 54.
88. *the previous occasion*: See page 22.
89. *Yin-Yang Masters*: See note 83.
90. *to twang the bow and keep the evil spirits at bay*: See note 83.

91. *I never saw her again*: The child was brought up in Sanekane's household. Years later, Nijō was in fact taken to see her daughter again (see page 93).

92. *the hundred days*: Women remained secluded for a hundred days after a birth or miscarriage owing to ritual pollution.

93. *depicting the poet-monk Saigyō's ascetic wanderings*: An illustrated version of *The Tale of Saigyō* (see Introduction).

94. *distressing events were afoot*: As a result of the decision to designate his son as the future emperor over Go-Fukakusa's claim, Emperor Kameyama established his own Retired Emperor's headquarters in anticipation of his abdication, which further upset Go-Fukakusa.

95. *joy hid within sorrow*: In order to accompany Go-Fukakusa's sad retirement from the world, Nijō too must take religious orders, thus fulfilling her cherished hope.

96. *The Imperial Priestess*: Two princesses were chosen as priestesses for the two imperial shrines of Kamo and Ise, where they served for three years. This Imperial Priestess was Kaishi Naishinnō, a half-sister of Go-Fukakusa and Nijō's half-aunt.

97. *the recent difficult political situation . . . the new Crown Prince*: The empress dowager, also referred to as Her Cloistered Highness, supported her other son Kameyama's claims to establish his son to succeed him.

98. *in the special red*: See note 1.

99. *the Saionji Counsellor*: Saionji Sankane, in private life her lover. She discreetly refers to him only by his title here because he is present strictly in his official capacity.

100. *This was a great shame, I thought*: Nijō is probably concerned for the priestess, who she guesses will be cruelly rejected by Go-Fukakusa if she fails to please him.

101. *the sake cups remained empty*: No sake was actually drunk, as the Imperial Priestess did not drink.

102. *The Saionji Counsellor has received his own personal cup from the lovely lady here*: This pointed remark hints that Go-Fukakusa is aware of Nijō's secret relationship with Sanekane.

103. *the triple robes*: This was only permitted to women of the highest status.

104. *a five-corded ox carriage*: The reed screens hung at front, back and sides of an ox-drawn carriage could be decorated with coloured cords, the use and number of which was dependent on rank.

105. *soothe myself with a visit home*: Her lover Sanekane could visit with ease if she was back in her nurse's home.

BOOK 2

106. *New Year's Day ritual herbs ceremony*: See the opening scene of Book 1.
107. *considerably upset His Highness*: See page xiii.
108. *gruel-stick games*: A game traditionally played at court on the fifteenth of the first month, in which people tried to strike each other on the thigh with a stick used for cooking gruel. If a woman was struck, she would bear a son that year, while if a man was struck he would father a child.
109. *Custodian Chief Minister*: A Chief Minister who took on the subsidiary role of Custodian to the young Crown Prince.
110. *the precedent of the Uji abbot*: Probably a reference to the story of an abbot whose filial piety to his old mother led him to catch and feed her fish, thus breaking his Buddhist vow not to kill.
111. *a family famed for its skill with the carving knife*: The Shijō family had a long tradition of culinary skill.
112. *the Lotus Ceremonies*: A four-day event devoted to chanting the eight chapters of the Lotus Sutra as a dedication to the soul of the dead on the first anniversary of their death.
113. *a certain exalted person*: He is unidentified because of his high status, but he is believed to have been Shōjo, the abbot of the imperial Ninnaji Temple (see Book 1, note 82), a younger brother of Go-Fukakusa. Nijō will later give him the private name of Ariake.
114. *the court football ground*: The popular aristocratic game of court football (*kemari*) consisted of keeping a soft leather ball in the air as long as possible by kicking it. The ground was set up in one of the palace gardens.
115. *More messages from him followed thick and fast . . .* : The lack of continuity here suggests that a section has been excised, perhaps to suppress a description of Kameyama's subsequent courting of Nijō.
116. *a Mandala Service*: A Buddhist service whose focus is a mandala.
117. *a garden competition*: A competition in which everyone is assigned a small garden plot among buildings where they compete to set up a temporary garden which is then judged.
118. *a suitable transference object*: An item of clothing belonging to the afflicted person, to which the possessing spirit causing the illness is transferred for exorcism.
119. *wearing soft silk*: He is trying to avoid detection by changing from the stiff rustling silk of his priestly robes.

120. *Flower Service*: A Buddhist ceremony held in spring and autumn, in which flower offerings were made.

121. *to select pines*: They may have been choosing pine trees to move to the new Rokujō Palace garden.

122. *piece of fan paper*: A fan-shaped piece of paper that is pasted to the ribs to make a fan.

123. *love like the curling smoke*: A reference to a poem in *The Tale of Genji* in which curling smoke represents hidden love that finds no outlet.

124. *'though I see the bright moon over other bays'*: A reference to a poem by Gishūmon'in Tango which begins 'I cannot forget / the autumn moon / over beautiful Naniwa Bay'.

125. *Tamagawa Village*: Code for 'depressing', derived from a punning poem about a village of that name.

126. *like a spider . . . grassy moor*: A poetic allusion that hints at her feeling of bewilderment and abandonment.

127. *a small lock of hair*: This indicates that she was preparing to cut her hair and take religious orders.

128. *'Ariake'*: 'Ariake no Tsuki' (the moon at daybreak) now becomes her private name for Shōjo.

129. *Flower Competition*: The players divide into two teams that present flowers for judging, together with accompanying poems.

130. *'Akebono'*: This is the first appearance of Nijō's private name for her lover Sanekane (see Book 1, note 5).

131. *the Izumoji area*: An area on the north-eastern edge of the capital, not far from Go-Fukakusa's palace.

132. *he clearly believed I felt the same*: The following passage is difficult to interpret, but it is implied that she goes to Izumoji as requested and discovers that a secret meeting has been set up by Ariake.

133. *'ambushed by love / before, behind'*: 'Ambushed by love / before, behind / I cower helpless / bolt upright in bed' (anon.).

134. *Kumano*: An important sacred mountain complex and pilgrimage site.

135. *the scene from* The Tale of Genji: Probably a reference to a scene in the 'Butterflies' chapter in which Lady Murasaki's gentlewomen ride in Chinese-style barges on the lake.

136. *the four marking posts*: Court football was played on a ground marked at the four corners by 'posts' in the form of a cherry, a willow, a maple and a pine tree, in this case cut branches.

137. *was presented as a Gosechi Dancer*: Young girls from high-ranking families were chosen to dance each year in the festive

dances held at the Gosechi festival in the eleventh month. The scene is being reproduced here as a form of entertainment.

138. *the scene from* The Tale of Genji ... *the ladies play music together*: An elegant scene in which some of the ladies in Genji's entourage give a musical performance.

139. *a thirteen-stringed* shō no koto: The seven-stringed *kin*, played by Onna Sannomiya, one of Genji's concubines, had by this time become obsolete.

140. *She is the aunt, after all, while Nijō is only the niece*: The recent arrival, who he insisted should play the role of Genji's primary wife Onna Sannomiya, is his daughter by a later wife, while the older Nijō is his granddaughter.

141. *that carriage ride when this principle of seating was reversed*: Probably a reference to the carriage ride to the Rokujō Palace in which she had taken precedence over her aunt, Lady Kyōgoku (see Book 2, page 67).

142. *a portion of the Lotus Sutra ... a letter my father had written*: Made as an offering for her father's salvation.

143. *the words 'I cannot leave this branch unplucked'*: There is no record of this poem.

144. *Abbess Shingan*: See Book 1, note 77.

145. *Kamo Festival*: The festival of the imperial Kamo Shrine in the capital, one of the most important events in the calendar.

146. *the sutra ... the burning house*: From the Lotus Sutra, which likens the unenlightened of this world to children playing obliviously in a burning house.

147. *that 'moonlit night' with its 'lingering sorrow'*: See page 70.

148. *he dreamed*: Spending the night at a shrine could bring a revelatory dream.

149. *Fujinomori*: An area south of the capital. A road connects it to Daigo where Nijō is in hiding, allowing Akebono to guess that the retainer may be coming back from there.

150. The Tale of Sumiyoshi: A story in which a girl who flees her mother-in-law's mistreatment and takes shelter with a nun at Sumiyoshi is united with her lover thanks to a revelation from the gods.

151. *Kiyonaga*: A retainer of Go-Fukakusa's who had a strong connection with her family.

152. *hototogisu*: A kind of cuckoo whose call is poetically associated with early summer.

153. *when the Yin-Yang Masters were consulted*: See note 26.

154. *the childbirth band ceremony*: See Book 1, note 53. There is no mention of a subsequent birth, suggesting that the child was either miscarried or stillborn.
155. *Mount Hōrai*: A mythical mountain where Taoist wizards dwell.
156. *the ex-Chancellor and Regent Okanoya*: His older brother Kanetsune.
157. *Nakayori who serves in my palace and is related to the family*: See Book 1, page 32.
158. imayō: A style of popular song sung by *shirabyōshi* (see the following note) that had become fashionable in court circles. Go-Fukakusa was particularly devoted to it.
159. shirabyōshi *performers*: Female entertainers who dressed in male court costume to sing and dance *imayō*.
160. *a certain private matter*: A secret meeting with 'Akebono' is implied.
161. *tree spirits*: Malign spirits of trees, embodied in echoes.
162. *So it was him*: Lord Kanehira, whose interest in her was implied in the previous scene.
163. *the song about the split statue of Fudō*: A popular song performed by *shirabyōshi*, which tells of an exorcism in which both the possessing spirit and the deity invoked by the exorcist to dispel it are the same Buddhist deity, Fudō. Torn between loyalties, the Fudō statue splits down the middle.
164. *cormorant fishing*: An ancient mode of fishing in which trained cormorants bring fish back to the boat. The Uji River, where the Fushimi Palace stood, was famous for cormorant fishing.
165. *the set of unlined gowns I wore*: These were the clothes that 'Akebono' had provided for her, a fact of which Go-Fukakusa was no doubt aware.
166. *known from of old to cause sleepless nights*: A reference to a poem by Minamoto no Shigeyuki containing the lines 'although I came to Fushimi / yet I could not sleep'.
167. *a mere empty shell*: Probably a quotation from a love poem depicting the unhappiness of being left after love, though the context lends it added ironic force.

BOOK 3

168. *It was around the middle of the second month*: 1281. No events are recorded for the years 1278 to 1280. She is now twenty-four.
169. *Nyohō Aizen*: A powerful deity worshipped in esoteric Buddhism.

170. *the Ursa Major deity*: This constellation (also known as the Big Dipper) is considered a deity in esoteric Buddhism, able to avert misfortune.

171. *that night of his 'lingering sorrow'*: See page 70.

172. *his sacred five-pronged vajra*: A hand-held metal implement used in esoteric Buddhist ceremonies.

173. *his bitterness over those events at the Fushimi Palace*: See page 100.

174. *the iris stems are picked for the fifth-month ceremony*: It was the custom at this time to give long-stemmed water iris as a symbol of longevity.

175. *that house where no one's on guard*: A reference to his secret entry through the broken wall to visit her early in their relationship (see Book 1, page 91).

176. *he turned into a blue demon*: See page 103 for a slightly different version of this story. The text may be corrupted here.

177. *'left and right each sleeve / soaked with differing tears'*: See Book 1, note 19.

178. *this 'moon of dawn'*: The private name she uses for him, 'Ariake no Tsuki' means 'moon of dawn'.

179. *a quiet ceremony . . . the tying of my childbirth band*: This signified that Go-Fukakusa accepted the coming child as his own.

180. *Flower Offering Ceremony*: A Buddhist service for the dead at which offerings of flowers were made.

181. *the ceremonies for the dedication . . . that were held here*: A series of ceremonial lectures on the Lotus Sutra held here in 1270, at which her father and other close relatives had been present.

182. *in my longing for the past . . . sobbing voices raised with mine*: Poetic quotations from the classics. The waves are pictured as returning again and again, evoking a past we cannot return to.

183. *the Yamamomo Captain Kaneyuki*: Fujiwara Kaneyuki, a close retainer of Go-Fukakusa.

184. *the little princesses*: The princesses were imperial children who were being raised at the empress dowager's residence.

185. *Kinhira the* shō, *and Kaneyuki the* hichiriki: The *shō* is a wind instrument similar to a panpipe. The *hichiriki* is a small, shrill reed flute.

186. *the Chinese poem 'over the citadel's tiled roofs'*: A poem by Sugawara no Michizane that goes on to describe the sound of temple bells.

187. *imayō*: See Book 2, note 158.

188. *Kameyama's young princess ... the future Imperial Priestess*: Princess Toguchi, Kameyama's daughter.

189. *which added to my woes*: See Book 2, page 81, for her quarrel with him.

190. *How close to you ... ruined hut*: The poem fancifully uses stock romantic imagery of a secret lover hidden away in a dilapidated house.

191. *the Five Great Sutras*: The five key Buddhist sutras of the Tendai Sect.

192. *the great sutra storehouse of the Dragon Palace*: Said to contain all the sutras that did not find their way into the human world.

193. *a mandarin duck*: Mandarin ducks, which are said to pair for life, are a symbol of lovers who cannot be parted.

194. *my own sense of guilt*: Her guilt is for the part she has played in encouraging him to stray from the path of rebirth in paradise.

195. *'I yearn / for revelation of that moment / when this dream's fulfilled'*: For this and the following poem see Book 2, pages 68 and 70.

196. *the robe I had exchanged for his that day*: See Book 2, page 69 (around the *kanashisa nokoru* poem).

197. *'the spring passed before I was aware'*: 'Shrouded within my room / the spring has passed / before I was aware / and now the blossoms that I waited for / have scattered and gone.' (Fujiwara no Yoruka)

198. *the forty-ninth day of mourning*: The final day of official mourning, when special rites for the dead are performed.

199. *The usual full moon Repentance Ceremony*: Ceremonies of repentance for sins committed were held on the nights of the full moon and the new moon.

200. *Lotus lectures*: Special lectures expounding the teaching of the Lotus Sutra.

201. *seemed to foretell this child*: The boy seems an incarnation of his spirit, which had entered her in the dream.

202. *reluctant to part*: It was the custom for a wetnurse to raise the child for its early years. Under normal circumstances, feeding and looking after a child oneself was unheard of for a woman of her class.

203. *that man who now belonged to the past*: Akebono.

204. *that man who had forsworn bitterness*: Akebono.

205. *my heart's prayers are offered to the gods*: 'Fruitless though it is / and my words unheeded / there is no moment / when my heart's prayers / are not offered to the gods.' (Priest Jōshō)

206. *the Five Lotus Rites*: Rites such as chanting and prayers based on the Lotus Sutra.
207. *the Thousand Chants*: A practice in which the petitioner chants a sutra one thousand times.
208. *Her Highness Shinyōmeimon'in*: Kameyama's consort.
209. *religious banners and delicately carved decorative plates*: Cloth banners with Buddhist images, and round or oval metal plates carved in various designs. Both were common decorations in worship halls.
210. *In secular life*: She had taken religious vows after her husband's death, as was the custom.
211. *the Reader*: The submitted poems were read aloud by a designated Reader.
212. *elsewhere*: No record remains.
213. *A number of pieces were played*: The list of names is omitted.
214. *the poetic illusion . . . 'cloud and mist'*: References to and quotations from well-known poems by the Chinese poet Bai Ju-yi.
215. *into such distance may your time continue*: Nijō is invited to add a line that plays with and continues the previous quotation, which she does by shifting the image of distance from space to time to create a suitably felicitous statement. The felicitous addition of lines continues below.
216. *that dawn moon shines still in those endless tears*: The dawn moon is a reference to her deceased lover Ariake.
217. *that river where heavenly lovers meet*: An allusion to the legend of the Herd Boy and the Weaver Maid, two lover stars who meet across the heavenly river of the Milky Way once a year.

BOOK 4

218. *I set out from the capital as the second month's waning moon was rising*: The story is taken up late in the second month of 1289. No events are recorded for the previous four years, during which Nijō evidently became a Buddhist nun. Now thirty-two, she is embarking on a journey from the capital to Kamakura, along the Tōkaidō Road.
219. *even the moon reflected in those drops seemed to me a tearful face*: The last two lines of poem 756 from the *Kokin wakashū*.
220. *the Barrier Gate of Ōsaka*: The first pass to be crossed when leaving the capital on the Tōkaidō Road, near present-day Ōtsu. The barrier gate, famous in poetry, was no longer functioning. Here and

below, Nijō's poetic account of the journey traces literary precedents that had established poetically important places (*utamakura*).

221. *Semimaru*: A semi-legendary early Heian period poet and musician of noble birth who was said to be blind. He was believed to
have lived in a hut in the hills near the Ōsaka Barrier Gate. The
quotation is from poem 1,851 of the *Shinkokin wakashū*.

222. *linking it with love*: The poem cleverly hinges on the *suru* of *koi
suru* (to love) and the place name *Suruga*.

223. *he would always send a sacred horse*: Horses were a common
though extravagant form of offering to a shrine's deity.

224. *the poet Narihira . . . still lying even in the fifth month*: Here and
below, there are references to a famous scene in *The Ise Tales*
(ninth century), centred in Narihira's poem on the strange sight
of Fuji's dappled snow in summer.

225. *Fuji's smoke too was now no more, it seemed*: Mount Fuji had
become an inactive volcano in the intervening centuries since
Narihira visited.

226. *so thronged this road with words*: Here and elsewhere, she is
visiting a place that is famous in poetry, where travellers traditionally paused to compose a poem to add to its poetic store.

227. *the Kumano pilgrimage*: The pilgrimage to the Kumano Shrine
in present-day Wakayama Prefecture was immensely popular
down the centuries. Today the pilgrimage route has become a
World Heritage site.

228. *the late Shogun Yoritomo*: Minamoto Yoritomo (1147–1199),
who established the military government in Kamakura.

229. *Brief nights are cause for sorrow*: A reference to a poem in
Shinkokin wakashū that laments the brevity of the night spent
with a lover.

230. *'long-worn robe'*: A quotation from another well-known poem
from *The Ise Tales*.

231. *the poet's 'two thousand miles from home'*: Here and elsewhere
in this passage, the description weaves in quotations from Chinese poetry.

232. *the Genji clan*: The clan of the Minamoto family who were currently in control of Japan's military government in Kamakura.

233. *Ono no Komachi*: A ninth-century poet renowned for her
beauty. The source of the following quotation is unknown.

234. *the forthcoming Zenkōji pilgrimage*: From Kamakura she was
planning to make a pilgrimage over difficult terrain to Zenkōji
Temple, in present-day Nagano prefecture.

235. *Yin-Yang Masters*: See note 26 (Book 1).

236. *Ceremony of Release*: A ceremony in which birds and animals were granted life and released, as a means to accumulate merit.

237. *the waters of that lineage*: A reference to her Genji inheritance, with a pun on the flowing water of the shrine's name ('Iwashimizu' means flowing spring).

238. *given the place*: Kamakura was still looked down on in court circles as countrified and uncivilized.

239. *return to the capital*: The Shogun was at this time merely a figurehead, the role being filled by young imperial princes. Prince Koreyasu, the current Shogun, was expelled from Kamakura on a whim by the powerful Regent Hōjō Sadatoki and forced to return to the capital.

240. *matting-sided palanquin*: A palanquin with straw matting for roof and side-blinds.

241. *Hōjō Sadatoki*: See note 239.

242. *turned to face backwards*: A humiliation that his father had also been subjected to when he was expelled.

243. *not just some upstart barbarian who had seized power by brute force*: Nijō is contrasting the Shogun's imperial lineage with that of the present rulers in Kamakura, who came of warrior stock.

244. *the Mikado Go-Fukakusa*: This formal title was only given to Go-Fukakusa after his death in 1304.

245. *daybreak on the snows of Kitano*: 'Daybreak on the snows of Kitano / seeing you I pray / the groundless blame that buries me in shame / should be washed thus clean and pure / by you, oh gods.' Composed at Kitano Shrine by Koreyasu's father Prince Munetaka when he was expelled from the role of Shogun after being accused of plotting against the ruling Hōjō.

246. *an exile*: An exaggerated description of the disgraced former Shogun Koreyasu, who had travelled along the more usual route through Hakone.

247. *The Viewing of the Horses*: A ceremonial parade of horses before the Shogun.

248. *The page has been cut . . . what had been written below*: Comment inserted by the copyist.

249. *a session of continuous composition*: An event at which a small gathering of poets chose a subject and composed a series of thirty, fifty or a hundred poems on it.

250. *the sutra*: The Mahasamnipata sutra.

251. *the Ten Thousand Recitations*: It was believed that ten thousand recitations of the prayer for salvation would ensure rebirth in paradise.

252. *far and wide behind and before me as I went*: The plain of Musashino, famous in poetry for its bush clover, is where Tokyo now stands.

253. *'as from the grassy moor / the moon emerges'*: 'Far in the distance / plain and sky merge as one / here in Musashino / as from the grassy moor / the moon emerges.' (Fujiwara no Yoshitsune)

254. *the robe is with me now*: Genji in exile was looking back to the great scholar-poet Sugawara no Michizane (845–903), who carried with him a scented robe the emperor had given him as a keepsake.

255. *the famous Sumida River*: It features in a famous scene (referred to below) in *The Ise Tales* (see note 224). Nijō is visiting sites famous in poetry as she travels.

256. *he declared that this name was the problem*: It is unclear why this name might have caused the rice to fail, but substituting 'rice field' (*ta/da*) for 'grassy plain' (*no*) in the name evidently solved the problem.

257. *this way . . . 'guards that bar the way'*: She resists turning north to visit the remote Oku region, following in the footsteps of the poet Saigyō and others. The quotation is a loose restatement of a famous poem, here intended to elegantly suggest that it would have been difficult and foolish to travel that way.

258. *the River of Tears*: A poetic conceit. No such river exists.

259. *'life has brought me back'*: 'Life has brought me back / to this dark pass of Saya. / Little did I think / grown old / I would pass this way again.'

260. *Atsuta Shrine*: See page 151.

261. *the Grand Shrine of Ise*: The Ise Shrine in present-day Wakayama prefecture was for many centuries one of the most popular pilgrimage sites.

262. *the Tsushima Crossing*: A crossing at the mouth of the Kiso River where it enters Ise Bay.

263. *the Kegon sutra*: The sixty-volume Kegon sutra was one of the five great sutras whose copying she had undertaken as a prayer for salvation.

264. *not being a descendant . . . seldom had reason to go there*: The two great religious centres of Kasuga Shrine and Kōfukuji Temple in Nara were associated with the aristocratic Fujiwara family.

265. *manifestation in this sullied world . . . the truth*: A reference to the belief that the Buddha chose to manifest in the world in the gentler forms of native deities such as the god of this shrine,

and to the allied idea that the 'empty words and specious phrases' of song and poetry could be a means to bring people to enlightenment.

266. *Minister Fuyutada's daughter*: For Fujiwara Fuyutada see page 103 (Book 3). He had been her mother's lover, and Jakuen may have been her half-sister.

267. *the five colours of salvation*: It was believed that a twisted thread of green, yellow, red, white and black, strung between the fingers of an image of Amida and the fingers of one dying, would lead the soul to paradise.

268. *'In this place . . . spared all suffering'*: It was believed that the mountain beside Taima Temple was a fragment of the mountain where Kashō (Sanskrit Kāśyapa) once preached, and his later bodhisattva incarnation, Hōki, came to practise on nearby Mount Kongō.

269. *Prince Shōtoku*: 574–622. A key political figure and scholar in early Japan, later revered as an incarnation of the bodhisattva Kannon.

270. *the building overlooking the riding grounds*: This building was used as a temporary residence both for the visiting administrator and for members of the imperial family on pilgrimage.

271. *when I left my aunt Lady Kyōgoku's apartments . . . to beg formal leave from him*: This event is not recorded in the text. It may refer to the customary visit to request permission for formal release from employment in order to take religious vows.

272. *the darkness of the world to come*: Her fierce attachment will condemn her to rebirth without attaining salvation.

273. *to see how different he looked now in his monkish robes*: Go-Fukakusa had taken Buddhist vows a year earlier. Their previous meeting occurred at night, so he had been barely visible and she was seeing him clearly now for the first time.

274. *a fire broke out*: Scholars question whether she could have been at Atsuta at the time of the fire, since it is recorded as occurring immediately after her pilgrimage to Hachiman Shrine.

275. *the sacred sword*: A sword that was the embodiment of the shrine deity, Kusanagi no Mikoto.

276. *the Yatsurugi Shrine*: Literally the Eight Sword Shrine. A large subsidiary shrine in the Atsuta Shrine complex that housed the sacred sword. The sacred altar area of a shrine building is normally sealed.

277. *the tenth year of the reign of Emperor Keikō*: Keikō was the legendary twelfth emperor of Japan. The following story refers

to the fact that the deity of this shrine was an incarnation of Keikō's son Yamato Takeru, who was sent to defeat the eastern tribes. Yamato Takeru was in turn a reincarnation of the god Susanoo no Mikoto of Izumo, the younger brother of the sun goddess Amaterasu no Mikoto, of the Grand Shrine of Ise.

278. *the words of my dream*: There is no earlier mention of this dream.

279. *the New Shrine . . . the Plain of Yamada*: The present-day Outer Shrine. The Plain of Yamada is the area surrounding the shrine.

280. *'here I will take my stand'*: Saigyō's poem is: 'Here I will take my stand / to wait out the silence / before the *hototogisu*'s call / in this cedar grove / on the Plain of Yamada.' The first call of the *hototogisu*, a kind of cuckoo that calls in early summer, was eagerly awaited.

281. *the sacred Thousand-Boughed Cedar and the sacred pond*: The Thousand-Boughed Cedar by the sacred pond in the grounds of the Outer Shrine was the closest place from which those in Buddhist orders could worship.

282. *Third Priest Yukitada . . . a man called Tsuneyoshi*: They were both members of the illustrious Watarai family of shrine priests, known for their poetry.

283. *sacramental mulberry paper . . . sacred sakaki*: Sacramental mulberry paper (*yufu*) cut in a zigzag ribbon is offered as a prayer at shrines, frequently tied to a sprig of the *sakaki* tree (*Cleyera japonica*), which is sacred to the gods.

284. *Second Priest Nobunari*: A man renowned for his poetry, who had died twelve years earlier.

285. *the projecting cross-beams . . . 'May no harm befall his sacred person'*: The roof's ridge pole ends in two crossed poles whose ends are cut either horizontally or vertically, with differing symbolic meanings. Her spontaneous prayer for the emperor's safety refers to Go-Fukakusa.

286. *'you live in the sun's brilliance'*: The deity of Ise's Inner Shrine is the Sun Goddess, Amaterasu no mikoto.

287. *this place that had meant so much to the deity*: Futami Bay, famous in poetry, is not far from the Ise shrines. The name Futami, which means 'look twice', was said to derive from the legend that the deity who first visited it returned to look again.

288. *Purification Beach, the Gold Lacquer Pines*: Local features made famous in poetry.

289. *'us "cloud-dwellers"'*: 'Cloud-dwelling' was an elegant term for the court and its inhabitants.

290. *Watarai's shrine*: The Outer Ise Shrine, which was in the Watarai area.
291. *the long ninth month*: The elegant name for the ninth month
was 'the long month'.
292. *the real prayer that was in my heart*: Her poem includes the conventional prayer for the emperor's long life, though privately her
prayer is for Go-Fukakusa.
293. *salting hut*: A hut on the beach where salt water was boiled
down for salt.
294. *that pass where lovers meet*: The Barrier Gate of Ōsaka (see
above note 220). The name's literal meaning led to its poetic use
to refer to the meeting of parted lovers.
295. *Tsuneyoshi*: See note 282 above.
296. *that far bay of Narumi*: Narumi Bay is near Atsuta Shrine where
she is going.
297. *the Ten Guardians of the sutra*: Ten female demons (Sanskrit
raksas) who protect believers in the Lotus Sutra.
298. *A year later*: This would date it to 1292, but according to historical evidence she is more likely to be referring to 1293.
299. *the mournful waters of the nearby Uji River*: This plays on the
double meaning of *Uji* (the river) and *ushi*, mournful or unhappy.
300. *the old poem . . . seem to turn the bright moon dark*: 'The sea
breeze that blows / across the moon-bright waters / of Akashi
Bay / stirs waves that rise / seeming as dark as night.' (Taira no
Tadamori)
301. *That man who discovered his River of Tears . . . Mimosuso River
in the ninth month*: See pages 166, 170 and 182. Mount Mikasa
is directly behind Kasuga Shrine. It seems highly unlikely that
Go-Fukakusa knew of these situations. Nijō is probably taking
the opportunity to borrow his voice in order to address the reader's possible suspicions.
302. *that embodiment of the two ways*: The bodhisattva Dainichi
Nyorai, the Buddhist avatar of Ise's deity Amaterasu, was
said to embody the dual aspect of compassion and virtuous
knowledge.
303. *the Eight Impediments of the Three Hells*: The impediments to
contact with the Buddhist teaching, encountered in the three
lowest hells.
304. *the fundamental obligations of this life*: Obligation to one's parents, to the ruler, to the people and to the Buddhist treasures.
305. *ruffian renunciates*: Men who called themselves renunciate
monks but were more like thugs.

306. *the awaited dawn of that new day*: She is quoting the poem that Go-Fukakusa wrote to her father as he was dying (see Book 1, page 22).

307. *the deity 'looked twice' here*: See note 287 above.

308. The text seems to have been interrupted at this point.

BOOK 5

309. *the shrine of Itsukushima in Aki province*: Itsukushima Shrine, one of Japan's great pilgrimage sites, is on the island of Miyajima near present-day Hiroshima.

310. *Emperor Takakura*: 1161–1181. He made the pilgrimage to Itsukushima in 1180.

311. *Toba*: a river port to the south of the capital from which boats travelled to the mouth of the Yodo River in Osaka Bay.

312. *Yukihira ... 'gathered the salt-hung seaweed / soaked with tears'*: A reference to a poem by Ariwara no Yukihira (818–893), who was exiled to Suma: 'If anyone should chance / to ask of me / tell them of my sad life here / gathering the salt-hung seaweed / soaked with tears on Suma's shore.'

313. *the 'thousand, nay ten thousand beats'*: From a poem by the Chinese poet Bo Juyi.

314. *slipping away in morning mist / lost among islands*: From a famous anonymous poem.

315. *how Prince Genji felt ... back to the capital*: A reference to a poem in Chapter 13 of *The Tale of Genji*.

316. *Bingo province*: Present-day eastern Hiroshima prefecture.

317. *the one that the famous Chinese beauty Yang gui-fei performed for her emperor*: Yang gui-fei (719–756) was the adored consort of Emperor Xuan-zong (r. 712–56). The dance was said to be one that he had created from a dream of an angel dancing. It reminds Nijō of her own life as the former emperor's favourite.

318. *The formal brocade clothing ... just like that of bodhisattvas*: Performers representing bodhisattvas in temple performances wore heavily brocaded clothes.

319. *Ashizuri peninsula in Tosa*: Ashizuri is the southernmost tip of the island of Shikoku. The following omits any description of visiting Ashizuri, replacing it with a story that repeats a common legend about the place. It is ostensibly told to her by someone she met there, but this awkward addition seems to be an afterthought.

320. *Kannon's Fudaraku paradise*: A fabled mountain off the southern tip of India, believed to be the home of the bodhisattva Kannon. The medieval Japanese cult of Fudaraku induced some believers to sail to the south in search of Kannon's paradise, often from the tip of Ashizuri peninsula.

321. *the thirty-three manifestations of Kannon*: Kannon, bodhisattva of compassion, was said to appear on earth in thirty-three manifestations to save all sentient beings.

322. *Satō Shrine . . . the Gion Shrine*: The description apparently follows her journey from Ashizuri around present-day Shikoku. The Cow-headed deity is also enshrined in the Gion Shrine where Nijō performed a thousand-day retreat on first leaving the Palace (see page 133).

323. *Shiramine and Matsuyama . . . the exiled emperor Sutoku*: Sutoku (1119–1164) was exiled to this area in 1156 for his part in the Hōgen Uprising, and died there. His vengeful spirit was thought to have caused subsequent calamities. The poet Saigyō famously visited his grave at Shiramine and composed a poem there.

324. *the poem Saigyō composed . . . and his poem 'fated to be thus'*: The poem Saigyō composed at Sutoku's grave is: 'For all / your jewelled palaces / of old / what now / is left you / in this after-life?' Tsuchimikado (1195–1231), Go-Fukakusa's grandfather, chose voluntary exile after an uprising in 1221, where he composed: 'Fated to be thus / in the life of this sad world / and yet my tears still fall / as if I have not grasped / why I should suffer.'

325. the Five Great Sutras: See note 191.

326. *mired deep in sin*: Buddhism prohibits killing and the eating of flesh.

327. *Kumano*: See note 134.

328. *Iinuma*: See page 159.

329. *Prince Munetaka . . . Lady Komachi*: See pages 158 and 155.

330. *Ebara in Bitchū province*: In present-day Okayama prefecture.

331. *Kibitsu Shrine*: An important shrine in Bitchū (present-day Okayama prefecture).

332. *settled down to stay in Nara with occasional forays . . .*: There seems to be some textual corruption at this point, with likely mistranscription and some words missing. This is one possible interpretation of the text.

333. *The Imadegawa Minister of the Right*: Saionji Kinhira, the oldest son of Sanekane.

334. *Her Highness*: She was now the primary consort of Retired Emperor Go-Uda.

335. *Enma*: The deity who sits in judgement on the dead.

336. *Transcribed as found ... from the cut page*: Inserted by the copier. The previous sentence is difficult to interpret, but seems to suggest that the deity conveyed a message that Go-Fukakusa would not recover. The removal of what follows may have been because it described an evil omen.

337. *the Kitayama retreat of Saionji Sanekane*: Her former lover, now fifty-six, had retired from the world five years earlier and lived in a villa north of the capital.

338. *The Crown Prince had already left ... and moved to the Nijō Palace*: The Crown Prince, who later became Emperor Hanazono, and others had moved to a different building to avoid the ritual pollution of proximity to the dead.

339. *the Rokuhara Constables*: The North and South Constables were local representatives of the Kamakura government who oversaw law and order in the capital. Their base was in Rokuhara, in the south-east corner of the capital.

340. *Heichūnagon*: An aide to Go-Fukakusa.

341. *Retired Emperor Fushimi*: The second son of Go-Fukakusa and Genkimon'in, who reigned 1287–98.

342. *'It wouldn't have been able to go past Inari Shrine'*: Owing to the pollution of death, the procession would have taken another route to avoid the shrine.

343. *how deeply dyed*: The mourning robes of those close to the deceased were dyed a deeper black.

344. *When His Cloistered Excellency Go-Saga passed away*: See page 17. He died when she was fifteen.

345. *Tennōji Temple, renowned as the place where the Buddha preached the Law*: Tennōji is an ancient and important temple in present-day Ōsaka believed to be the site of entry into paradise and the place where the Buddha preached.

346. *The time of the forty-ninth-day ceremonies*: See note 199 (Book 1).

347. *before he became Crown Prince*: He became Crown Prince in 1275, when Nijō was eighteen.

348. *'Why should autumn hold such special sorrow?', as the old poem has it*: 'Evenings end each day / knowing no season / yet why should autumn / hold such special sorrow / above other times?' (Fujiwara no Saneo).

349. *the Miidera temple complex*: A large and important temple complex at the foot of Mount Hiei near Lake Biwa.

350. *a circular design in gold dust of a loving pair of mandarin ducks*: This design was the family crest of the Shijō family. The crane in lozenge design was the crest of her father's family, the Koga.

351. *the Three Jewels of Buddhism*: The Buddha, the Buddhist Law, and the priesthood.

352. *The first twenty volumes of sutras . . .* : The rest of the sentence is missing, probably due to a copyist's error.

353. *the* nenbutsu *invocation*: See note 60.

354. *go up to Yokawa on Mount Hiei . . . the paper and water I needed for copying*: Water for the ink used for sutra copying was traditionally sourced from the holy well at Yokawa.

355. *The page has been cut . . . what had been written below*: A copyist's inserted comment.

356. *the recent imperial anthology*: Shin Gosenshū: The thirteenth of the great imperial anthologies of poetry, which had been completed the year before. Imperial anthologies were considered the definitive poetry collections of their age.

357. *every imperial anthology since the* Zoku Gosenshū: A total of five of his poems were included in three imperial anthologies.

358. *our princely ancestor*: Her father's Koga line was descended from the imperial prince Tomohira (964–1009), known for his poetry and scholarly accomplishments.

359. *imperial poets*: It was the culmination of recognition as a poet to have at least one poem chosen for inclusion in one of the imperially commissioned anthologies.

360. *Hitomaro*: The early poet Kakinomoto no Hitomaro (d. 708) was considered a kind of patron saint of poetry. He is the old man who appears in her dream.

361. *Tsukushi*: An important province in the north of the westernmost island of Kyushu.

362. *Prince Shōtoku's grave in Kawachi*: See note 269.

363. *Go-Uda*: (1267–1324), reigned 1274–87. He was Kameyama's second son.

364. *he had been moved to his Saga Palace*: His move followed the custom of moving to another place as death approached to spare others being exposed to the pollution of death.

365. *Kumano*: See note 134.

366. *the Shōkō shrine building*: One of the buildings in Nachi's Kumano Shrine.

367. *deformed*: Go-Fukakusa had a mild congenital deformity of the lower spine to which this scene may refer. Physical deformity

was understood to be a result of past karma. (See also Book 4, page 172, where she asks the same question of the dwarf.)

368. *nagi*: *Podocarpus nagi*: A conifer related to the yew tree, sacred to the Kumano area where Nijō presently was.

369. *The fan is a manifestation of the thousand-armed bodhisattva Kannon*: A version of Kannon whose many arms work to save sentient beings. The association is derived from the fan's many ribs.

370. *memories of the past*: She is remembering her unexpected meeting with Go-Fukakusa there (see page 172).

371. *basketweave palanquin*: A plain palanquin with basketweave sides.

372. *a Lotus Tribute*: A service in praise of the power of the Lotus Sutra.

373. *The copy I have used ... If only we knew what was written below*: Inserted by the copyist. In fact the work appears to end here. Perhaps what followed was an addition such as a supplementary collection of poems.